Final Fire

FINAL FIRE

A PHOTOGRAPHER'S TALES
FROM A VERY SMALL ISLAND

A MEMOIR

MICHAEL MITCHELL

Published by ECW Press
665 Gerrard Street East
Toronto, Ontario, Canada M4M 1Y2
416-694-3348 / info@ecwpress.com

Cover design: David A. Gee
Author photo: Ken Straiton
Cover photograph: Michael Mitchell
Fire raft: John McEwen with installation assistance by Kerry Mews

To the best of his abilities, the author has related experiences, places, people, and organizations from his memories of them. In order to protect the privacy of others, he has, in some instances, changed the names of certain people and details of events and places.

LIBRARY AND ARCHIVES CANADA CATALOGUING IN PUBLICATION

Mitchell, Michael, 1943–, author
   Final fire : a memoir / Michael Mitchell.

Issued in print and electronic formats.
ISBN 978-1-77041-481-5 (softcover)
ISBN 978-1-77305-345-5 (PDF)
ISBN 978-1-77305-344-8 (EPUB)

   1. Mitchell, Michael, 1943–.
2. Photographers—Canada—Biography.
3. Photography. 4. Autobiographies. I. Title.

TR140.M58A3 2019   770.92
C2018-905321-6   C2018-905322-4

The publication of *Final Fire* has been generously supported by the Canada Council for the Arts which last year invested $153 million to bring the arts to Canadians throughout the country, and by the Government of Canada. *Nous remercions le Conseil des arts du Canada de son soutien. L'an dernier, le Conseil a investi 153 millions de dollars pour mettre de l'art dans la vie des Canadiennes et des Canadiens de tout le pays. Ce livre est financé en partie par le gouvernement du Canada.* We also acknowledge the Ontario Arts Council (OAC), an agency of the Government of Ontario, and the contribution of the Government of Ontario through the Ontario Book Publishing Tax Credit and the Ontario Media Development Corporation.

Ontario
Ontario Media Development Corporation

ONTARIO ARTS COUNCIL
CONSEIL DES ARTS DE L'ONTARIO
an Ontario government agency
un organisme du gouvernement de l'Ontario

Canada Council for the Arts
Conseil des Arts du Canada

Canadä

PRINTED AND BOUND IN CANADA   PRINTING: COPYWELL   5   4   3   2   1

Several of the following chapters first appeared, in somewhat different form, in *Descant* and *Canadian Art*. The section on photographer Douglas Clark is adapted from a catalogue essay written for his posthumous exhibition at the Art Gallery of Ontario, which is reproduced with permission from the Art Gallery of Ontario. First published in the exhibition catalogue *Sweet Immortality: Douglas Clark*, © 2005 Art Gallery of Ontario. Several camera-related incidents told in *The Molly Fire* are retold here as this is a book about life as a photographer.

For Sheila, Jake and Ben

Memories are not carved in stone but scratched in sand.

"There are three sides to every story, yours,
mine and the truth. No one is lying.
Memories shared serve each differently."
ROBERT EVANS

"We can't resist this rifling around in the past, sifting
untrustworthy evidence, linking stray names and ques-
tionable dates and anecdotes together, hanging on to
threads, insisting on being joined to dead people and
therefore to life."
ALICE MUNRO

"Though nothing truly escapes us, memory and mind
from the moment of our birth are notoriously, almost
hopelessly, selective, elliptical, and inventive. And
memory and mind, for expression, perhaps for their
very existence, depend upon language — than which,
of course, there is no more evasive
and deceptive a medium."
RUSSELL BANKS

"Copying the truth may be a good thing, but inventing
the truth *is better, much better."*
GIUSEPPE VERDI

EXCUSES

"We are the guests of life."
MARTIN HEIDEGGER

"The blues, the blues ain't nothing but a cold gray day,
and all night long it stays that way . . .
the blues is a one-way ticket from your love
to nowhere; the blues ain't nothin' but a
black crepe veil ready to wear."
DUKE ELLINGTON

The big question is: how to live? We all take our own paths. This book is about mine. Several times in my life I arrived at a doorstep leading to a secure and predictable future. Each time I hesitated on the threshold but didn't enter. I chose, instead, to be a cowboy with a camera and a keyboard. It has been a rough road for decades but I survived and, best of all, I was never bored.

This is also a book about the corollary: how to die. Most of my friends have made wise and patient exits but a few have destroyed the quality of their last months or years by being irritable, angry and fearful. They left a mess.

While this is a book about being a photographer, a worker in a medium with an important role in memory, it is also a book about losses — lost times, lost landscapes, lost animals and, above all, lost people.

I would have liked to have written a book that runs like a Swiss watch but life and death are really messy and much of that mess has spilled onto these pages. I wrestled with them for several years and can't really claim victory. However the great thing about attempting to write a book like this is that it gives you a chance to try to be bigger than you are.

"There is no answer.
There never has been an answer.
There never will be an answer.
That's the answer."

GERTRUDE STEIN

"The place in which I'll fit will not
exist until I make it."

JAMES BALDWIN

ONE

THE EDGE

"It was exciting, confusing and scary.
It was all the good things in life."
MELISSA FRANKLIN

1984

"Canadian photographer, we're coming in the dark to cut off your head."

A slash of static from Contra Radio, some broken martial music and then the return: "Canadian photographer. we're coming in the dark . . ." Cut to martial music and repeat. The three Sandinistas sleeping beside me on a rooftop, a mere mile from the Honduran border, are fast up and wide-eyed. They roll for the roof edge with our radio and vanish over the eave while waving me back. Gone. My Jeep driver's face reappears and he skids a hex-barreled pistol toward me. "Sleep well *corazoncito* — little heart —" He smirks before vanishing again. I'm alone for another long, dark Nicaraguan night. The gun he leaves is pitted with rust.

———

A quarter century has passed. I stand by a small northern Ontario river that descends to Georgian Bay not far from the French. It's in full melt-water flood, glassily snaking over a pair of abandoned bridge piers on its race to the Sweet Sea. A big hemlock torpedoes out of one fork and vanishes around a curve. A white pine soon follows. The spring river's

I

5 a.m. A teenaged Sandinista fighter prepares for the day's combat on the Honduras border

big shoulders can't be contained — it bullies whole trees out of the banks. I skid my aluminum skiff into the current, secure it to a tree and begin to load.

In Nicaragua, far to the south, Daniel Ortega, once a sleek revolutionary in designer sunglasses, is now a balding, middle-aged social democrat, reconfirmed Catholic, accused estate embezzler and pervert. He's now struggling to hold onto power. We met several times but circled like strays. Now we're both tired and dogged by time but still alive.

I ease the boat into the current and drop it into gear. Eddies work the hull making it torque and twist while gathering speed on the run down to the Bay. We've all made it through another winter. An illusion of hope and promise lies ahead.

A mixed forest of leafy scrub and small conifers slowly unrolls and shifts along the banks as I descend. Three miles down the first great pines thrust above the bush — a small Temagami. In time I will watch them burn.

TWO

CALLOW

"Liar, liar, pants on fire!
Your nose is longer than a telephone wire."
CHILDREN'S CHANT

"It ain't braggin' if you really done it."
DIZZY DEAN

1955

Our little gang slouches home from school, circling around the girls, torturing and teasing, laughing. At the top of the hill descending beside the town's buckle factory, Ronny peels off from the group to enter his house, a shabby old red-brick tragedy on the corner. He runs in the open front door and climbs the stairs to his parents' second-floor apartment. His dad slumps in a press-back wooden chair at the kitchen table with a gun barrel in his mouth. We are in grade five.

SCHOOL 1958

I pull a wide plank of clear white pine from stock at the end of my high school's wood shop. While the girls across the hall bake cupcakes in home ec. the boys are each charged with building a fireside bench. Wood shop followed a drafting class that was easy. There, in collective secret, we'd combined our shabby skills to produce a single technical drawing of the Arts and Crafts bench we were each now building. One by one we'd go to the head of the class to present the same drawing and get our grade. Brecky, our short fat shop teacher chain-smoked,

3

so his teeth were baby-shit yellow and his breath stank. He made each of us sit on his knee. "Now Mikey, what nice little picture do we have from you today?" Both of us were looking at the name box on the sheet of drafting paper. It was not only now smudged gray like a November day — I was already the tenth person to erase a classmate's name and block-letter in my own — but it was getting flocked, like fancy wallpaper, from so many erasures.

As Brecky bounces me on his knee I glance back into the shop classroom. The left wall is a row of full-height industrial lockers. While I undergo this ritual humiliation my classmates have retreated into those narrow cabinets. By folding the doors back against each other they had created a series of little triangular hideouts. Their feet poked out the bottoms while columns of smoke rose from the tops — we were all hooked on Exports or Players Plain. We and Brecky were caught in an ageless game. We cheat. He knows we cheat. We know that he knows that we cheat. He knows that we know that he knows. It's our collective dance of pretend — the real-life lesson of the classroom. We will all eventually be future small emperors in our gotchies bravely, or not so, faking our way through grown-up life's many performances.

––––––

2011
I have slipped out of the city and settled in for the long hum north on Highway 400. Light industry gives way to suburban crescents of foolish facades — Tudor, Georgian and veneer Victorian. It's another world of pretend — where crown moldings are made of petroleum derivatives, square windows have function-free stucco keystones and garden rocks are made in molds.

Soon the last real estate signs are behind me and free-ranging cows feed on new grass. The highway loops over the moraines, heedlessly slashing through the Holland Marsh before climbing the gravel hills again. In an hour the gneisses of the Shield will hump up beside the road and the first great pines will soldier through the second-growth bush. My skiff awaits me on the Reserve where the little river slides to the Sweet Sea. I park there and load.

On this trip down my boat disturbs a heron. It takes flight downstream, running just ahead of me, banking through the turns of the river's course between the trees, waiting for me to give up the chase. Finally it escapes the channel through a break in the alders walling the banks and I finish the little journey alone, reach my cabin and build a fire. The dark will drop soon — it could last a few hours or prove permanent.

Our woodworking skills are even shabbier than our drawing ones. The end gables of the bench have scalloped cut-outs between the feet and an elaborate handhold in the centre of the board that is also scalloped. It will have to be cut by hand with a coping saw. Tricky. However the biggest challenge proves to be getting the end gables and the side rails all at the same height in order to support the top. The difficulty is compounded by the fact that none of these members are perpendicular to the floor — they approached it, by design, at a rakish angle.

Well, not a single one of us managed to get it all level. One foot would always be shorter than its mates. The top of one end gable never lined up with the rails that led to the other. Brecky's rule was that everything had to be done with a sharp tool — a chisel or a plane — never a file. As soon as he slipped out for a smoke we'd be at those suckers with an industrial belt

5

sander. It could take down an offending gable in seconds. In fact it would always overtake. Then you'd have a vigorous go at the rails to get them to match the newly reduced end member. We had to work quickly before Brecky returned. Each session was timed by his burning, unfiltered roll-yer-own. The piles of sawdust got higher. The benches got lower. There's an old carpenter's saw about how he's measured and cut this damn board five times and the sucker's still too short. It was just like that. At the end of term when Brecky made us put our pathetic benches all in a row they made a roller-coaster line that looked like those performance graphs you get from your mutual fund provider. Our families would each get a view of their burning home fires from a different perspective.

We moved on to metal shop. As I kept many tropical fish and had never been able to afford more than a five- or ten-gallon tank I decided to weld me up a hundred-gallon number so that I could get into some seriously vicious fish. It was a bit like making the bench — getting all those pieces of angle iron to line up perfectly to evenly support the big sheets of glass was tricky. But by the second last day of term I'd pulled it off. After all the caulking and sheets of glass were installed I filled it with water to test for leaks over night. When I came in next day to get my grade the whole shop was flooded. So lemme see: Latin's finished, a woodworking career is out, I won't be a draftsman, I failed as a glazier and I'll never earn a living welding. What's left?

———

This week we're running two new docks down to the island. A big flatbed from a lumber company in the Sound slowly backs down the muddy ramp to the river. Its hoist swings 32 feet of heavy, floating dock down to the water. I tie them off to a tree, slide an eight-foot length of pipe through thick galvanized eyes on their ends and join both docks. We're ready for the run.

My older son has come to assist. He's a vegetarian cook, activist and landscape architect. My other helper, Danny, directs an executive program at a university business school. I know I'll never be able to tow these docks and maintain steerage, so we're going to rely on spring runoff to ferry both docks miles down the river. It's our Canuck homage to Huck Finn — two wooden rafts on foam billets. The rapids run so hard around the first bend that we have to line the docks through them from the shore. After that success Danny and my son, Jake, board the docks while I run interference from the skiff.

We make magisterial progress down the river — so stately that this trip will take four hours instead of the usual twenty minutes in a fast outboard. The intricate forest on both banks slowly unrolls like a pair of scrolls. A muskrat crosses our path and dives. A jay calls. We round a bend and a river otter reclines on the north bank. It calmly watches us drift past. Cumulus clouds are building in a blue sky. Swallows flit across the river. A snapper sunbathes on a deadhead.

But my son Jake and Danny see little of this from their positions at opposite ends of the raft. Jake attacks corporate globalism while Danny mounts a vigorous defence of free-market capitalism. A bear peeks at us through a screen of alders. The two Hucks are getting louder. One of them slams his steering oar on the dock's deck to better make his point. They're now shouting at one another. The big raft thumps against the bank and the debate stops. A northbound V of geese honks overhead. A mink dives from the

bank. There's a minute of silence. Then it begins anew
— youth versus middle age, left opposing right, ideal
against the real, a father versus another's son.

Our little gang is wading up 10 Mile Creek in the ebbing
spring flood. We have all been to see the town blacksmith and
put down our paper route money so he'll make us new trident
spearheads. We now carry them upstream fixed to the ends
of stout six-foot cedar poles that we have cut ourselves and
stripped of bark. An old Chinese couple trails us by several
hundred feet. They carry burlap sacks.

Ostensibly we are here to kill lamprey eels, those supremely
ugly parasites that have been devastating the Great Lakes fish-
ery ever since the Seaway let them in. In truth we kill absolutely
everything that moves — suckers, eels, mudpuppies, muskrats,
frogs. The big carp-like suckers race up the rapids as we splash
through the shallow waters in our rubber boots in excited pursuit. After lancing them we toss them on the banks and leave
the thrashing coarse-scaled bodies for the Chinese to recover.
None of us wants to think about what they do with them. We
all drink cherry Cokes and eat mysterious dishes in our town's
only Chinese restaurant.

After several miles of wading in bone-chilling water we
encounter a half-dozen strands of old barbed wire sagging
across the stream. We duck under them and are now on the
farmland of one of the guys. Donaldson is a big-boned country boy with awkward movements and huge raw hands. His
dad grows corn on the flats above the river valley and raises
sheep down where we shuffle through the mud. They also have
chickens scratching behind the mean little brick Victorian their
large family lives in. They've got to be three or four to a bedroom but none of us knows for sure. We're never invited in.

Pete spotted it first — the cop cruiser creeping along the

concession road parallel to our upstream trudge. What we are doing is illegal. The round light on the cop car roof illuminates and begins to rotate. The car stops just upstream of us and two cops get out and wave us over. Donaldson puts his big foot on the shoulder of his trident and pulls up hard on his pole. The shank slips out of the wood. He signs us to do the same. We follow him up to the car with our sticks on our shoulders leaving the spearheads buried in the muck. The Chinese disappear in the thickets.

We all tended to think that Donaldson was not the sharpest axe on the woodpile but sometimes he'd come out with a good one and fool us all. This was one of those times. After getting the conservation lecture from the cops Donaldson told them that we were all just poor shepherds tending his father's flock. There'd be hell to pay if we lost any sheep so we'd have to excuse ourselves and get back to work. His dad's temper and violent rages were legendary. Nobody wanted to confront him for confirmation, not even the police. They glared at our poles. We kept the ends with the telltale shank holes down in the mud beside the road. The lead cop finally closed his book and climbed into the driver's seat. His red-faced partner gave us an evil eye and climbed in beside him. We were left to do God's work on the banks of our tiny Jordan River.

———

It's early June but the river still runs high. When I bail out the skiff it's got minnows and huge water bugs in it. I load quickly and set off down the river. The banks are screaming with invisible life. It's as lush as a tropical forest. Four miles down I bank around a bend in the river and encounter a mother bear rushing her cubs up a Manitoba maple. They go higher and higher with their mum in panicked pursuit. The impossibly slender top branches sway and bend under their weight. Mum watches from the last fork on the way up. They're smart animals. They push limits hard but always seem to know what the branches will bear. After I pass all three shimmy down after this close call with a noisy, dangerous hateful mid-sized mammal — me.

1956

Fred is the biggest guy in my grade six class. He shaves 'cause he's also the oldest, this being his third try at getting to grade seven. Fred doesn't do English, math or social studies: he spends all day slouching in the back row by the windows making what he calls "art shit." For months his creative project has involved drawing in nipples, underarm and pubic hair on little white bisque-fired nude girlie figurines. Fred took the money he got stealing hubcaps and bought a whole box of these beauties down at the gas station on the bad part of the main street. In every corner of Room 6C you could hear the scratching of his 2H pencil on the little clay crotches. Our skinny spinster teacher said nothing. She was afraid of Fred.

But Fred was no one-note Johnny. On various fetes and holidays he'd switch media and make coloured drawings. For Halloween he drew a pumpkin framed by crossed swords dripping blood. He did the swords with a ruler. For Remembrance Day the dripping crossed swords framed a blood-red poppy. There was even more red at Christmas where the swords crossed a yule tree they must have cut down. For Valentine's both heart and swords dribbled blood. If you were an art person you might have called Fred a primitive serialist.

Fred never did get out of grade six on account of the fact that he got Lottie Gamble's panties down by the back wall of the Methodist church across from our school. The day our year ended I ran into Fred pushing an occupied baby carriage into the pool hall. Then I saw Lottie come looking for him. She'd put on a lot of weight. She looked tired. She'd also flunked out of grade six. This was the same year that the *Toronto Star* did a front-page story on Ontario's teen pregnancy epidemic and named our town.

The muskrats are raising a family under my new docks. All night I can hear those relentless rodents chewing tunnels in the foam billets that keep the docks afloat. Drinking early morning coffee on the rocks I watch the busy little bastards swim into my small harbour with their groceries. I want to evil-eye them to oblivion. The principle of peaceful coexistence is being severely stress-tested.

Early on a sweet Sunday morning I carry my first espresso in a glass cup out to the high domed rock that guards the harbour entrance. Within seconds of sitting down a muskrat comes paddling in from the inlet. As it follows the shore I spot a mink snaking along the rocks in parallel. Once the muskrat gets within a couple of meters of the water's edge the tiny mink vaults into the air, lands on the muskrat's shoulders and rips its throat open. The savagery of the attack is numbing. The morning's music is gone.

1955

Every year there was a town parade. I forget now exactly what it was celebrating but I think it was for the incorporation of the town in the mid-19th century. Members of all the service clubs marched — the Kiwanis; Odd Fellows; all the wild animal orders like Lions, Elks, Moose; as well as the elite that owned their own businesses, the Rotarians. Some people sorta knew how to play instruments so there was a marching band but for kids the best part was on account of the town having a mental hospital hidden away behind trees down near the lake. Every kid in school knew somebody with a parent who worked there. Stories were told about how many patients died getting shock treatments administered by somebody's dad and how those who survived it were sort of hollowed out in the head. You'd see them wandering around town looking vacant and confused. Since this was pretty scary we all looked forward to the town parade where a few of the better-known out- and ex-patients would amble in the parade dressed in clown suits. It made people watching from the curb laugh. All that was some half a century ago and it seems that now people have made some progress in attitudes but probably not enough.

The great thing about going to school in a small town was that there really wasn't all that much stratigraphy. You knew everybody from the guy who lived in an earth hut cut into the railway embankment at the north edge of town to your school buddy whose dad was the mayor. Kids like models and life in this town was a good model of how the bigger world worked. That too was scary.

SCHOOL 1957

Three grubby fourteen-year-olds crouch breathing hard in the dusty dark. We've crawled under our new high school's stage, struck a match and are now unscrewing a vertical grate beneath the wings of the proscenium. Four large screws fall and it's free as are we after years of heavy discipline in junior school. Our little trio shared a proud history of detentions, the slap of the strap and are now like small pack animals fleeing a cage. We're beginning high school. We steal, swear, swagger and smash. We cheat, snigger, torture and tease. We get caught, punished, escape and repeat. We're proud of our recidivism. The adult world is all darkness and anger — big shoes, stiff bodies, dark suits and shadowy hats.

During this first fall of grown-up school we have been in constant trouble. Our homeroom teacher has had numerous closed-door sessions with the principal so the secretaries watch us anxiously. We push on, explorers in an expanding universe. This grate was our far shore — a New World. We slid it aside and slipped into the mysteries beyond leaving a trail of spent kitchen matches as we slithered through the concrete service tunnels beneath steam pipes and bundled BX cables.

A few hundred feet in we hit a secondary tunnel branching off to the left. As it was faintly illuminated from its ceiling some dozen yards ahead we decided to investigate. A thin rim of light fell from what was obviously an access hatch giving to the world above. We huddled in the faint gray light beneath it holding out collective breaths. You could hear voices. The loudest was that of Terrible Taft, the school's principal. A scrape of chair legs on the hatch above our heads revealed a scary truth — we were directly beneath the big man's office desk. You could hear every word the enemy uttered.

In this war between students and staff we soon became the chief intelligence officers. We made our moves in the bright world above and then retreated underground to listen as the enemy laid its counterterrorism plans. That fall we scored victory upon victory, our schemes and exploits ever more daring and the administration's ever more desperate. Our status in our tiny world was rising. Even girls looked at us with admiration. We became a triad — the Gang of Three.

So the Christmas term ended in triumph. Not only had we saved our skinny asses repeatedly but were able to dispense largesse to older criminals and save theirs. Lofty footballers and track stars from the stratospheric heights of grades twelve and thirteen became clients of the three sages of a dawning information age. We were invaluable. We were heroes. We felt invincible.

In early January our triad shambled up the hill and back to school in the lambent light of an Ontario winter. The Terror Trio had no chance to reconvene until the first week's end. We loitered about after the first Friday's gym assembly and then snuck beneath the stage as janitors put away chairs. We gathered outside the grate and lit a match. It revealed a grim truth. Each screw had been replaced with a weld. Our triad had been ratted out. We were now nobodies.

———

I round a bend four miles down the river and spot the heads of three moose protruding from alders on the bank. When they see me all three withdraw. After I cut the motor the three heads re-emerge, dark, sleek and healthy. We regard each other for a dozen heartbeats before they calmly shamble off into the bush.

1957

The Terrible Triad is slouched in adjacent seats for our classics class. While our teacher conducts a declension drill we busily draw jock straps and pushup bras on the statuary in our *Living Latin* textbooks. We pass notes with crude Latin jokes — *Semper ubi sub ubi* — *Always wear underwear*. Snigger, snigger. Miss Wilson catches this and asks our member Pete to translate a Latin passage. He shambles to his feet and says, "Jeez, I dunno. It's all Greek to me." The class laughs. He gets a detention. Sandy and I snigger helplessly. We get detentions. Class dismissed.

2011

This river run is another screw-up. I've just gotten up on plane in the skiff when I go crashing over a submerged deadhead — those sneaky buggers that lowly slide downstream like sleeping manatees. They hide just beneath the surface in the tea-coloured water, feeding on motor skegs and propellers, pitching our boats into the banks. Their message is that this is canoe and kayak country, a land for the slow and watchful not the noisy and rushed. I tilt the outboard motor, grab some pliers from the bilge and rebend the prop blades into something more like a pinwheel than a closed fist. I restart and resume the trip down leaving an oily moiré on the water. I see no animals but I know they watch and wait. They're always there, alert, patient, quiet.

1958

The Triad — me, Sandy and Pudgy Pete Pen-hooker — are prying a board off the high wooden fence surrounding the huge, abandoned leather tanning factory on the main street of town. Once inside the boarded-up block we'll creep around, peeking through windows at shadowy machinery and spooky tangles of plumbing and cables hanging in mysterious, soot-gray light.

We're putting off our real mission — the terror walk across *The Pit*. The northern half of the site was occupied by an enormous waste reservoir planked over with rotting 2x10 timbers. If you peered down between the boards you could just make out the viscous black liquid filling the block-long toxic lake that was rumoured to be bottomless. You'd gotta prove yourself by nonchalantly ambling hundreds of feet across the pit's decaying wooden cover all the way to the far end. Otherwise you're a pansy scaredy-cat.

We'd tied each other to tracks, run around the woods shooting each other with pellet guns and rolled used four-foot heavy equipment tires downhill through the downtown four-corners at night but nothing was as scary as falling through the dark into a vast poison pit. This was a recurring trial. Twice my foot broke through crumbling planks and I'd had to casually extract my leg and saunter on. I'd made it!

Does anyone today parking their minivan in the lot of a big chain grocery store now on that site have any notion of what is below the tidy, painted parking spaces?

Directly across main street was another 19th century dark, satanic mill. The Malleable Iron & Brass Works was still operating in the 1950s. Mr. Nichols, the bald and pudgy choirmaster of the Anglican church, was office manager and bookkeeper of what the townies called the Buckle Factory. I knew him not only from choir practice but also because this mill was on my paper route. After I'd delivered the local Thomson broadsheet to inmates of the county jail I'd drag my canvas news bag up the stone steps of the mill office building and hand Mr. Nichols and his pair of desiccated female assistants their newspapers.

If fussy old Nichols had any business on the factory floor he's occasionally let me tag along as he made his way through the blackened halls of the mill's many wings. Even by the standards of small-town 1950s the place was astonishingly archaic. Long drive shafts hung from cast iron bearings in the ceilings. Big iron pulleys drove leather belts looping down to machinery on the oil- and grease-soaked dirt floors. Dark men in blackened bib overalls ran spinning, reciprocating machines. Fires in the melting heaths supplied the lighting. Our job, on the way home from school, was to break that factory's windows.

Pete, Sandy and I wade through the grain fields down to

Highway 401 to meet CN steam locomotive 5031 where the tracks cross the big road. The engineer and fireman know us so they wait until we climb aboard for the ride back into town. This spur line runs through fields up to a big lumber-yard where they drop a load, pick up some grain and chuff back to the city. There are never much more than a half-dozen cars to the train but there was always a caboose with a cast-iron stove. The caboose cupola was a favourite place to ride and feel big. Sometimes we got to drive the locomotive when it was deep in the fields and nobody could see.

One summer a long strange train crept up our spur line. You could spot its lurid cars far out in the yellow fields long before we could read the big red banners painted on their sides. The whole foreign outfit came to a clanking stop only two blocks from my house and a door opened on one of the long silver cars. A wrinkly trunk snaked out of the darkness inside. Shit, there was a jeezly elephant in there! A ramp was dropped and another elephant and another and another and more club-footed down onto the cinder road. Soon a long line of elephants, trunk to tail, were lumbering down Highway 2 toward the small city where they still make cars and pickups.

———

This night, as restless waters grumble outside, I have a dream. I'm walking along Bloor Street in Toronto carrying a bear cub. No one pays us any attention as I try to find something for it to eat. A woman stops me and suggests a can of cat food. I continue to walk, and walk, and walk — Bloor is a very long street and the cub is heavy. I fail to find food. The dream gradually fades.

Next morning after coffee I pull on a sweater and jacket and descend to my aluminum skiff. The engine hard-starts in the morning cold. I reverse out of my little harbour, twist the shift and accelerate up the inlet toward the river mouth. I've left a few things in my van six miles upstream on the Reserve.

Once on the river I round the first big bend and spot a bear cub high in a north bank tree. I cut the motor and glide toward it. As I close on the tree I realize that there's not one bear but three. The over-burdened tree protests. Three pairs of bright black eyes stare. The middle cub begins to descend, scram-bling over its kin, grounding and disappearing into the alders. The lower one follows while the top-most cub visibly debates — freeze and wait? Ignore and eat? Flee? Reluctant and resentful, it gradually descends and shambles off into the mysterious bush. My boat drifts back the way it came.

1957

My entire troop is lined up in our public school gym. As a patrol leader I've been told to stand before them all in my best uni-form. My shirt is stiff with badges — I've even got the bronze and silver Arrowheads. I should be exemplary but I'm up here as a bad example. We'd gone camping the week before. I'd filled my canteen with my homemade apple wine. I'd kindly shared it with the boys in my tent. I got caught.

It was now only a decade since the Second World War's end that most old soldiers only wanted to forget. Deprived of com-mand, a few martinets had moved over to scouting and one of them stood before me now, red-faced and trembling with virtuous rage. Scouting had been my father's idea — his understanding of boyhood. I thought it ridiculous — the animal hooting of cubs, the paramilitary ranks, all the parades and marching and those minor military men who loved bossing boys.

My crime is announced. I brought booze on a camping trip. *Rrrrrip*. My silver Arrowhead is torn off my shoulder by raging-red-face. I smirk. I gave fermented apple cider to twelve-year-olds. *Rrrrrip*. My bronze is gone. I don't repent or apologize. *Rrrrrip*. My leader's stripes are torn away. Now I'm free.

———

I've cut the motor and drift alone, slowly spinning, down the river. I'm trying to learn the patience of plants.

1955

"Smelly *Telly*, stinking *Star*, *Globe and Mail*'s the best by far."

A dozen grubby 12-year-olds slouch in the shadows as vans from Toronto enter the backside of town's main commercial block to drop off the day's big city newspapers. We are divided into tribes based on the paper delivered. Bundles are broken into routes, stuffed in cotton shoulder bags and dumped in the heavy steel carriers on our handlebars. The carriers disappear into the December darkness. It's collection day — hours of slogging through slush, ringing doorbells and waiting in the damp chill to collect payment from delinquent customers. There are many deadbeats.

Tonight I'm the last one out. I sit under the only streetlight — surrounded by pickups, old Chevys and garbage cans — gawking at photographs of distant wars, movie stars, hockey goals and car crashes. Someday I'll see these things for real and make the pictures.

———

Last night a flock of jays flirted around my island for an hour before moving on. This morning the only

bird is a big black crow stiff-legging from log to log
at the water's edge.

1959

Our fall term French exam is being held in the school gym
where beige desks are ranked in long rows on a beige floor
between beige walls. I'm hanging with a small group of panicked crammers outside the entrance doors. At the nine o'clock
bell the staff march us in and I distractedly stuff my declension
cram-sheet into my back pocket and shuffle up to a desk near
the stage. The big doors close with an echo.

Teachers patrol the rows distributing exams. The room falls
silent and we're ordered to begin. We have two hours. Pens
scratch, paper rustles and shoes scuffle — we're fighting for our
lives. Just past the halfway mark I hear a footfall at my back and
feel a hand slip into my back pocket. The forgotten cram-sheet
is withdrawn and shoved under my face. I'm marched out of the
room by my old Latin teacher. Court is The Principal's Office.

Terrible Taft is triumphant as is the Latin teacher who
crosses her arms in smug victory. They'd never been able to
nail our trio but one is better than none. They will have their
revenge and they do. When our graded exams are returned
before Christmas each of mine — French, Latin, history, geography, algebra, geometry, chemistry, physics, even health — is
defaced with a fist-sized crimson zero.

My father knows Terrible Taft and was not impressed.
Perceiving an injustice he decides to act. An appointment is
made and we face down Taft in his office. These two tall men
in dark suits angrily circle each other but Taft has all the cards
— the seat of office, righteous indignation, ethics and the rule
of law. We leave in defeat.

Despite my criminal mind I'm a decent student. The grades
of the following two terms carry me through the year and I

survive. Taft resigns at year end to take a similar post at a high school in southwestern Ontario. With time my world brightens and the Taft years gutter and die. Another grade passed and I'm free. I get a summer job in the bush and prepare to ride the train all the way to the Pacific where I'll ferry up Vancouver Island and become a logger. The universe expands.

At Union Station I pay 50 borrowed dollars for a seat from Toronto to Vancouver. Then I pause at a newsstand to buy four days of train reading — with no berth the nights will be long. A huge and very black headline in a big Toronto daily stops me dead. An Ontario high school's star student having unexpectedly failed his provincial exams has been denied university entrance. Upon appeal his papers were re-evaluated and the failing grade stood. A further appeal has resulted in an inspection of his exam papers and the discovery that they are not his but rather those of the principal's son. An illicit peek at student papers had confirmed what that principal feared — his son would fail. Some paper palming secured one boy's future and damned another's. That midnight switcher had been Terrible Taft.

———

Two-thirds of the run down the river on an overcast day I hit something with a soft thump and the motor quits. I lean over the gunwale and peer into the dark tannic water. The bloated body of a buck hangs in the silty river just below the surface. As I stare it slowly rotates and four legs, stiff with rigor mortis, rise out of the water. The hooves glisten with the wet. The body looks like bagpipes.

1955

The death business has always been with us. My grade six

class is being marched down the last street on the edge of town to visit the county's brand new jail. Our giggling group is led into the processing area and counted before getting a tour of the shiny new cells. Then we are subjected to a lecture about law and punishment. After a pee break we are taken to a final area. It's a small square room with shiny cream walls and gray lino tiles. There's a steel-framed interior window on one wall flanked by one door in and another out. Once we've assembled two-deep around the room's periphery the friendly policeman directs our attention to a hook and pulley system centered in the ceiling. Then he points to the floor. A square section of tiles is framed in a metal molding. We are shown how beneath the floor it's hinged on one side and supported by a sliding bar on the other. Each side of this trap door is as long as our height. Better watch out. We are not shown the rope.

———

When I take my coil of rope down to the dock it is no longer *rope, cord* or *string*, it becomes *line*. I step off the dock into my little sailboat's cockpit and pre-pare for my annual spring humiliation. I always do this alone because many friends consider me the one real sailor in their lives. They know that my father had been a ship captain and naval commander. They know that he taught me how to use a sextant, how to splice an eye and tie knots. What they don't know is that every winter I forget it all and every spring I must sneak off with a book to relearn and practise. So lemme see — a *common bowline* begins with a loop in the standing part, then . . . And there are bowlines *on a bight,* the *flying* bowline, the *running* bowline, the Spanish and the Portuguese ones and special bowlines used by climbers. There are *hitches*

and *bends* and *lashings* and *loops*. When I have
to bypass a line weakness or shorten it I'll need a
sheepshank. My father taught me this one and years
of Cubs and Scouts involved me tying hundreds of
them but once again I'm stymied. What did I learn in
Baden-Powell's little army?

SCHOOL 1958

My poor high school classmates: every time we have an essay
assignment they have to slouch wearily in their seats and listen
to the English teacher read my latest effort aloud to the class.
I'd hate me too.

This time the stakes are higher. There's been a regional
essay contest and our teacher has submitted one of mine. It
has won. The prize comprehends a little cash and a book. Both
are now forgotten but a last-minute addition remains memorable — the judge has invited me to his house. It's a very pretty
white clapboard cottage on a treed lot in a small town on the
big lake — Ontario. I arrive alone, bang the knocker and am
admitted by a cleaning lady who directs me to the basement.
It turns out to be one that's, as we used to say, "finished." This
means wall-to-wall carpet, acoustic tile on the ceiling and dark
Weldwood paneling — a beta version of all the suburban family rec rooms soon to come. This one differs in that wherever
the wall space is not covered with framed photos signed by
forgotten celebrities, the paneling is obscured by many running feet of sagging bookshelves. I meet the judge and we have
a little chat about the writer's life while I sip a Coke and he has
something more adult. When he goes upstairs to answer the
phone I scan the bookshelves. The library is very eclectic. It
features none of the classics I've been taught to admire. Most
puzzling is a substantial collection of Hardy Boys adventures
and Carolyn Keene mysteries. Why would a grown-up, an

established literary adjudicator no less, bother to read these teen entertainments?

When he returns bearing refills for both of us I somewhat jejunely enquire. He changes the subject and describes his life as a young poorly paid reporter for a big city daily in Chicago. My English teacher had always made withering remarks about mere journalists so I was barely listening to his reminiscence when a sentence caught my attention.

He had worked the four p.m. to midnight shift on the news desk. He would then go home to his tiny apartment and while brewing a large pot of coffee open his mail. Twice a month there'd be a letter from the Stratemeyer Syndicate with a flat-fee contract attached to a one-page book outline. He'd start writing by one a.m. and two weeks later mail off the completed book. That's how Leslie McFarlane came to write a score of Hardy Boys adventure books and the first dozen or so Carolyn Keene mysteries. Now he had the house of his dreams with a finished basement and I had a tiny start.

―――――

There are low voices on the wind. They're water on stones, a breeze through pines, the distant gargle of cranes. Footsteps sound along the shore. The waves speak and the wind sings, sighs, whispers and moans many small secrets.

1964

Four of us ran an undergraduate interdisciplinary research project. We — a future physicist, an engineer to be, an upcoming baboon ecologist and me, the anthropologist/archaeologist — planned to sample every drink on the bar menu of the Embassy Tavern's Starlight Lounge. We were young enough to believe that understanding a zombie, a pink lady or a banana daiquiri was essential adult cultural knowledge. This large room off Bellair just north of Bloor in midtown Toronto was a subterranean, tropical paradise. Its high dark-blue barrel-vaulted ceiling, sprinkled with hundreds of tiny lights twinkling like southern stars, was supported by columns disguised as palm trees. A glowing bamboo bar levitated along one wall while the far end had a stage framed in coco fronds. We'd pay a two-dollar cover, descend the wide stairs and enter this magical place to hear a galaxy of fading stars — the Everly Brothers, Bill Haley and the Comets, Bobby Curtola.

However, for us the main attraction was the drinks menu, a bible featuring numbered illustrations of complex cocktails, their coloured layers oh so lurid and alluring in that basement tropical night. We knew that serious research had to be systematic so we began at page one. Each week we'd work our way through three or four new cocktails. We'd have seconds of favourites to test repeatability. The goal, over a hundred drinks away, was our liquid Eldorado. We never did quite make it.

But for several years we explored global geography via Singapore slings, Manhattans and Moscow mules. One night I showed up with a half-dozen friends to celebrate the birthday of finally reaching drinking age. My first legal drink was delivered by the bartender himself as a gift to an established regular — me. On another night we excitedly showed up after an evening class to see Louis Armstrong and his band play our lounge. The cover charge was out of our reach and the place was jammed. All but one of my friends sulked off to the Colonial Tavern downtown. Our remaining sad little party of two slouched into the licensed pool hall a floor above the lounge. We grabbed the last booth at the back and ordered a draft. We were counting our change to see if we had enough for seconds when a deep voice asked, "You boys mind sharing your table?" Louis Armstrong and a couple of sidemen slid into the booth with us and ordered drinks all around. They small-talked with us for 20 minutes before going down the back stairs to play their final set. That lounge is now a suit shop.

During my undergraduate years trudging through slush on King's College Circle the central visual event was the slow rise of the first TD Centre tower. When Mies's elegant structure finally opened I went up to the top and was stunned to realize that I could see the far shore of what had always been to me a vast sea. The U.S. was right there, just a hop and skip across a mean and cold pond. It forever changed the geography of my childhood.

Last night I visited that lake in a dream. Its entire shoreline was ringed with 200-storey buildings. My freshwater sea was further diminished. It had reverted to the smelly, stone-shored graveyard for alewives, algae and gray oil-slicked water with a great aggressor looming on the horizon.

THREE

GET A JOB

"I don't like work — no man does — but I like
what is in work — the chance to find yourself.
Your own reality — for yourself, not for others —
what no other man can ever know.

JOSEPH CONRAD
HEART OF DARKNESS

1958

"This is the last time that bitch is going out in a powerboat. She's a fucking squaw so she can drop her big ass in a canoe." Archie, a crippled-up old white guy, is talking about his wife, Edna. She's Ojibwa, from the local reserve. Edna had been out all night on one of her binges, drinking and fooling with the boys in town. On the seven-mile trip out of the inlet for home she'd fallen asleep and her old varnished Peterborough runabout had gradually run itself into a weedy back bay and partway up the shore. The tired Johnson 25 had eventually quit so the boat just sat there for hours with its 300-pound cargo slumped in the stern in her latest screaming dress from the Eaton's catalogue. She really loved her bright colours and beer. That huge wife was some sight moving through the pines in those dresses with her copper skin and shiny black hair.

This was my second summer working for them in their small Georgian Bay marina beside the lighthouse. It wasn't much. They had a 100-foot dock on cribs supporting a 900-gallon fuel tank and an old Texaco gas pump. There was a rack of plastic 2-cycle oil bottles beside it that I had to look after. Archie would buy a case of them at the beginning of the season. One of my jobs was to make a big show of opening one up and dumping the whole fancy quart into the customer's five-gallon outboard tank before pumping the gas. It was my responsibility at day's end to refill those bottles of luxury oil from the 45-gallon drum of bulk utility oil behind the shed. The virgin oil in the sealed bottles was popular with the customers so you had to be careful not to spill on the paper labels. If you were, you could get a whole season of refills out of each bottle. Every cent counted.

At the other end of the dock was their little general store and post office. That's where I stole the Burnt Almond chocolate bars that I mostly lived on. In this business you got pretty good at sneaking around.

So Archie was as good as his word. A couple of days later he turned up in his ancient inboard utility with a canoe balanced in the cockpit. It was a terrible looking thing — blackened varnish peeled off the gunwales and the canvas was torn and sagging. Got it from an old customer.

"You boys is gonna fix that boat up for the bitch."

Mike, who was also from the reserve, and a year older than me, stared at that ruin of a boat and then at me. He made a secret face.

"Yer gonna strip her right down, re-canvas and then paint her up. Let the cunt choose the colours."

So for the next few days Mike and I scraped and stripped between customers at the gas dock. After about a week we called Archie over for an inspection. Passed. He gave us a two-minute lesson on how to canvas and then hobbled off to his post office in the back of the store. You could hear the canceling hammer.

That canvas was sure heavy. We tugged and pulled, tacking it on with little copper brads. When she was all covered over we trimmed the excess. After another inspection Archie gave each of us a galvanized pail.

"Throw water on it and soak her good."

We did. And the canvas started to steam in the hot sun. It soon tightened right up.

Now for "the cunt and the colours."

We called Edna over while Archie hobbled off to his stamps. Yesterday her big dress was a cardinal flower. Today's was someplace between banana and pumpkin. She rocked back on her stumpy legs squinting at the boat. Some gulls called overhead. Small waves broke on the shore.

"I want the gunwales, them thwarts and ribs on that outfit to be coral pink. You can do the canvas in turquoise."

Mike made another face.

And I was having trouble imagining this — trouble seeing what Edna did. But we'd been ordered to do what she wanted. We both got in our little seafleas and raced off for town. At C.C.'s big general store we bought the paint, a couple of pad eyes in brass, even a paddle. It had an Indian head, headdress and all, burned into the blade.

On the way back out we stopped at the bootleggers for a couple of Molsons. Shit I was almost 15.

We got back to work, selling gas during the morning mail rush, making nice to the girls. We all, them and us, kept our T-shirts and jeans tight. After lunch Archie came out, scoffed at the paint colours but told us to put in on thick. We spooned it on the canvas like plaster — didn't finish until after eight. As the light failed I cranked up my 10-horse and raced off in my eight-foot boat for our home island. I warmed up a can of stew on my little coal-oil stove and then went to bed in the cabin.

Next morning I was in to work by eight. Islanders later told me they'd know to put the percolator on when they heard me go by each morning. When I got to the marina Archie, Edna and Mike were already staring at the canoe. In the morning light it was really fucking beautiful. Just fantastic.

"Take 'er down to the water."

We did and that huge woman slipped into it ever so lightly,

took the paddle and disappeared. Dress that day was lime green. Try to imagine all those colours together and the blue of the sweet waters, the swept pines and the glittering granitic rocks.

Some sight.

So Edna, having been pretty much fired from her own business, went fishing. That's all she did for the rest of the summer. We'd see her all over the place in that boat while we were out doing the propane deliveries to the islands. You'd look up while dragging a hundred-pounder up a rock face and there she'd be across the channel, line over the side. You'd grunt the empties into the steel workboat and take way off for the next customer and she'd be there already, line over the side. She was everywhere all at once. It got spooky.

And did she get fish! In a couple of weeks she was a legend with every fisherman on the northeast shore. Small mouth, perch, pickerel and pike, even the odd muskie showed up in the bottom of her boat. Once she came home with a huge sturgeon. And some lake trout. I began to eat better.

I did eventually find out how she got hold of those deepwater offshore fish like the trouts. One full moon night when the wind was up she came whispering over to Mike and me after work. Would we take her out in the big steel boat after Archie went to bed? He always went early on account of the pain in his crippled-up back. We dove for the two-four we kept cold in a dozen feet of water off the gas dock and brought up half the case. Then we gave Archie time to fall asleep and the three of us took off with the beers. She showed us how to line up the homemade ranges and get out through the shoals without hitting a rock. When we were a few miles out in the failing light she told us to slow down. There were a bunch of spars bobbing way out there in the big water. We closed on them. Then Edna leaned over the side and began pulling up the neighbor's gill nets. Those commercial guys had got a good haul of lake trout. We soon had scales all over the deck.

We got back in pretty pleased with ourselves but when I got in to work the next morning and tried to pump gas there wasn't any. While we'd been out lifting the fish tug crew's nets they'd been on top of our 900-gallon tank helping themselves. Pretty expensive fish.

———

I have an American neighbour far across the inlet. I dread his arrival because, like the few other Americans in the township, he blows the silence away. Within five minutes of arrival he's got a gas-powered water pump going. Most Canadians have silent solar ones. No sooner is his water tank filled then he starts a generator so that he can vacuum his log cabin. When the vacuum is full he gets out a gas weed-whacker and attacks the disorderly Canadian wilderness. Then he fills the remaining minutes before dark with a gas leaf blower driving offending pine needles off the rocks of the Shield. Now that his property is under a cloud of two-stroke engine exhaust he vacates to guzzle hard liquor with another sockless giant a couple of hundred feet away. Most of us would paddle there. He roars over in an outboard.

1959

Mike comes in for work at the marina with a great sparkling sweep of water as his seaflea comes off plane near the dock. He steps out of his little boat with a shoebox under his arm, signaling to me to quit the gas dock and meet him in the motor shed. I finish refilling the case of quart oil bottles, wipe the labels clean and stack them in the rack. I walk landward on the long wooden dock toward the shack where we repair motors and water pumps.

I love that greasy little temple to guy stuff — love the oily black planks of the floor and workbench, the silvery glow of the chrome vanadium sockets, wrenches and drivers, the dirty light seeping in through the panes, the hanging gaskets and the big white girls caressing tools on the calendars.

Mike puts the box on the bench and motions me over. He's conspiratorial. "Fell out of a tree last night on the Rez." I knew he'd gone home overnight to see his folks on the reserve. His mum needed some support.

He starts to pry up a corner of the carton; I hear some scratching inside. He slips his hand under the lip, fishes about and withdraws a really ugly little chick in his hand. Sensing that I'm under-awed he stage-whispers, "It's a baby hawk, stupid." I look more closely. Is he shitting me?

"Mike, what are you going to do with it?"

He doesn't say, "We, honky," but I can tell he's thinking it.

"Go in the store and buy something for it to eat. We're gonna raise a killer."

Jeez, now I gotta go in the marina store and skulk around under big Edna's X-ray vision. She'll be right up front, a huge lump in a bright dress, sitting behind the cash. I pass her by and go to the back of the store where they shelve the pet food. I don't know what hawks eat but I figure this one's gonna be a pet so that's how it'll eat. I chose a flat can with cute kittens on it. They've got pink ribbons around their scrawny, fluffy necks. Edna's watching me.

"What you boys up to?"

"Nothing much. Changin' the plugs on the Simpson's motor." I add that so it'll sound like work.

"You gotta pay for that," she says beady-eyeing the kitty can. "I don't want no cats peeing in the store. You better give 'em away or drown 'em."

I slap down a dime and she sweeps it into the till and looks out the window toward the gas dock where I'm s'posed to be.

I go out to the motor shed where Mike pries open the can lid with a screwdriver. He takes the spark plug gap gauge off the bench and uses a flat feeler to spoon out some food. The little chick that's been squawking up till now clamps its beak shut. It's not gonna eat this shit.

"Go get something else!"

"Jeez Mike that tin cost a fucking dime. You give me the money."

So for much of the day, between customers' boats, we tried feeding that little-squawky-bitty-thing different stuff so it could get big and vengeful.

Nothing.

Edna's eagle-eyeing us but says dick-all. We're blowing all our beer money on different tins — tuna, cat and dog, even those teeny cocktail weenies. Ugly little head always turns away. Edna's moving the merchandise so she don't care. She likes getting the money back that she give us — we're the day's big customers. She still doesn't know yet what we got.

On toward five o'clock I got sent back into the store — remember Mike's older than me — to try one more thing before going home. Only thing left is something called Devilled Ham. Turns out that the little bugger loves it. Now what we gonna do? This is the smallest tin in the store and the most dear. We got stuck with some sort of elite hawk.

Next morning when Mike and I get in and check the box on the bench Edna shows up in that dirty shed. She knows a baby hawk from a chicken — she's more Native than Mike who's only a 50-percenter.

"I can order a case for you boys. Save you some money."

We're committed now — up to our eyeballs in hawk shit. We say yes if we can we pay on time.

That little bugger grew real fast. I got in one morning and

Mike was banging up a perch for it — put it between the store and the shed for our baby's future. It wasn't long before that bird was using it to supervise our work out on the gas dock. And customers were coming to admire the hawk what didn't fly away. It was only nearly a lifetime later that I learned about hoods, jesses, creances, bells and bewits — all those falconer's fancy terms. I didn't even know that raptor meant robber even though I was taking Latin at school.

Once *hawk* could fly it got interesting. When we were coming in to the marina he'd fly out to escort us in. He'd also send us off at night. Soon he gave us rewards. When the big American cruisers came in for a final fill-up before off-shoring it to Killarney they'd see Mike or me with *hawk* on a shoulder running the gas pump. They'd pay us to pose for a picture — two Native guys with their pet eagle. You'd think they'd know from their own propaganda that *hawk* was no bald eagle and I was just a Scots/Irish Canadian choirboy but they didn't. I thought they were dumb racists but took the money anyway. *Hawk* had to eat and we needed beer. Come summer's end Mike took *hawk* back to the reserve where he'd have more authority and could be his self.

———

A column of Canada geese has been solemnly cruising down the inlet for weeks. They debuted as a family of six — four goslings steaming tandem between their parents. Every week or so the parade shortens as predators and disease take out the young. Only a week ago the parents were protecting a single gosling. Today the elders swim by alone. A season has been lost.

1964

Students always need money. While my fellow undergrads drive cab, wait or wash dishes, I work as a pair of eyes. On Huron Street, near the university, an old Chinese Canadian, Mr. King, runs an entertainment service from the living room of a Victorian semi. He books singers, dancers, musicians, comedians, magicians and jugglers for conferences, conventions and corporate parties. He manages to run a successful business despite being totally blind. I've been called over on this wet November evening to accompany him to the Imperial Room of the Royal York. He's booked a new act.

We've phoned Co-op Cab — he's a socialist. I help him into his coat and guide him to the door. I pop his umbrella and help him down a set of slippery, foot-worn wooden steps and out to the curb and the cab. This is reversed at the hotel. Once we're in the Imperial Room we stand together at the back of the hall. When his act comes on he leans toward me.

"Is the lighting nice?"

"Yes, they've got a blue spot on her."

"Is she attractive?"

"Yes, Mr. King. She's a redhead with a full figure. She's striking."

"Big boobs?"

"Looks like it."

"What's her dress like? Respectable? It's not too low at the top is it?"

"No, Mr. King. It's right up to her neck," I lied. "It's dark blue with sparkles."

He relaxes a bit and listens to her sing.

"Are people watching? Can you tell if they like her? It's very quiet."

"That's because they're all listening. Don't worry, they're paying attention."

Applause.

I guide King to the washroom then find a few of his friends for him. Soon I'm back describing the rest of his acts. He wants to know every detail of their dress, their presentation and reception. He requests an exhaustive description of the room. This job is teaching me to be visually alert, choose my words carefully and be a storyteller.

At 5 p.m. every weekday I trudged across King's College Circle to my undergraduate job at the main University of Toronto library. We were a group of perhaps a dozen students and indigent scholars who convened every evening to enter new acquisitions into the cataloguing system. As it was the mid-1960s the system was still based on paper file cards that required accurate sequencing in banks of varnished hardwood drawers. We filed in many languages including Mandarin, Greek and Arabic. There were also three different cataloging systems at play — the Library of Congress, Dewey Decimal system and a unique U of T system left over from the Upper Paleolithic. It was a nightmare.

The group was entirely female but for two males, me and a garrulous Eastern European, middle-aged scholar named Dr. D. Upon arrival each night we were each given a stack of cards to file. The women flicked through the files efficiently — it was like knitting — while Dr. D. and I bumbled through the various languages and systems. We always finished last, me due to basic incompetence and Dr. D. because he was always distracting the group with lectures on the glories of Hungarian history and culture. It seemed that all human advances, from agriculture and animal husbandry through writing and rocketry, were the invention of Hungarians. The Greeks, Romans, Incas and Aztecs, Brits and Americans were all brainless slackers. No Hungary, no civilization.

While I daily distinguished myself by being last to the last card, I soon discovered that this job also helped me to be first. After a year of filing I understood how the system worked far better than any of my fellow graduate students. I could research in circles around all of them. And I did.

A final thing. One of the attractive female filers had a most curious name — Felicity Pickup — delightful but I never did.

Filing cards in a paper card catalogue is now an obsolete skill, one of many jobs victimized by technology in my lifetime. When I worked one summer in my grandfather's cigarette company there was a guy in a suit who once a week toured the offices disassembling the big black telephone handsets in order to disinfect them. That was his profession — telephone disinfector. He's gone as are the blacksmiths I used to visit, the bell-ringing gypsy knife-sharpeners, boat caulkers, gas pumpers, typewriter repairmen, X-ray shoe fitters, elevator operators, locomotive firemen, gandy dancers, whistle punks (I've been one) and bromide men — the guys who worked the big commercial black-and-white darkrooms. These old jobs shaped the cityscape. In the west end of Toronto, between College and Davenport around Dufferin, the late 19th century city maps reveal that narrow, block-long buildings used to occupy the lands that are now back alleys. They were rope-making sheds where workers did Maypole-like dances up the blocks pulling hemp strands. I'm sure it was hard work but the idea is beautiful.

FOUR

THE DISCOVERY
OF PHOTOGRAPHY

"A photograph is a secret about a secret."
DIANE ARBUS

*"Photography fascinates the greatest minds and
yet can be carried out by any fool."*
NADAR

In 1952 I was given a Kodak box camera for Christmas. It
had two viewfinders, one for taking vertical photographs and
a second on the side for horizontals, like landscapes. The lens
board had a vaguely Art Deco design screened in black on its
nickel-plate face. The balance of this primitive machine was
covered in black simulated leather. A small red window at the
rear allowed you to see the frame numbers printed on the 620
film's backing paper as it scrolled through. With its fixed focus
lens and lack of any shutter or aperture controls it was as basic
as a working camera could get. I loved it.

For a reason known at the time only to my nine-year-old
mind I decided that my first picture would be of my father. As it
was too dark inside for my slow lens and film we had to go out
for this freighted portrait session. I say "freighted" for a reason.
My father, a man never easy with his family, himself or even
the world, didn't want to pose. My mother fetched his long
dark wool coat and fedora and pleaded with him to indulge me.
It was also freighted because years later that first photograph
became the most troubled photograph I ever made.

We stepped out into the tarnished pewter light of an overcast December. A cold and hostile wind tore at our coats. He stood on our gravel drive and I framed him between our brand-new yellow brick house and the Beaver Lumber kit garage that he'd erected that fall. That house was just an 18-month stopgap while he found a location for his new business. He hated the house, the raw postwar development it was in and the future Toronto suburb to which it was attached.

My naive, full-length portrait of a gray man on a gray day in a dark coat under a shadowy fedora proved to be a transparent witness to his deep unease and unhappiness at that time. His ambivalence about his life was reflected in his face. Each side was different. Two people were struggling behind it. The women of the family all remarked on it in whispers.

He knew it too so when years later I used it as a component of a new image he hired a lawyer and threatened to sue me even though only five people in the world — his immediate family — knew the image was of him. The reborn photograph became part of a widely toured one-man show, it entered the collections of several museums here and in Europe and, worst of all, became the cover of a very successful American rock album. It was suddenly everywhere, even life-sized, in London and New York record store windows. It was another lesson in the potential power of a photograph.

———

I'm awakened at first light. It's barely past five and already everybody's at work. A beaver pair churn around an abandoned dock behind the cabin, assessing its potential as the basement for new lodgings. Twenty feet away a hooded merganser protests, a heron lumbers overhead and a merlin shrieks. But none of these creatures is the reason I'm awake. As usual I've slept

with the exterior door by my bed wide open. Only a
light frame and screen separate me from the world of
the woods with its many smells and voices. One of
them has pulled me from sleep — a large and glossy
black bear. It calmly eyes me as it chews its way
through the only small tree between me and the water.
I grab a camera as I rise and quietly open the screen.
The bear shows me its backside as it casually saunters
away becoming a black hole in the landscape.

Think about how radical photography is. You point a small
black box at the subject of interest and the appearance of that
moment is instantly preserved in time. Without the photograph
one's memory may eventually drizzle the event with maple syrup
or smear it with shit. However, the photograph can stand as
memory's rebuke and corrective. You recall graduation as happy
and heroic but the photograph shows someone looking rumpled and insecure. The new car you were so proud of now looks
primitive and stupid. Myth and memory are skewered by fact.
    The California photographer Edward Weston believed that
photography was basically an honest medium. Hard work and
devious ingenuity were required to make it lie. Weston's position reflected the medium's analogue period. Digital imaging
has made that assertion much easier to challenge, not only
because of the ease with which pixels can be manipulated in
post but also because of the very nature of image capture in a
digital age. The process involves considerable extrapolation.
You might liken the lens-based image captured on a digital
array to a sketch on a napkin. That sketch is then processed
and interpreted by embedded software that "guesses" what
probably happens between the recorded pixels and then fills
in those spaces to construct the much larger file recorded on
flash memory. As a result, a significant portion of a digital

photograph is made up, is guesswork, is actually a fiction. In any other medium this level of evidence tinkering would never be accepted in court.

———

Several bass boats mutter past my island. Their occupants hunch over the screens on their electronic fish finders. Little pixelated fish symbols hover as the Bay's jagged bottom scrolls by. This is their reality: cartoon fish, a graphic bottom, not the freshet rippling the water, the screech of gulls or the intense blue of the sky. We inhabit a world of symbols and images.

Photography just *had* to be. For centuries Europeans had been toying with simple imaging devices like the pinhole-based *camera obscura*. Rival devices such as the *camera lucida* employing mirrors or prisms were soon developed and in time lenses replaced the original's pinhole thus dramatically improving the sharpness and brightness of the *camera obscura* image. However all of these instruments simply projected what was before them as ephemera. They could not freeze and fix the image. The "gentlemen" who tripped out across Europe to record the sights with these gizmos were limited to using them as a drawing aid. They weren't yet photographers: they were tracers and copyists.

When Fox Talbot, the future English co-inventor of photography, took a *camera lucida* to Italy in 1833 he described his experience with that instrument: "For when the eye was removed from the prism — in which all looked beautiful — I found that the faithless pencil had only left traces on the paper melancholy to behold."

Many tried to directly fix what Talbot called "fairy pictures, creations of the moment and destined as rapidly to fade away." By the 18th century it was well understood that certain materials, especially silver salts, responded to the light of the sun. However the images captured using them were as evanescent as a passing bird. By late in that century the race to cage that bird was on — Western culture needed and demanded it. How else could we record the developing individualism within the masses, market the products of the industrial revolution or celebrate foreign conquests and globe-spanning empires? Advancing science and increasing materialism required the visual exactitude that only photography could provide.

Curious and inventive minds, like the son of English potter Josiah Wedgwood, came close in the late 18th century, but, as far as we know, the earliest surviving photograph was made by France's Nicéphore Niépce in the mid-1820s although he claimed to have fixed an image as early as 1816.

As with any urgent idea whose time had come there were simultaneous inventors in many places. Aside from Niépce's work at Chalon-sur-Saône, the Parisians Hippolyte Bayard, a civil servant, and the showman Louis-Jacques-Mandé Daguerre both developed their own successful photographic processes. Bayard's direct positive method was a paper-based system as was Talbot's contemporaneous but negative-based process in England. There were even successful experiments as far away as Brazil.

However, the first practical photographic technology was Daguerre's. Announced in 1839, the daguerreotype consisted of a silvered copper plate developed in mercury. It was, in Oliver Wendell Holmes's beautiful phrase, "a mirror with a memory." Instantly embraced, it was just what Western culture had been waiting for. Now that the mirror's memory had been fixed, we could accurately record and inventory the world around us. The new technology quickly jumped the English Channel and, a heartbeat later, crossed the Atlantic.

It was a wonder; it was transformative; it destroyed myths; it changed everything. It was the perfect visual technology for an age of imperialism. We could now take possession. To photograph something was to master it. At last we knew.

By the mid-19th century practical improvements to the medium allowed it to go on a tear and nobody embraced the new medium like Americans. An estimated 30 million photographs were made there between 1840 and 1860. As might be expected in the land of extreme individualism, 95 percent of those images were portraits. But photographers also set out across the globe to record the world's wonders. And the world has never been the same since. Truly.

Photography was the perfect image-maker for the New World because it was free of history. The many visual traditions that dogged European painters of landscapes, the *nature morte* or the portrait didn't have the same hold on photographers. While traces of those traditions clung to the work of many picture-takers, on the whole it was a fresh medium that encouraged new ways of seeing. Cameras encouraged viewing from new angles — from below, from above, even within. And the edges and corners of photographs seemed to almost arbitrarily slice through objects in a way that was foreign to pictorial traditions but soon came to be liberating. Photography and photographers have also enlarged our sense of what is significant and what is beautiful to now include: crushed cans, cigarette butts, industrial units and even the dead. The medium also allows us to edit the world, to break it down into manageable pieces that can be possessed and controlled.

Western culture was the perfect incubator for a medium like photography. A culture that fostered literacy conditioned people to privilege the eye as the main sense organ for interpreting the world. Some cultures and many animals rely on the nose, the ear or touch. And a culture that had laboured long and hard to perfect the clock so that time could be subdivided and measured set the stage for a medium that could arrest it. Moreover, a culture that was busy mechanizing and industrializing what had traditionally been the work of the hand both needed and was prepared for a medium that automated picture-making. It made perfect sense that France, and especially England, were the cradles of photography.

The relationship to time and the recording of the moment created images that were unprecedented. The new medium created a revolution for the eye. Vision was disrupted and industrialized. American photographs of the Civil War showed the true face of battle — the muddy disorder, the ugly banality of death, the pointless destruction. The myths and heroics of painters were hooked off the stage. Reality was thrown in the face of myth.

1968

As a graduate student in anthropology during the late '60s I just accepted the poorly printed, journeyman photographs that illustrated ethnographic and archaeological reports. However, one day while leafing through a well-known Meso-American archaeologist's report on the ancient city of Teotihuacan outside Mexico City, I turned a page to a photograph he'd made of the so-called Pyramid of the Sun. I'd seen photographs of it many times before but this one was different. Although not a photographer, he had the benefit of decades of work in its shadow. He'd ascended it many times and viscerally understood its mass, how high and steep it was. And through archaeology he'd deepened his knowledge of its builders. Consequently, his photograph of it managed, without the crutch of dramatic lighting or tricky perspective, to give it a presence that I'd never experienced before. It was enormous, it was the culmination of the tremendous effort of a people. It confirmed power and faith. It was so *there*, so *present*, so *incredible*. It was not just a pile of rock. It *was* belief.

I was all too familiar with the way the painters in my family enhanced the presence of their subjects by altering the position of elements in the scene before them and by concentrating on details of the central subject in their paintings. But I'd never seen this done in an apparently mechanical and indifferent medium such as photography. The decisions that archaeologist had made while taking the picture were subtle but revelatory. I'm sure that many photographs he made during decades of field seasons had informed this final triumphant vision of this ancient culture's greatest monumental achievement. He'd managed to distill all his knowledge and experience into a single revelatory photograph. It was unforgettable. I began to get more curious about the medium.

The camera imposes a vanishing point perspective on vision that isn't necessarily cognate with our experience of the world as we move through it. This becomes obvious when one reflects on all the global cultures, past and present, which ignored or failed to develop perspective in their visual arts. The Paleolithic cave painter clearly didn't experience space like Canaletto. He saw game, he saw the hunter but not the mountain, valley or plain. They were incidental, non-essential, irrelevant and hence effectively invisible so they weren't rendered.

Photography caught me by surprise. Picture making was almost a family business. My mother's businessman father had been an accomplished Sunday painter, friend of A.Y. Jackson and, at one time, employer of Casson. Two of his daughters, my mother and her younger sister Barbara, graduated from the Ontario College of Art in the early 1940s. My mother painted and taught art her whole life while her sister Barbara became an art teacher at Central Tech and longtime Arctic travelling companion of painter Doris McCarthy. Even my sister became an artist and teacher.

When I began exploring with a camera in the early '70s it became a way of escaping the self and embracing the outside. Freed, in a sense, from myself, I could engage with the world and connect with my fellow human beings. Many beginning photographers find it difficult to photograph people on the streets. They fear confrontations, a fist in the face. Street photography is perfectly legal but invasive. In order to get over this anxiety I devised an exercise for myself. I borrowed a wide-angle lens for the Pentax I then had and walked early one morning to the Royal York Hotel in downtown Toronto. At the west end of the hotel there's a revolving door through which patrons exited to get a cab or board a bus for the airport. I positioned myself right in front of it so that the doors filled my viewfinder — very close. For an entire day I remained in that spot. I photographed every single person who emerged from the hotel.

By day's end only one individual, a businessman rushing with a briefcase, had questioned what I was doing. I briefly explained my exercise: he shrugged, got on the airport bus and disappeared. I had learned how to be confident but non-threatening. Over the next four decades I photographed politicians, business leaders, revolutionaries, soldiers, famous writers, actors, athletes, musicians, artists, heroes and criminals without incident. The only people who could never handle it were cops.

My next confrontation was over 40 years later in Kensington Market. I had staked out a position at a key intersection of the market and was photographing faces on the street with a very long lens. If people seemed disturbed, turned away or covered their faces I lowered the camera and let them pass. A corner coffee shop there had seats in the window. A half-dozen rough-looking guys sat watching me while they nursed their coffees. As I could see them getting agitated I avoided pointing the lens in their direction. Nevertheless I could sense that they were working themselves up. Finally the woman who owned the shop came toward me screaming. What was I doing photographing people without their permission? Those weaselly window guys didn't have the guts to confront me and make their own trouble — they got this woman to do it.

Faces on the streets of Toronto's Kensington Market

I still take photographs nearly every day but seldom carry a camera everywhere. Not only does the staggering volume of images one can generate with a digital camera become unmanageable but the camera and its viewfinder/screen eventually becomes an interface that can distance one from the world. It's like an earbud for the eye. And drive-by shooting rarely yields anything more than anecdotes and fleeting curiosities. It takes greater planning and intention to make an enduring photograph. Most great photographers' life's work can be summarized in a score of images — or less. Making a memorable photograph, one that engages a number of people over time, is very difficult. It takes years. It rarely happens.

———

This is a morning of flying fours. As I watch four elegant terns circle and dive I realize that four Canada geese are paddling single file westbound beneath them down the inlet toward the open Bay. Then a low chortling makes me look up from the water and I watch four sandhill cranes fly across the inlet toward me. They pass directly overhead: their calls have been echoing across this planet since the Pliocene. They are the most ancient and beautiful of birds. Their survival is both a miracle and a mystery.

At the very heart of photography there is a mystery, not just the old magic of silver nitrate responding to light — although that is seductive enough — but also a photograph's function as memory, as a marker in time. The decision to press the shutter release can be as important a marker as the resultant image itself. Without doubt most images that result from that act, especially in the digital age, are never looked at again. It was the act of taking the picture that was important. The taker is like a dog pissing on a tree, staking out territory, taking possession of place and time to declare *you are my lover, these are my children, my house, my car, my life. I saw. This was, I am.*

There are also temporal and spatial mysteries. What happened just before and after the picture taking? Whose hand is that on the frame's edge? Whose boot is at the bottom? What took place behind the photographer? Why record this subject at all?

Students frequently get stuck and take the same photos repeatedly. Whenever this happened while I was teaching at Banff we would often grab a student about to make a picture and turn them 180 degrees before they made their exposure. It was a good habit breaker and occasionally it was revelatory.

———

I just want this evening in Georgian Bay to go forever — the soft warm wind sighing through the pines, a burble of small waves, a distant whippoorwill and Bill Frisell's *Good Dog, Happy Man.* Solitude.

A photo supply salesman enters my studio with a delivery and looks around. When he spots two large Infinity speakers hanging on either side of the set he remarks that every busy photographic studio that he's ever been in has a great sound system. It's true. And the intense connection between photography, photographers and music is one of the medium's many mysteries. Surely one reason is that both are time-based media — music deals in time's flow while photography is based on arresting it. Music gives photographers some continuity.

Ansel Adams played piano and dreamed of being a concert pianist. Aaron Siskind played violin, Lee Friedlander has long been passionate about jazz and gospel and made photographs about Charles Ives and New Orleans funeral bands. The Canadian painter Charles Gagnon, who also took many photographs, had a recording studio. Geoffrey James plays jazz trumpet. Another photographic friend played both cello and piano. Arnaud Maggs, who loved jazz, designed the original cover for *Jazz at Massey Hall* and made a large photo piece about all the jazz albums on the Prestige label and another based on the Köchel catalogue numbers of Mozart's compositions. Maggs once told me about taking a piece he'd written to Oscar Peterson and his band at a club in Montreal. Peterson was gracious but his band started to play Arnaud's piece in such a way as to gently show him how derivative and banal it was. Arnaud went back to graphic design and photography.

The great Czech photographer Josef Sudek would exclaim, "*A hudbe hraje* . . ." ("And the music plays . . .") from under his dark cloth whenever he felt he was making a great negative. And nothing has given me more pleasure than working my way through a large orchestra in rehearsal to make photographs.

When various members of the Toronto Symphony asked me to photograph them in Vienna's Musikverein during a tour I didn't have a large enough format camera to ensure that all 100 or so players would be identifiable. I borrowed one from a string player in the band and had the larger format film shipped in from my supplier in Frankfurt. So it goes both ways.

My island is little more than a rock. At 0.374 acres it is much smaller than the islands 20 miles to the south that I inherited from my mother's family. Down there I had a hundred-year-old cedar board and batten cottage with three bedrooms and a big stone fireplace in the living room. The building huddled on the east end

The TSO in the Golden Hall at Vienna's Musikverein, photographed with a borrowed camera

of a four-acre island — early summer people had seen
the west wind and open water as a threat. The island
had never been logged so the white pines of its interior
were majestic. Perhaps once a year I'd scrabble my
way around the island getting scratched by junipers
of the understorey. It took me years to realize that I
didn't need to own all that land. I really only dwelt
on the point where the building sat. There was also
a big uninhabited island immediately south. I owned
several acres of it as well. It was famous for its blue-
berries and rattlesnakes. I didn't need to own it either.
I picked berries there once a year, usually to the protests of my American co-owners who would leap into
their boats and run over to tell me to get off. For me
they were foreigners kicking me off my own land. For
them there were no borders. They owned the world.

So I sold the family place to a friend and eventually gave my part of the second island to a charitable
land trust. Now its snakes could live in permanent

peace and I sought refuge farther north where there were few people and even fewer boats.

I'm now the custodian of less than half an acre but have a much more intimate relationship with it. The tiny pockets of soil in its declivities support one alder, three white birches, 22 cedars, 26 white pines and one jack. I know every one of them and can look after their welfare. The shoreline is barely a dozen feet from the lip of my big screen porch. I know it intimately too. Now, after many successive years of low water, the level has risen a couple of feet and presented a new coast. Not only is its contour different but so is its music. I knew well the songs of the waves when they reached my small shore. This year they're all different as they break on new mini headlands and curl in different hollows. It's a whole new songbook.

2000

The Austrian cellist Clemens Hagen and I are stuck at the back of the bus. We're racing with the Toronto Symphony Orchestra from concert hall to hall across western Europe — Germany, Hungary, and his Austria. At every stop I have the wincing experience of following him as he crashes his Stradivarius cello down the bus steps in a plastic case. Here is a guy who plays beautifully but is seemingly indifferent to the noisy beating he gives his instrument at each disembarkation.

Great musicians can be incredibly narrow in their perceptions and appreciations. Their skills have demanded such unrelenting focus since childhood on the development of a small set of finger, tongue, lip and lung skills that they can be very underdeveloped in other areas — they've had no time. In Budapest I made a portrait of Clemens playing that members

Clemens Hagen, cellist

of the TSO administration thought wonderful. When Clemens saw it he was completely indifferent. He was all ear, not eyes.

And similarly photography isolates sight from all the other senses.

1984

It's five a.m. on a February morning. I've just spent a night on the ground a few hundred feet from the Honduras border. The high buzz of insects has tensioned the tropical night as rats run over us as we try to sleep. The several hundred Sandinista soldiers lying around me are getting up and preparing for a firefight in which some of them will die. Many of them are still in their teens. I rise, load a half-dozen Hasselblad magazines, and begin prowling through our camp taking photographs. The men briefly face me, their minds focused on the perils just minutes into the future as the sun climbs to illuminate a soon slaughter.

I work, totally focused on the moment and the men. The world seems trapped in ice as I make pictures for precious minutes before the commanders call and the troops form units that quickly slip off into the bush. When I'm left alone in the camp the world suddenly rushes back in like a breaking wave — smells, rushing sounds, transforming sights. It is no longer suspended in secret silence. It breathes, sighs, sings and moves. Touch returns. I'm no longer a mono-sensed photographer, both celebrant and prisoner of the eye, but a medium-sized mammal swimming in a complex sensual surround — immersed, buried, overwhelmed by the business of the world. All my senses are now awake.

The hunter in a preliterate culture lives in a rich, multi-signal, synaesthetic sensorium. He makes his way through the forest keenly aware of sound, smell, temperature and air movement in addition to sight. All his senses are fully developed and on high alert — operating in concert. But we have learned to fragment and isolate our senses. When fully engaged in making a photograph I've always been conscious of senses dropping away as I slipped into a space that's purely visual. It's like being an athlete or performer entering the "zone."

I still have a basement full of enlargers and darkroom gear. There's also a cupboard-load of film camera bodies and negative files to remind me of the shift from analogue to digital. Like many older photographers I half miss the dim rooms with amber light, the sound of gently burbling water and the image slowly swimming up — unforgettable! A certain alchemy is forever gone with digital. Not only are the fluid sounds gone but so are the smells of stop and hypo and the tactile tooth of photo papers. All are superfluous, superseded and superannuated along with obscure skills like feeling for sheet film code notches in the dark and spooling fragile film blind onto reels for processing. The romance of process is gone as well as a certain magic. Now only the eye is triumphant.

Originally photography had, in a sense, a foot in magic. Daguerre, the Parisian who gave the world the first mass photographic process, was a showman in the business of large public illusions. His dioramas wrapped his audiences in evolving, fantastic landscapes. It was theatre with elaborate sets but no actors. He thought a perfected photography would be an aid in their production.

With each technological change there are losses and gains. In a crude way digital has restored the old view camera experience of the world swirling with life on the camera's ground glass. The new cameras' small screens don't have the mystery of image being reversed right to left and upside down or the theatre of the dark cloth over the head, but they do give a sense of what the world made flat in a picture is going to look like.

My many long assignment flights up the spine of the Americas, across the Atlantic or the long Pacific grind home from Asia were returns to a great unknown. Had your eyes been acute, fingers fast, your meters accurate and had the film moved through the gate? Would there be static flashes from the arctic cold, film fog from aggressive airport X-rays or degradation from the heat? To return to YYZ was to pace exhausted in a lab while your stock was dipped and dunked or roller transported through the soup. And then the final hunch over a light table louping dozens of processed rolls and sheets for dirt, scratches and careless focus. Did you have the shoot?

Digital removed all this. The fast feedback allowed more focus on the idea and the purely visual. It accelerated one's development as an image-maker as one could refine one's approach shot by shot rather than shoot by shoot. It permitted risk as failed exposures no longer meant successive dollar bills cranked through the camera back by a motor drive. Now there were few costs. And it was also easier on the back as there was less to carry. A bag of loaded 4x5 sheet film holders weighs a thousand times more than an SD card and stores less information. A hard drive can store hundreds of fat albums. The packs of light balancing gel filters have been replaced by the white balance button. Overall, there is less stuff, fewer consumables and poisons.

Many had gotten sick in the darkrooms of the world — weird cancers and respiratory inflammations. We were all playing with acids and heavy metals so this was predictable. While I needed the observational discipline imposed by photography as I moved about the world it was severely limited by the demands of the darkroom. The world roared by outside the dark door while one was agitating film, rocking trays and pouring toxins down drains. Analogue did have the advantage of being physical and tactile — burning and dodging by hand, chemical mixing, tray rocking and interleaving the wash. Now photographers stare at computer screens. This too is isolating but less alienating. There is light, people pass by and the big world flirts just beyond the window. Today digital's wastes kill electronics recyclers in China rather than here. We've off-shored the poisonings.

However, the computer and the various image processing and manipulation programs developed for it have led to a lot of over-processed imagery — too much total contrast, too edge-enhanced, oversaturated and too cleaned up. Honest images of the world's wonderful messiness are being rendered down into tidy graphics. This impoverishes our experience of the world and makes us less capable of dealing with its complexities. The quiet, disordered beauty of the world is being superseded by contrivances that shout. These screeching, supersaturated pictures tire the eye.

Our burden as a species is our big brain and too much consciousness. We are astonished by our existence and the world's but also know we are going to die. Our family histories tell us it will be at 45, 60 or a decade later or more or less. Both my parents went at 81 so there is a good probability I will leave the building then too. Now 71, I can reasonably count on a decade — 3,600 or so mornings filling my espresso machine, checking email, phoning friends, doing the dishes, planning for my 10th last summer, making pictures and procrastinating. Here lies one of the miracles of photography. Every photograph of me answers an "Am I?" with an "I am!" And every photograph I take is an affirmation of being, of both myself and my subject and our world. The release of the shutter is an existential act.

———

The wind sifts through the pines hissing like poured sugar.

I love this landscape but I can't photograph it. This is probably for the simple reason that it's been the great constant in my life since childhood. I don't have the need. I *know* it.

Yet another photographer colleague has invited me to help select his work for a show. This always dismays me: it seems essential if one is to claim to be an artist in the medium of photography that one be capable of confidently editing one's own work. We are not painters or sculptors or writers, people who manually create their statements: instead we do it by machine. The art is in the selection — from the moment one interrupts the flow of time with a shutter while choosing a tiny rectangle from the great dome of physical reality that surrounds us. This act is an edit and editing is all that we've got. If you can't do that from the first step on through to selecting from contact sheets or digital files then your status as an artist is seriously diminished. It's as if you don't recognize your own themes, your own take on the world and experience. It's the edit that clarifies what your work is about. Without that you have little to contribute. You are a cameraman, not an artist.

———

I carefully walked my 0.34 acres this early July morning and counted 29 different species in bloom. They range from chives, bluebells and a pair of orange poppies that have reseeded annually since a planting over a decade ago to the balance which are wild and indigenous — white and purple iris, columbines, daisies.

1979

We're gathered in a classroom at Banff. I'm trying to teach about 20 photographers for the summer. Most of them are recent grads from art schools right across the country. They're smart, ambitious and arrogant. Each morning we gather to discuss one another's work. Generally the women take photographs with traditional female themes — children, gardens, domestic life and portraits. However their takes on these subjects can be quite fresh and arresting. Today the presenters are all guys. They've been out photographing the mountains and their pictures are terrible. At best they look like postcards — scenic, remote and affectless. The women stare at these pictures in silence. They are utterly unmoved as am I. These images are dead.

As I begin to talk about them I start to get a notion of what has gone wrong. I began showing them photographs made by the first photographers of the American West — Jackson, Weed, Muybridge and Watkins. Those 19th century men had ridden out on the new rails being driven through a raw landscape in quest of the Pacific. When the tracks ended somewhere on the

Great Plains or the Great Basin they got off and mounted horses or walked westward. It was hot, dry and dusty. They were thirsty and their legs ached and their feet hurt. If they decided to make a view from an eminence they climbed it on foot dragging huge view cameras and crates of glass plates up slope with them. Every plate was precious — making an exposure was a commitment to hours of darkroom work after all the gear had been lugged back down to safety. You didn't fool around.

Their pictures were terrific. The mountains and valleys had a gritty presence that took you right to them and held you there. These photographs were vivid and intelligent because their makers had a real body sense of just how desiccated it all was, how hot, how steep, how threatening and overwhelming. My 20th century students were driving along the Trans-Canada in air-conditioned cars, pulling over whenever they recognized a nice view. Their cameras had motor drives that pulled long rolls of film through the gate. They could expose now and think about it later. They were drive-by shooters. Their photographs were betrayed by inexperience. I told them to put on hiking boots. They told me they didn't have the time.

While retrieving my bags in the Calgary airport a few years later I discover that the big guy beside me has the same destination that I do — the art school at Banff. On the bus ride through the foothills I learn that Smith is there to teach paper-making while I'm to do the same for colour photography. At Banff I discover that the school's colour lab and darkrooms have not been replaced since a big fire several years earlier. Not only are there no photo facilities but there are also no photography students. And the handful of visual art students present have little interest in my medium. Rather than spend 10 days drinking beer while staring at Mount Rundle I elect to team up with the paper-maker.

We decide that any deficiencies of the Banff Centre will be overcome if the school's main staircase is enriched with a large mural created by both of us. As we set to work I soon realize that the paper guy is a much better long-term strategic thinker than me. The vast quantity of fibrous pulp required for this three-dimensional work of genius will be cotton. The cotton will be obtained by grinding up the jeans and shorts of consenting young women in the program and the coloured batches will be derived from their blouses and panties. This pulp will require screening in a large water bath. The school's Jacuzzi will suffice. Unfortunately one cannot enter this therapeutic pool with clothes on. We eagerly anticipated surmounting this limitation.

Much to my surprise a handful of beautiful young women agree to participate, no doubt figuring that we are just a pair of entertaining, but harmless, geezers — we are at least the age of their fathers. When the horrified administration discovers our plan we are banned from the Jacuzzi on the grounds that ground-up girl shorts will plug up the pool pumps. To ensure the administration that cotton pulp is harmless Smith enters the president's office and drinks an entire quart of watery panty pulp. The boss is too slack-jawed to say no.

To give our near-naked romp in the jet pool some current cultural cred we program Philip Glass's *Einstein on the Beach* over the centre's P.A. system. Then we jump in the pool with the girls and start screening. A few hours later we have produced a 10-foot-long abstraction, a lumpy hybrid of Frankenthaler, Rothko and de Kooning. It is so thick that it takes several days to dry. The night of the day it does we sneak a ladder into the staircase and install our masterpiece high overhead. It was still there the next day and the next and the day we both departed for Ontario. Its fate remains one of Canadian art history's great mysteries.

1979

When I was hired by the Ontario College of Art to teach students colour photography, I dove into the job but soon found it all a bit hopeless. The colour lab was equipped with the little plastic print-processing drums and plug-in rollers that were sold in photo hobby shops. This primitive gear didn't allow for the accurate temperature controls crucial for consistent results. Additionally the prints frequently emerged from the drums streaked and stained. The students were discouraged and demoralized. Another problem was that they worked in a historical vacuum. The library had few books on colour photography and no teaching slide sets. The students had no clue what serious photographers had done with the colour medium. There were no possibilities to show them and no tradition to build from.

I set about single-handedly and single-mindedly to address these deficiencies. As I had by then accumulated a studio stuffed with classic photographic monographs it was possible to address the school's image deficit. I began making teaching slides for my course by copying material from my books. However the print-making side of my classes was more problematic. There was no budget for the purchase of a professional processor. As I got more familiar with the institution I discovered that there was, however, a substantial budget for maintenance. My putting one and two together spanned the country.

I had recently taught for a summer at Banff. A few months after I returned to Toronto the building that housed the Banff Centre's colour lab had burned down. The head of the photography program, Hugh Hohn, had collared his staff in the middle of the night and they'd run into the burning building, disconnected all the cables and plumbing on the big Kreonite roller-transport, print processor and carried it, like pallbearers, out of the building. They staggered through the snow to an adjacent building and jammed it under a staircase. It sat there for months, homeless.

I got on the phone. Since the machine was orphaned and the photography program consequently suspended, could I make some arrangement to better shelter the precious machine? As the spring term drew to a close a deal was struck. The Banff Centre would lend the processor to OCA; OCA would use its maintenance budget to restore and repair it. I had almost solved the second of my big course dilemmas. Only a couple of thousand miles stood between the parts of my solution.

Once again I went tin-cupping to the OCA administration. If they would buy me a few tanks of gas I would drive my Chevy delivery van at term's end across the country to Banff and retrieve the Kreonite. I got the gas money.

The next phone call was to persuade my old friend Macbeth that a drive across Canada was the perfect tonic for his depression. I was very lucky that he agreed because he's the kind of guy you can stick in the driver's seat while you sleep for 10 hours knowing that you'll wake up far away from where you passed out. Anyone who has done that drive understands that half the trip is getting out of Ontario. As an Italian acquaintance who'd once come over from Rome to do that odyssey complained, it was a matter of a tree, a rock, a river, a lake and then another tree, rock, river and lake for hours and hours and days until the final release of the open prairie. He'd suffered acute spruce fatigue.

A meeting of the original Banff pallbearers was convened and beered. We gently grunted the big machine into my truck. It filled the entire space from the driver's seatback to the rear doors. I thought we'd lost our travel accommodations but there proved to be just enough top clearance to house a couple of occupied sleeping-bags — we were skinny guys then. The flat top of the processor became a double bed. We gassed up and set off for the East.

The program improved. However I was still stuck with a part-timer's Saturday class in addition to my degree-bound students. The weekend class was very difficult to teach. There were women in it who only wanted to photograph their kittens or do underwater shots of their synchronized swimming sessions. On the other hand there were a couple of people who had big view cameras, understood the Ansel Adams zone system and were seeking transcendence. One of them was the sophisticated head of an important publishing house. How can one be useful to such a diversity? I didn't want half the class to be taught up or down to while others were bored.

The classes for full-timers during the week were easier. My biggest challenge there was the latest tech toy from Japan — the Sony Walkman. Most students had one and so during the lecture portion of my classes I'd have to walk down the aisles plunking off headphones as I talked. *Sprong! Sprong!!* The worst offender, the self-proclaimed coolest guy in the whole school, ended up a server in a College Street restaurant.

1980

This year it's my turn to sit on the admissions committee at the Ontario College of Art. We convene in a large room with tables piled high with submissions from across Canada and the Caribbean. The latter are extremely difficult to assess. One is acutely conscious of the limited instruction they have had on their little island nations. How does one see past the basic and often obsolete exercises they have been given to some germ of talent?

This year the larger issue is the enormous number of applicants who want to become wildlife painters. The layperson often assumes that the essential prerequisite for success in the visual arts is something we call *skill*. In actual fact skill is all too common: it's original ideas and something we might call

63

vision that are rare. The tables before us are carpeted with skillful renderings of flora and fauna. These applicants have so much control over their pens and brushes that you can literally detect their source materials, their signature characteristics are so faithfully rendered. They usually work by projecting slides and copying them so faithfully that a photographer who really knows his materials can detect what type of film was used for the original source.

After reviewing so many dozens of these portfolios I begin to amuse myself by deconstructing the source imagery. So here we have a Kodachrome forest clearing in which an Ektachrome wolf stalks an Agfacolor deer. Every nuance of the grain structure of these emulsions along with their characteristic colour biases are reproduced in these paintings. It's quite mindless. Are these people artists, illustrators or copyists? Can these skills ever evolve into anything more than demonstrations of dexterity? The rendering talents of Frederick Verner, the 19th century Canadian painter of First Nations encampments and voyageurs running rapids devolved in the hands of his descendants into illustrations of dress shoes drawn for ads in Toronto newspapers. Do shoe artists, as they were known, deserve special nurturing by society? Is there any value in these skills in an age of photography? We're placing bets on the futures of these hopeful applicants and probably getting it wrong more often than right.

By my third year of teaching I'd had enough. I taught Thursdays through Saturdays. Inevitably I'd be finishing up some photo assignment in Vancouver, California or even Europe on a Wednesday night and realize I had to take a red-eye to Toronto to give a class the next day. I was enjoying one of those brief periods — they come and go — when I was the hot guy to art directors. I had lots of assignments and was being well paid whereas part-time college instructors are the gleaners of the academic world. They work very hard for a few droppings. When I looked around at the full-time faculty at the college they all seemed to be coasting downstream toward their pensions. I decided to freelance full-time and make whatever art I could in the interstices. I now had a wife and kids. I became a professional photo cowboy.

A sometime client had set me up with a new one who had a very special object to be photographed. I was sworn to secrecy until the job was over. Several days later a guy in a beautiful Italian suit rang my buzzer. He was hefting a very large aluminum portfolio case secured by numerous locks. Once inside, the door bolted by his request, he ceremoniously opened the huge flat case and revealed a large dark carefully packed grubby old cloth. I looked at this big mottled rag without comprehension. "What is it?" I asked.

"It's the Shroud of Turin. I need a good photograph of it — for postcards."

———

I kayak out through a back channel, round a small point and cut back in toward the mainland interior. It would appear to be an unpromising reedy back bay but I know its secret. It terminates in a wall of scrub where if you listen carefully you can hear water run. After grounding my boat I exit and hump it into the wall of scratchy bush and grass. In 30 feet I've climbed up 20 and can now see the curve of the hidden high beaver dam shouldering uncountable tons of water. There's a huge hidden lake up here, a score of feet above the Bay and dozens of acres in extent. It's not on any topo maps and doesn't really read in aerial photographs. It's another secret.

After re-launching the kayak from the dam's lip I begin to thread my way through the many small black water channels that lead to the open lake. The mossy hummocks that border these passageways are covered with rose pogonias, beautiful miniature pink orchids on half-foot slender stalks. There are many thousands of them lining my tannin-dark channel. Even when I cease paddling and coast, the boat glides too fast for me to see all that surrounds me. Once on the main body I make for the large island that crowns its centre and begin a watchful circumnavigation. Once this island was a heron rookery but the big birds were chased out a decade ago by a pair of biker bald eagles that began nesting atop the tallest pine at the island's far end. A hundred feet from that nest is a sentinel tree where the male runs guard duty. I want to see the male and stare contemptuously at its very ugly huge babies. I carefully round the far end, glide and surreptitiously glance up.

The trees are empty. The eagles have flown.

As analogue photography slips into the mists of history there are both gains and many losses. The beautifully machined bodies of Leicas, Hasselblads and Linhofs have been replaced by injection-molded plastics, leather by vinyl and exotic, even radioactive, glasses by coated crown glass or acrylic. A whole vocabulary, a nomenclature vanishes as well — contact sheet, pressure plate, darkroom, dark cloth, changing bag, safelight, push process, motor drive and so on. There are many more. We will never again develop, stop and fix our pictures. You can't wash and dry a pixel. And gone forever are the after-class, beer-soaked *sotto voce* conversations with your girl about the Scheimpflug correction.

Idling slowly under the bridge at the top of the river I'm down-bound for the Bay. Rounding the first river bend I feel watched. Forty feet up in a big pine two big-eyed horned owls glare down at a puny man in a tin boat. They remain immobile. I'm too large for lunch.

The old photography of plates and film had made off with many of our daylight hours. We laboured in darkrooms whose only poetry was the tinkle of wash water and the emerging image's sleight of hand. Meanwhile the world roared past outside the darkroom door. When the digital array finally freed us, photographers everywhere escaped blinking into the world's brilliance. We believed we'd been liberated from darkness only to discover that we'd all become office workers. We are now captives of the desk chair, the keyboard and a glowing screen.

I have five guests at the island. They sit — one man, four women — distributed along the 40-foot length in the cabin's main room in various chairs — pressbacks, wickers and a Mennonite bent-wood rocker. All are hunched silently over their devices, intent on tiny displays and touch screen keyboards, hour upon hour. Beyond the many-mullioned windows lies the world — roaring, singing, whispering, flashing, vibrating, scintillating, rippling, glowing, shimmering, radiating, beckoning and calling as they tap their keyboards, gone and oblivious.

Pewter sky with a pale blush descending to the treeline. I'm sitting on my big screen porch a dozen feet from the water's edge concentrating on the veils of sound hanging like successive flats on a barren stage. Near sound: water streaming off the roof and rattling on the hard gneiss of the Shield. Next the soft kiss of small waves driven by a freshet from the west. The following curtain is the sibilant wind through the pines with a faint dry crackle from the lone birch on my point some 40 feet away. And finally the ground bass of the big breakers on the foreshore a mile out to the west. All these curtains of sound interweave slowly with the wind, penetrating each other, changing places and perspective in an endless series of velvet variations. A round, guttural thunder enters as a refrain, calling up a new set of variations every few minutes or so.

They're a smart group of students — physicists from Chalk River, teachers from Sudbury, a clutch of alert and curious northerners and a few stragglers from the south. I'm to lead a two-week photography workshop, centered on a common assignment. The school, Canadore College in North Bay, has recently been given the decommissioned Bomarc missile base north of town. It still has its launch sheds, maintenance buildings and a structure designed to hold the guidance computer, a monster with vacuum tubes the size of garbage cans that had less computing power than a smart phone. The college had yet to figure out what to do with the whole installation.

But I have. It seems to me that this abandoned Cold War relic is the perfect subject for a class assignment. It's nearby, self-contained, and has an interesting history and freighted structures. When I announce the project to the students all hell breaks loose. "We didn't come here to get involved in politics!" screams one of the southern students. "I hate war!" shouts another. I guess students taking a summer course for their annual vacation don't want to think about realpolitik. They're here for Group of Seven picture fantasies. I back down but a few of the students, the smarter ones, pursue my suggested project anyway.

1972

The police in this Toronto neighbourhood pick up the local teenage boys, drive them down to Cherry Beach, beat them up and dump them. I've been told this repeatedly by local parents and now it's my turn. The cruiser has pulled up, blocking my view of the street and that of the houses across from it. I'm sitting on the curb this early Sunday morning, with both my Rolleiflexes on my lap as I spool fresh rolls of paper-backed film into them. I've been photographing for several weeks to illustrate a forthcoming book by journalist Graham Fraser on the Trefann Court urban renewal struggle. This low-income downtown neighbourhood lying largely between Queen Street East and Shuter Street east of Parliament, is threatened by urban renewal. The working-class residents of the many owner-occupied houses here don't want their houses razed and the neighbourhood flattened. They don't have much money but they do have a functioning community. They like it and are prepared to fight for it.

And they have allies. The local meetings I attend with my cameras are chaired by the likes of John Sewell and David Crombie. Both of these men will do stints as Toronto's mayor. But at the moment these cops are the issue in my life. They exit their car and tower over me asking aggressive questions and making crude insinuations. Knowing that what I'm doing is not only legal but supported by people more powerful than this pair of bullies I continue with my film change while quietly dealing with their abuse. There's always been a sizeable element of my city's police force that is out of control. There still is. As soon as you give guns and a certain authority to a group that is, by and large, lightly educated and trained, there are going to be control issues. I've always been struck by the quite extreme personality differences between the people who become firemen and those who go into police work. The firemen tend to be salt of-the-earth helping types; the police force seems to shelter many bitter, angry and aggressive personalities.

After a half hour of this interference I get to my feet and begin to walk away. When they demand to know what I think I'm doing I tell them I'm going to the phone booth down on Queen to call my friend David Crombie. They look at me, then at each other and silently decide I'm more trouble than I'm worth. They glare and drive away. This was not to be the last time.

———

When I awoke in the cabin this morning the world is gone. A paint-thick fog had rolled in the dark and "disappeared" the far shore, the islands between, even my point. Out on the front porch the night rain had left a million pearls and tiny lenses on the screens. The whole soundscape has changed as the mist greases the waves of sound. Far-off breaking waves are at my feet; birds sing in my head. The universe is once again made strange.

This is going to be a big photograph — a real mother of a picture. Toronto's Eaton Centre is nearing completion and retail tenants are preparing to move in. The provincial liquor board, the L.C.B.O., has leased a large space at the Dundas Street end of the block-long complex. It's one level below grade with an entrance presenting a long blank wall to the public area of the mall. I've been asked to come up with something to cover the wall. The architects are basically talking about custom wallpaper.

After making several presentations they chose my least interesting idea — a photograph of row upon row of stacked bonding barrels. I get on the phone to find a distillery that will admit me and a big view camera. Finally an old established one on the QEW freeway west of Toronto agrees to participate.

Before admitting me to the bonding warehouse they take me on a familiarization tour of the distillery. This may be a house of booze but the tour is sobering. We all believe that rye whiskey is made from rye, gin from juniper and vodka from potatoes. What really happens is that a long line of dump trucks from southern Ontario farms back up to the rear doors and unload tons of corn. A mixture of kernels, water and yeast fills up mash tanks and begins to bubble and ferment. This stinky mess is then boiled and a distillate collected. The resultant clear liquid, a mixture of alcohol and water is then pumped out through an overhead pipe. Before exiting the distilling area the pipe forks into five smaller ones. One goes into the vodka room, another the rye, the gin room and so on. In these rooms flavouring extracts are added and the finished product put in nice bottles with classy labels. It may all look different, taste different and have different names and reputation but it's all just hooch — corn liquor. This business is all mythology and marketing.

I make my exposures and then some large prints, which are mounted together in a long row on a heavy board. I hire an old photo retoucher from Toronto Island to disguise the seams and alter some barrel numbers so the repeats aren't evident. The whole mockup is then re-photographed with an ancient wooden 8x10 view camera to produce the enormous negative that will be projected onto a giant darkroom wall hung with rolls of black-and-white photo paper. The enlarger that does this work is yet another antique wooden 8x10 camera on rails.

The finished print is to cover a wall 10 feet high and a little over 40 feet long. Fortunately for me when I scout the site a construction foreman tells me that I should consider making the print somewhat oversize. How much? He says at least 10 percent. So I do. Installation is to take place overnight the day before the store is to open. When I arrive with a team of paper hangers and begin the midnight work I discover the wisdom of the foreman's advice. The Eaton Centre may look like a giant machine but it's not a precision one. The concrete floor at the foot of my wall is as irregular as the surface of a fast flowing stream. At some points in my 40 feet we have to trim off a foot of picture at the bottom; at others only the installation of baseboards hides the failure of my mural to reach the floor. The construction errors are staggering.

1973

One summer day I crossed Front Street on a whim and walked into the north building of the St. Lawrence Market. As it was Sunday, not a market day, the vegetables had been replaced by a miscellany masquerading as antiques. In the course of half-heartedly ambling around I suddenly spied stacks of photographs in a vintage bowed-glass display case. These cabinet cards, roughly 5 by 7 inches, were amazing. On one level they were typical New York studio portraits of the 1870s and '80s — the subject sat or stood before a painted backdrop accompanied by one or two overly elaborate pieces of Victorian furniture and an exotic plant in a pot. Every uptown photographer in Manhattan made similar portraits of local society types. But these were different. In place of a successful businessman or idle lunching lady was a giant, a dwarf, a fat lady, a naked obese man or an ethnic exotic. And there were rubber skin men, Siamese twins, a lobster boy, a lady with four legs. In short, all were freaks. The imprint on the base of these cards verified that they had all been made on the Bowery by the same photographer — Charles Eisenmann.

Who was this guy? I knew my 19th century American photography pretty well but I'd never heard of him. And who were these strange people? Were they real? Why had these portraits been made? Dry as dust histories of photography like Beaumont Newhall's failed to deal with vernacular images. They were predicated on a canon of waspy masterpieces. I couldn't get these images out of my mind. I wanted them. Their owner refused to sell. He enjoyed having people covet his stuff.

Over the next couple of years whenever I ran into that guy I bugged him to sell the collection. I couldn't tell you how many times I was rebuffed. Over time I gradually gave up but one day he called me. He'd recently bought a house in the Annex and in the course of preparing to move in had discovered that much of the plumbing was shot. He had to fix it or be homeless. He was out of money. If I paid the plumbing bill I could have the photographs, all 450 of them. I bought him his drains.

Over the next several years I spent my spare time obsessively researching that material. Slowly, in fits and starts, I figured out who Eisenmann had been and the identity of his sitters. It was a massive amount of work. This was before computers and the internet. Without any information online I had to drive to any place that could yield cues — New York, New Jersey, Illinois, Wisconsin and many points in between. I did. In time a publisher got interested and I had a contract and a year or so to assemble a manuscript. I set to work on it in my spare time.

Until one day the phone rang. It was my editor to be: she was totally wound up and screaming. It took me a few minutes to understand why she was so agitated. Virtually her entire list for the season had fallen apart and she had nothing to show her boss. Her solution was to bully me into finishing my manuscript in 90 days instead of a year. I can't deal with screamers so I caved.

A modest advance allowed me to decline photo assignments and concentrate on the project. I developed a routine. At the time I was living in a tiny winterized cottage on the Scarborough bluffs. I'd drive from there mid-morning to my downtown studio, make coffee and spend the next four or five hours reading through my notes for the next section of the book. I had shoeboxes of research notes on 3 by 5 index cards. By about six in the evening I'd have memorized the content of relevant cards and I'd go out to a local Chinese restaurant to have supper. More about that restaurant and its beautiful waitress later.

After dinner I'd return to my studio and write furiously for six or seven hours. By midnight or so I'd be exhausted and get in my car for the 45-minute drive back to the bluffs. Once there I'd be so wired I couldn't sleep. I'd pour a beer or a glass of wine, build a fire, put some music on the stereo and stand by the cottage's big picture window that gave on the lake. As the building perched precariously a mere 50 feet from the soft clay 200-foot drop to the water, the view was spectacular.

During that three-month period the music that helped me unwind and get to sleep became very important. I soon became addicted to a specific piece, Steve Reich's *Music for 18 Musicians*. It was then a relatively recent piece of minimalist music with a repetitive and overlapping structure that slowly built in complexity and then gradually unraveled itself. It was music to program your brain. I must have listened to that 50-odd-minute-long piece several hundred times while working on the book and waiting for the next call from the screaming editor. I finished the book.

So my supper "dates" with the beautiful Chinese waitress were also finished. I missed her grinning delivery at every meal's end of a porcelain bowl cupping a single fortune cookie. She'd stand by my side as I opened it and read the fortune. From the very first day they got better and better — fame, fortune, romance and adventure. It became a running joke with the restaurant staff. They began gathering to hear my escalating good news as other patrons tossed their bleak fortunes to the floor. When I finished the book I opened my last fortune: "Don't believe everything you read." I was struck dumb and helpless but the beautiful waitress leaned over and whispered in my ear, "Don't believe that either."

Decades later I was travelling around Europe with the Toronto Symphony. After several concerts in Germany and Hungary we landed in Vienna. The Musikverein is one of the great public music halls of Europe and one of the very first. Home of the Vienna Philharmonic, its past resident conductors are a who's who of the European classical tradition — Brahms, Rubinstein, Richter, Furtwängler, von Karajan. It's the ground zero of 19th century classical music, especially the Germanic tradition.

And now the TSO was going to play several concerts there with Jukka-Pekka Saraste on the podium. It was not uneventful. The band had played a set program across Europe. As there were a few changes for Vienna some extra rehearsals were required. One afternoon Jukka was taking them through one when the TSO musician who represented the union mounted the podium and took Jukka's baton from his hand. The union-approved rehearsal time was up. By this point I'd done enough drinking with Jukka to know him reasonably well and when I saw his expression at this intervention I knew he was going to quit. And he did. Classical musicians in big orchestras are among the most spoiled people in the arts. They can act more like unionized civil servants than artists.

A small hiccup in Vienna was the sudden illness of the TSO's principal percussionist. Russell Hartenberger, who was on the tour as part of the percussion section, had to step in as a replacement. The piece was Beethoven's Seventh, a highly rhythmic symphony with a very prominent role for the timpani. I stood on a corner of the empty stage while Russell sweated alone through the percussion parts on such short notice. This was not the rep that he usually played. I knew him best as a key original player on Steve Reich's *18 Musicians*. When he had mastered the Beethoven he approached me and asked if I would photograph him with one of the golden caryatids that fronted each column in the hall. These huge women had cantilevered conical breasts aimed aggressively at the audience. Their putative function was to disperse sound in a hall famous for its acoustics. The combination of those breasts with Hartenberger's small bald head made for a curious photograph.

We got talking and I told him how much his playing and Reich's piece had meant to me when doing that first book. I confessed that I'd several times been in a room with Reich but never felt comfortable approaching him about his composition and the role it had played in my life. Russell thought that was a shame, Steve would have liked it.

Almost two decades later I was having lunch in an Asian restaurant on Gerrard Street East when a posse of percussionists walked in. As I knew a couple of them well they stopped by my table. Russell Hartenberger and Ryan Scott, remembering how much I loved Reich's *18 Musicians*, told me that they were rehearsing that very piece only a couple of blocks away for a celebration of Reich's 80th birthday. "Come over after lunch; it's only three blocks from here." Ryan promised to leave the rehearsal hall door unlocked so that I could get in and Hartenberger promised to introduce me to Reich.

I went. I got to hear the entire piece twice before Reich told the ensemble, "You've nailed it." Then Russell made my introduction and I got to tell the composer that I'd listened to his hour-long piece over a hundred times in the space of three months some 40 years earlier. He looked at me as if I was deranged.

However that night in Vienna after I'd photographed Russell with the breasts there was a horrible moment when the orchestra stumbled in one of the Beethoven movements and the whole thing unraveled in front of a very knowing Viennese audience. What could be worse? They pulled it together after a few bars but it was humiliating. And this was the same band that had, only a week before, made Berliners in von Karajan's famous Philharmonie Hall cry.

———

We're told there is no longer a place on Earth where one can go and hear only natural sounds. The soundscape is invariably disturbed by a distant train, a passing plane or traffic roar. It is always shocking after hiking deep in the northern bush to reach a highway and experience the brutalist roar of tires on pavement until it again becomes familiar. We live in a river of noise.

I've been porch-sitting for several hours watching late afternoon become dusk before slipping into night. Last light licks treetops on the far shore before the overtaking night sips the final colours from the day. In two hours a full moon will rise. No loon calls, no gull cries, the air is still, there are no waves and no music from the shore. All I hear is the seashell noise of my own blood moving. I've found a place that doesn't exist.

When the TSO reached Budapest on its European tour we were installed in a modern hotel on the Pest side of the Danube. Then the whole orchestra was bussed to the residence of the local Canadian ambassador for a welcome reception. This diplomat proved to be an attractive middle-aged woman with a much younger boyfriend and an impressive collection of African art. The house filled up rapidly — the orchestra had over a hundred musicians. As I made my way through the crowded rooms two players from the bass section excitedly hustled me into the large living room to take a photograph. Four of the youngest female players in the string section were sitting in a demure row on a large beige sofa. Behind them on a window ledge stood a large African sculpture of a tribesman with an enormous erection. None of the young women had noticed. This juxtaposition was what I was to memorialize in a photograph.

There was a problem. I couldn't get a clear view of the sculpture's crotch as it was partially hidden by one of the violinist's big hair. The solution — reposition the figure. I passed my cameras to one of the bass players and unobtrusively slipped behind the sofa to inch the sculpture into a more revealing position. As I did so the huge erection fell out of its socket and rolled across the reception room floor and vanished under another sofa. The whole room burst into guffaws, the female fiddlers cottoned on to the setup and swanned out of the room no longer the butt of the joke. I was.

———

The frog's mouth opens and closes in a silent scream as its body slowly slips down the gullet of a four-foot black water snake. I watch this execution from my skiff halfway down the river. The frog's glassy eye shouts terror and pain. The snake's say nothing.

In Budapest it was my turn to find the après concert entertainment for a cabal of players from the string section. I wandered the streets of Buda, occasionally collaring a likely looking local and explaining my mission. Most suggestions were dull but a young woman suggested a bar deep under the Danube as a surefire evening's entertainment. When she explained why I knew it was indeed the spot. After the evening's performance was put to bed I led a dozen players down a winding set of stairs beneath a plaza by the river. Deep underground was a large cave-like room with a bar, stage, lights, loud music and the wildest drag show I'd ever seen.

2007

A call from a former colleague at the Toronto symphony office takes me down to the rehearsal hall of Toronto's new ballet/opera house, the Four Seasons Centre. I'm to observe a young conductor from Quebec, get acquainted and take a few photographs in preparation for a subsequent studio portrait session. One of the photographs will be on an album cover. I've photographed a number of conductors at work but this new guy, Yannick Nézet-Séguin, is different. He's tremendously musical, so full of song and wonderfully persuasive and charming in front of an orchestra. The hall's players seem completely seduced and work hard to please.

Some days later we do a studio session. Yannick arrives with his boyfriend and we work hard for an hour or so. Although I suspect he's somewhat of a musical conservative it strikes me that Yannick is just what the TSO needs — someone youthful, charming and dynamic to dilute the rows of gray hair in Roy Thomson Hall with a younger audience. However, in no time at all he is scooped up by the London Philharmonic Orchestra, then Rotterdam's and by 2012 he's fronting the legendary Philadelphia Orchestra. Soon he will direct the orchestra at the Met. We don't move fast in this country. And we still wait for our own to be validated elsewhere.

Everyone knows that Nashville is a music town. What most don't know is that it's not just ground zero for the commercial country music industry, it's also home to blues, folk, rock and a very respectable symphony orchestra. As a result of work in Toronto with the TSO I've been flown down to Tennessee to photograph for a Nashville Symphony fundraiser.

They need a new hall. The current one is located in one of those mid-20th century brutalist cultural centres that mix spaces for the visual arts, books, theatre and music in a singularly compromised facility. When I climb to the high seats at the back of the concert hall during the first rehearsal I instantly understand the problem. With every forte passage in the music the ribbed metal pan ceiling rattles on the open web steel joists supporting it. It creates a junkyard clatter. Horrible.

The band's conductor, Kenneth Schermerhorn, is a former Leonard Bernstein protégé. He's chosen to mount a performance of Beethoven's Ninth Symphony as the cornerstone of the big fundraising gala. It will also be a sunset performance for him. He's in his 70s and retirement looms. He dies not long afterward at 75.

I will photograph for a week as he marshals and rehearses the substantial forces — full orchestra and large chorus — for the realization of the performance. It's hard work for them, it's a pleasure for me. Compared with Toronto, Nashville's players are young and the band is small, only around 80 players. But it has vigour and it's wonderful to feel the performance come together hour by hour, day by day. Toward the end of the week the chorus joins rehearsals and the whole endeavour begins to cohere. I spend the evening hours after daytime rehearsals at the country music bars downtown or at the Bluebird Café where songwriters and players from the region come in to introduce their newest songs and test audience reaction. It's another kind of rehearsal.

My first job is to visit the town's best tailor with Schermerhorn to choose the clothing for photography. As the hall is dark and I'll work with long lenses I'll have to push process the black-and-white 35mm film to extreme speeds, often over ISO 6000. Despite this, when the commemorative book is eventually printed the pictures look wonderful. Even more surprising is their impact when these miniature camera images are used to fill whole billboards along the interstate. From a moving car at 50 yards they manage to be arresting.

When the big performance arrives on the final weekend I get to see one difference between Americans and Canadians. Nashville's elite step right up to the plate. Within hours of the gala launch they've already written cheques for well over a third of the total millions required. Canadians would have sat on their wallets waiting for government to pony up most of the dough. It's not long before all the required money is raised. A great little orchestra will get the hall it deserves.

2000

I come from a long line of Anglican ministers on my mother's father's side. These Irish protestants went to Dublin's Trinity College for generations and then joined the clergy. Some of them crossed the Atlantic to establish parishes in the New World. Thus as children my sister and I were marched to service every Sunday at 11.

I had a brief career as an altar boy. I'd rise at 6:30 and rush to church on my bicycle, slip into my cassock and surplice and meet the minister in the little room beside the organ bellows. The seven a.m. communion service required me to kneel beside the altar for three quarters of an hour and then abruptly rise to my feet to assist with the wine and wafers. Almost invariably I'd stand, see stars and sparks, then faint dead away. After a year of disrupting the service I was seconded to choir duty at 11. That summer it was decided that I should get some polishing at Trinity College Choir School with the great ecclesiastical composer Healey Willan. I went. I hated it. After a subsequent brief career groping choirgirls in the organ bellows room I finally quit. The minister's rage at my departure was such that my parents ceased to be churchgoers.

Decades later I was sitting in a bar on the outskirts of Vienna drinking with the bass section of the Toronto Symphony. Being the tour's photographer is a job I love. I'd been the orchestra's photographer on and off for a number of years. My first assignment was back in the early Andrew Davis days. I was to photograph him for overhead transit ads on the subway and streetcars. As it was early December I was to do it during a Messiah dress rehearsal minus the chorus. The orchestra launched into the Handel and I launched into the string section to get a good angle on Davis. After 30 minutes someone in the back desks of the section raised her hand in complaint. Andrew stopped the band and turned to her.

"I can't concentrate. The photographer is singing."

The concertmaster stood up and turned to her.

"Yes, I can hear him too. He knows the music and he's in tune."

Andrew waved his stick and the rehearsal continued.

In the Vienna bar I'm sitting next to bassist Ed Tait who hasn't drunk for years because of health concerns. This evening as we're near the end of the tour he's decided to have a wee dram. We get to talking and discover that we'd been classmates many decades ago at Healey Willan's Trinity Choir School. As the drams got less wee it was decided that when we return to Toronto we'll attend a choir service at St. Mary Magdalene, Willan's old parish.

Some months later this we did. Ed drove in from the country and picked me up. We parked his car on Manning Avenue and walked to the church. The minister was greeting a long line of parishioners at the door. When we reached him he stared closely at each of us.

"Welcome back, my sons."

This gave me the whim whams but Ed managed to get up during the service and go for a nostalgic communion. I remained slouched in the pew with my eyes closed, hiding if not from the Lord at least from the reverend and my past.

———

I spend a lot of time now just simply being. I sit on my island's point, clear my head and watch the wind carve the water and choreograph the pines. I witness the sun polishing the wind's work. I smell pine resin and dead needles. I feel the mother-touch of moving air and listen, listen, listen. I'm content to be alone.

1968

Composer David Tudor sits at a grand piano. The keyboard cover is flipped up but he doesn't play. All the sounds generated come from a glass dipping duck that pecks away at a bowl of water on the Steinway. Tudor has attached a tiny mic to its beak — *blup, blupp, blurpp* — the stupid top-hatted bird with the bright red bottom goes up and down, dip and dunk, dip and dunk, a perpetual motion machine. A mic cable runs from the bird to the piano leg to an amplifier to a mixer that's connected to a chessboard. Gordon Mumma and a couple of other musicians are also wired to the board. Each of its squares houses a photocell. Every time the chess players, John Cage and Marcel Duchamp, make a move the music is remixed. The performance goes on for hours and hours. Chess is a slow game.

Duchamp had long been one of my heroes. Toward midnight the Toronto audience gets restless and begins to drift out of the hall. I turn to my future wife Annick and remark how much I'd like to meet Duchamp. She looks around at the dwindling audience and stands up. She heads not for the door but for the front of the house. I follow. We slip through a narrow door beside the stage and walk into the middle of the performance. Tudor smiles and nods before going back to his duck. I sit beside Duchamp and his wife Teeny while Annick joins Cage. They are very gracious and we strike up a rambling conversation between their moves. After a half hour or so other audience members do the same. Soon the stage is jammed with people and Tudor throws a hissy fit. He kicks everyone off but us. The performance goes on — one o'clock, two and then toward three. We're still there.

Finally the two masters declare a draw. Cage packs up the chess pieces. It is one of those cheap sets in a softwood box with a sliding lid. He closes it and then offers it to me. What I should have done is gratefully and gracefully accepted it and asked each to sign it. Instead I modestly decline it and kick myself for the next 40 years. A few months later Duchamp is dead.

———

After stepping out the door I hear a dragonfly rattling in its death throes. The pitch is high and unusually loud so I bend over to have a closer look and spy a creature vibrating its way out of a large cocoon. As I bend in closer I realize that the cocoon is attached to a snake. The rattler's body — middle-thick as a radiator hose — moves with the slick slowness of slime — warning, warning, warning. I'm instantly cold, vulnerable, alone. It's as if Eternity is at my feet.

The model is like a coffin. North York is getting an arts complex with a gallery, a theatre and a concert hall for recitals. Garth Drabinsky will program the theatre and hall so I'm on the job as photograper having done work for Drabinsky's Livent. I'm told that part of my appeal as a photographer for Garth is that we're both polio survivors. Although I'm seldom aware of it, people tell me I limp some when tired. Garth was not so lucky. He will limp and drag a foot for the rest of his life. We never talk about this.

Advance marketing for the North York venues is underway even though construction is ongoing. A beautiful model of the hall has been commissioned and shipped to my studio. Russell Johnson of Artec in New York has been commissioned to do the acoustics. Being a master of sound, he's wisely decided not to reinvent the wheel. He'll work with the classic shoebox shape of the Musikverein in Vienna, Amsterdam's Concertgebouw and Boston Symphony Hall. If you limit the seats to under 2,000 and have some nice wood and plaster forms to absorb, reflect and disperse the sound you'll get a beautiful instrument to put an orchestra in. The ranks of gigantic gold women with improbable conical breasts does this dispersal job at Vienna's hall but good Toronto won't do brassy Amazons. Our diffusion panels are more redolent of a suburban rec room.

You can't fool much with the formula. When touring with orchestras I've always gotten a great seat, centre orchestra level, a dozen rows back so I could shoot without obstructions. Stuttgart has an asymmetrical Rudolph Steiner–inspired hall that has acceptable acoustics when you're in the audience but goes bad for musicians on the stage. If you're back with the brass or tympani you can't hear the four dozen string players less than 20 feet away. All the players at rear can do to keep the beat is watch 50 bows. Onstage in the fan-shaped hall in Budapest you could hear every note twice. Weird doesn't work.

The North York shoebox model is two feet wide, twice that long and open at the audience end so you can see toward the proscenium. It's beautifully done, even down to the tiny Steinway grand at centre stage. Despite parts of the ceiling being removable, the model is difficult to light. And every time I stare at the upside down and reversed image on the camera's ground glass something bothers me. The hall plans undergo various changes weekly so the model leaves and returns several times for modifications and more photography. It continues to unsettle me.

I repeat the photography several times so the big brochure will be current. My pictures go back and forth to the graphic designers, the music producers, to Garth and his gang at Livent. Despite many opinions and small setbacks the publicity machine grinds on. Finally the promo book is in paste-up. Press time is imminent. I have a final troubled squint into the back-end of the model when the problem finally hits me. All those meetings, discussions and opinions and nobody had noticed that the micro Steinway had the bass strings on the right and the short ones on the left. The teeny piano was built backwards. Architectural model-makers are not musicians.

As this was before Photoshop the mockup went back once again to the architectural model studio to get fitted out with a new mini nine-foot grand and I got to light and photograph it one more time.

For the time being my model photos satisfied the marketers but when the hall was actually finished and in operation Russell Johnson called me from New York. He wanted it photographed for his portfolio and he had very specific ideas of what he needed. Could I make a photograph during a performance in a larger format that would show the audience, the performers and the hall all at once, sharp, clear and perfectly illuminated? Again, since this was before digital and Photoshop it was going to be tricky but I agreed to try. Shutter and SLR mirror noise ruled out using a Hasselblad and the light levels were too low for slow view camera lenses. Fortunately I owned a couple of curious Fuji cameras. Those things were like huge Leicas — no clanking mirror, just a rangefinder viewer. Quiet. And they made a negative that was 6x9 centimetres, a reasonable substitute for sheet film. More difficult was getting permission to shoot during a concert. But Johnson's name carried the day. I got in, I did it, I got it. I'd arranged for the house lights to come up during the closing bar. I had a window of a few seconds. It was enough.

I couriered the pictures to New York. When I got a letter and a cheque back within days, Johnson said he'd asked for that photo for every hall he'd ever done anywhere in the world. This was the first time he'd gotten exactly what he'd requested. And it was the first and only time in 35 years of freelancing that I got a thank-you note from a client.

The challenge had come from the slow emulsions and low tolerance for high contrast subjects inherent in the film stocks of the day. Today's digital shooter can crank the ISO up to 3200, even 6400 and beyond to deal with the low light and shallow depth of field issues. And now even a simple amateur program like iPhoto can open the shadows and flatten highlights. Composing photographs while viewing a directly projected image that is inverted and flipped right to left is now a lost and unnecessary skill. Today I'm somewhat amazed that I'd been aware of the piano reversal when viewing a ground glass image that had so little relation to conventional seeing. Of course our eyes work the same way as a camera lens and focus an inverted image on our retina. We actually see upside down. It is our brains that automatically erect the eye's image and restore the correct handing — a nice little piece of unconscious software that proved quite difficult to make conscious.

After Livent blew up in a storm of papered performances and bubble books Garth was reborn as a resort marketer. We convened at the Muskoka Sands one winter weekend morning. His gang — girlfriend and associates — are all tricked out in brand-new white snowsuits. They look like urban polar bears. A brace of identical snowmobiles is lined up outside reception. After a blue smoke rev-up we're off, Garth in the lead, on a photo reconnaissance. First stop is a small cliff with Christmas card icicles decoratively dangling. "See that? Shoot it!" he growls. The convoy thunders off over the snowy Shield. "See that!" he barks. A log cabin with smoke spiraling up from a stone chimney makes another postcard. "Shoot it! Get the woodpile!" We race over frozen lakes, plow through drifts, skid across frozen streams and rocket down forest trails. "See that: shoot it. And that!" In a couple of hours we've catalogued every possible winter wonderland cliché and head for home. Nobody can keep that guy down, not polio, not even the courts.

———

With historically low waters in the Bay my small island is separated from the much larger empty one behind by little more than a metre of water at one point. I keep a compost pile on the back island as defence against unwanted visitors — coons and bears to my little rock. As I leap over the gap with a compost pail in each hand I realize that a fox snake swims in mid-crossing below me. It's as big as they get, closing in on six feet, and so elegantly scaled and patterned that it looks like glazed ceramic. As it's in the water it can't do the rattler imitation that always gives me chills. I carry on and dump my load of peels, shells and moldy bread. It will all be gone in hours unlike the bleached coffee filters I used to add to the pile. I haven't done that for a half-dozen years and they're all still there in defiance of sun, rain, freeze and thaw. I gather and burn them.

When I return I see the snake scaling the rockface onto my island. It glides like grease up the rock face and into my junipers. Now I'm sharing a very small island with a very large sneaky snake. Where is it?

During the 1980s I was constantly on the road, flying back and forth across Canada and up and down America. When I was in town I put in long hours at my studio editing, filing and working in the darkroom. While I was absent with busyness my children were growing up. I was missing it like a '50s dad.

Returning home late at night my two sons and their mum would be asleep. We were living at that time in a wonderful Darling and Pearson turn-of-the-century bank building. That neoclassical building, bow-fronted with Ionic columns, keystones and pediments had the address carved in stone over our entrance door. I would climb the stairs after midnight to confront a dozen silent rooms littered with evidence — of the day's work and my sons' play. These traces of the ongoing family life that I was missing were often mysterious.

In order to understand and in some way participate in my family's life I began to photograph this evidence. It was frequently very dense so I soon began to use a large format view camera the better to describe the complex tableaux that were the days' witness. I was always a purist in this work — never touching or adjusting what lay before the lens and always honouring the available light. The late-night lighting dictated complex camera movements — tilts and swings, rising fronts — as well as very long exposures. The resulting photographs were exhibited and collected numerous times and published in books and art magazines. They found an audience but one that wasn't always amiable. There were some women photographers who specialized in domestic and family themes. They protested that their work was often ignored but when a man — me — explored the same territory he was listened to. Upon eventually publishing part of the series as a small book called *Staying Home* I wrote a short introduction in an attempt to explain myself.

"Making a photograph is an act of recognition. What we chose to exclude and retain is based on what we know. If we are working well, not photographing intellectually but intuitively, we can sometimes catch up with ourselves and pull together strands from the past or even from the future. It is a visual way of making personal sense of what is probably truly random — the whole mess of life.

"We seldom know much about ourselves. We go about, acting and reacting, being pulled by strings that were attached in childhood. A child's life is the experience of causes. Then we grow into forgetfulness and usually only desperation makes us attempt recovery. Sometimes we have small moments of recognition.

"These pictures have now been around for a while. They have travelled my country and crossed an ocean masquerading as a family diary. This was a partial truth. Some of these pictures are still travelling while others have found homes in what must seem to my children to be very strange places — a doctor's waiting room, government buildings, a brewery head office, the homes of friends and strangers, several museums and, undoubtedly, a few basements. During the past half-dozen years I would think that anyone who is curious has had time to make them theirs. Now it is my turn. I want to know why I took them. Why I spent so many nights labouring in the low light with a big awkward camera when I really needed sleep. For three years.

"This is a small book about meaning. It traffics in recognitions. It claims to make recoveries. The stories are all true."

———

The first of summer's convection storms catches me on the river run. Gore-Tex is no match for the downpour's violence and after a couple of miles I'm completely soaked and shivering. The rain drives so hard that my face stings and I can't see. When I reach the beginning of the inlet the seas are high and the skiff begins to pound. I plough along pathetically until I reach my harbour and turn in. I run into the cabin and build a fire. A leak in the cupola drips on the dining table and pings on the kitchen pots. I find a dry corner and sleep.

1986

This is another cruel November rain. Photographer Doug Clark has been assisting me all day on a difficult location shoot — tricky lighting, an impatient client and extremely difficult subject matter: transparent acrylic furniture on an arctic white background. We're both exhausted. I offer to drive Doug home in the rain.

Halfway there he changes his mind — he wants to go to his gym. I turn the van around and begin grinding through the dark, drowning rush-hour streets. After we negotiate a few blocks in heavy downtown traffic he realizes that his plan is unrealistic — he wants to go home. I backtrack once more and soon we're approaching Bay Street from Dundas West. So much water streams down the windscreen of my Chevy van that the wipers can't keep up. I see the road briefly after each sweep before it disappears in a greasy moiré of coloured lights and reflections. The rain is hard-driven by wind.

We're in the curb lane making for a green light at Bay Street when the truck in front of us suddenly cuts into the centre lane leaving us facing an enormous orange construction sign that has blown down during the storm. I skid to a stop.

Looking in the mirror I see a TTC streetcar approaching a block behind us — more than enough time to back up from the sign, switch lanes and get through the intersection before the light changes. Seconds after I start this reverse maneuver the van cants up steeply on its curbside wheels and we're showered in glass shards and splintered wood. We wheeze to a halt and so does the vintage 1948 Toronto Transit Commission Presidents' Conference Committee car that was supposed to be a block away. My van is now balanced off its side at a 45-degree angle. Scrambling out the downside passenger door feels like leaving the *Titanic.*

The intersection is instantly invaded by maroon-jacketed TTC inspectors mumbling into little collar radios. It's amazing — there are at least a half-dozen of them hatched somewhere in the Chinese restaurants and donut shops lining the street. In minutes their mutterings have effect — a police cruiser pulls up. The cop gets out in the downpour, looks at my yellow van hanging off the side of the PCC and the already long line of rush hour streetcars backing up behind and starts shouting. He's so angry that after venting for three minutes he jumps back in his cruiser and drives away. By the time more cruisers arrive the PCCs are backed up across University Avenue. The maroon mumblers call a tow truck.

The streetcars are lined up past McCall when the tow vehicle pulls up and a big tattooed biker gets out. He stands akimbo in the rain. His head turns toward the streetcar, then toward my van, then toward the construction sign, a lamp post and finally toward me. He then reels off a hundred feet of cable with a snap hook at the end, feeds it around the lamp post, a telephone pole and then around my van. He cranks up his winch and deftly lifts my vehicle off the side of the trolley — beautiful!

I push my way through the gaggle of inspectors and admiringly ask for his bill. He looks down at me pityingly. "Buddy, you're in so much shit I don't got the heart to charge ya." He climbs into his cab and disappears as the inspectors close in like pack animals. A cop breaks in through their circle and shoves a clipboard into my face. I have a choice: I can sign a guilty confession now and agree to pay damages or I can choose to be charged and go to court and lose points. I looked at the now doorless rusty streetcar with its broken windows and long crease down the side. I look at the heaps of splintered glass and rotten door wood scattered through the puddles. I confess.

Decades earlier my father had gone car shopping with a friend, a juvenile and family court judge. The justice bought a brand-new top-of-the-line Buick and the pair of them set off along the Danforth to go home. While they waited at a red light a streetcar behind them failed to stop and demolished the Buick. Both men were slightly injured. The judge told my father that he, the judge, would be charged and the TTC driver would be blameless. Traditionally the streetcar tracks were legally a rail right-of-way. Anyone driving along a street with trolley tracks was effectively joyriding down the mainline to Vancouver. You had no rights. The judge was indeed charged.

It would be years before the law giving TTC lawyers so much pleasure would be changed. My embrace of the PCC came before that change.

Confession supposedly liberates but my trolley-abuse relationship only gave me months of anxiety. Every week or so I'd inquire about the health of my victim. She was an outpatient in the yard for several weeks while waiting for an appointment in the welding shop. When she eventually recovered from that operation she moved on to rehab in carpentry and got fitted with new doors. After convalescing there for a few weeks the poor dear moved on to glazing. A couple of months later she was still collecting full pay in the paint shop. She still needed decals and a boot stripe.

When New Year's rolled around my personal PCC car was still on sick leave. I trudged into 1987 with a feeling of dread. I was going to lose my house, my cameras and my children. I should have gone to court and raised hell about the collapsed construction sign.

In late February I was in a restaurant after a Friday of tidying up things before flying south on a holiday assignment. On my way up from the basement washroom I stopped at a pay phone and called in for messages. This was the first time that the TTC had actually called me. Here was my second public-transit life crisis. The rainy night confession had been bad enough but now I was faced with either being a whimpering whinger worrying about the size of the bill all the time I was away or I could man up and face the music — now. "Have some gumption," my father would have said.

I sided with gumption and called head office. The official assigned to my case conducted an extended reading from my invoice. Each department had left details of hours spent, materials consumed, duty lost. The whole thing ran to a half-dozen pages. I steadied myself by leaning on the pay phone. Finally he came to the money shot.

"I think there may be a zero missing here, possibly two, probably three, even four. But it's Friday afternoon and I want to go home. If you come up here right now and settle your debt to society we'll just close this thing off and end the week."

"What's the damage?"

"It says here that you owe the Toronto Transit Commission thirteen dollars and sixty-four cents."

The VIA train from Toronto rocks and rumbles over a frost-heaved roadbed en route to Ottawa. I've got one whole car as a studio for the complete return trip. My light stands are heavily sandbagged, my strobe cables snake down the aisle and more gear is piled on the seats. While the models and assistants gossip in the forward section, I work hard in the rear of the car to execute a long shot list for a concertina-fold VIA promotion piece that will be mailed to every house in Ontario. In it a pretty business woman will daydream out the window, a vigorous old couple will have geriatric fun on a train ride, a mother will travel with her perfect child and so on. It will be a very long day.

At Cobourg the train stops so I can set up a platform tableau of a perfect young couple kissing goodbye prior to boarding. When I finish the photograph the rail crew are anxious to get rolling as there are paying passengers in the other cars and a freight thundering up to rear. But I can't find my crew. My film loader, my makeup lady, the wardrobe mistress and hairdresser have gone missing. A loiterer at the station claims they've all jogged into town to buy smokes. I run after them, peeking through store windows all along King Street searching for the renegade women. I finally spot the vagrants at the counter of a convenience store. It's piled high with cigarette packs; its elderly proprietor looks harried. When I enter I discover that each member of my gang is trying to buy a pack but none of them wants to get throat, tongue, lip or lung cancer let alone heart disease so they've rejected all the packs that illustrate those pathologies. They keep the counterman busy opening new cartons to expose the pack illustrations. There will be a late train but no ugly deaths.

After four evenings of high winds the weather has fallen off a cliff during a very long night. Eighteen hours ago the barometric pressure went into a free-fall so severe that in less than an hour it dropped right off the scale into an unknown place and stayed there, invisible, unmeasurable by any of my devices, for 13 hours. The accompanying downpour was so extreme that water sluiced down the interior walls, cascaded off the big oak table centered under the cupola and pooled on the floor. Everything got soaked. By dawn all the windows are opaque with condensation and the world outside was gone. I mopped up the water and built a fire. Angry breath and a great wet finger had reminded me that I'm not in charge. My place in this universe remains very, very, small.

1980

It's midweek in late November. The month has been true to itself — gray, cold and damp. Rain was falling when I made coffee in the dark at seven this morning and now that evening rush hour has arrived it still falls. Outside my studio door on Queen Street East is a streetcar stop. It is always busy, being the point at which people riding east on King from downtown on King disembark to wait for the Queen car which will carry them to their homes in the Beaches and beyond. From here the King car swings north to rumble up Broadview all the way to Danforth and the subway.

I'm in my third floor darkroom printing an assignment when the doorbell rings a few minutes before five. I shut down the wash water and descend to street level where I open the door to a rush hour crowd hunkered resignedly in the rain. A small gray man in a trench coat stands by my door. Am I Mr. M. Mitchell? "Yes," I reply. He reaches under his coat and withdraws a long tractor feed printout that he allows to unfold until it reaches the sidewalk. The paper rapidly darkens in the downpour. "This," he says, tapping the soggy paper, "is your life."

The TTC waiting crowd begins to take an interest. Dripping-Trench-Coat points to the top sheet. "January 1976: late! February 1976: late! March 1976: late again!!" And so on all the way down the soggy printout until we reach the present lying in a puddle on the sidewalk.

"This is your record!" he shouts in the rain. Again he reaches under his coat and hands me his business card from the provincial retail tax department. I do not hang my head in shame.

Those were my days as Sisyphus. I was working 60, 70 hours a week, doing labour-intensive assignments, spending most of my meager returns on new equipment to better execute my jobs as well as realize my own projects. I bought my first Nikons and Hasselblads in those years, my first large format Linhofs and enlargers as well as aluminum travel cases. Optimistically I had incorporated, a legal move that added yet another layer of calendrical tax obligation to my life. At one point I stopped to count the number of tax filings I was obligated to produce each year. There were monthly provincial and federal sales tax returns. A palimpsest of quarterly returns lay over both those as well as quarterly income tax filings and the dark tower of the annual one. Somehow, as addendum to my 70-hour weeks, I was to file taxes a total of 32 times a year. I was a one-man operation, I had a small child at home, I was exhausted, I couldn't keep up. As it often took several months to get paid for jobs I repeatedly applied to have the filing periods reduced to quarterly or less. However, as soon as I had a good run of getting paid promptly or extra business, the computer systems would automatically return me to monthly filing and the 32 returns. I was endlessly rolling the return rock up the tax mountain that would then roll down over me. Then I'd spring up like Road Runner, my third dimension restored, and put my shoulder to the rolling return and begin the uphill push once again. I felt like the victim of a protection racket.

Yet another corporate assignment. This young company has somewhat unexpected roots. Founded by the son of a Scarborough heavy equipment mechanic, it grew out of the operations of a large Canadian life insurer that has since gone bankrupt through risk-taking management. This division was hived off in time to survive. Its business was simple — finance the acquisition of tangible hard assets in low risk enterprises.

It began with dentists. At the time it cost about $100,000 a chair for a graduate dentist to get set up. One knew that the personalities attracted to dentistry were going to be basically stable and conservative ones — all those small town WASPs and ambitious Hong Kong immigrants and Jews just wanted a secure place in the middle class. And you also knew that people's teeth were going to rot. If you bought a newly graduated dentist his gear and set him up, chances were pretty good you'd get your money back plus your fees and interest for doing so. If the odd one proved to be a nut-bar then you only had to repossess the chair and drills and X-ray gear and peddle it to the next grad. It worked like a dream.

To expand beyond this model you had to cultivate political and corporate connections. By the time I started working on their annual report, Newcourt Financial was buying whole trains, fleets of buses and flocks of huge aircraft for different enterprises. I've never had an interest in being one of those aggressive guys who set up businesses like these and makes them prosper long enough to cash in and cash out. But it was always intensely interesting to be a fly on the wall watching their moves and figuring out how it all worked.

I have to say I thought some deals seemed to lack client utility. At one point I was sent out to a wintry field an hour east of Toronto to photograph its contents. When I got there I discovered rows and rows of Grumman step vans lined up in the snow. All were painted up in Canada Post colours and ready to go. Now I had done considerable work for Canada Post — shooting pictures for stamps, writing and researching various commemorative booklets and I knew some of the people in Ottawa. Thanks to email Canada Post is now a shadow of its former self. But in those days it was wallowing in cash and André Ouellette, its boss, had built a specially furnished and ventilated cigar smoking room at headquarters for himself and his political buddies. One can only guess why they chose such an expensive way to acquire delivery trucks.

Today we're going off to inspect Newcourt's latest acquisition, Xerox Capital. We are four: Newcourt's founder Steve, his leggy secretary, his chubby chairman and this photographer. We boarded a small plane at Pearson and lifted off for Indianapolis where a limo glided us to headquarters. Once there the Newcourt trio sweep through the offices like a juggernaut, wheeling around corners in the corridors to take yet another division. At one point I linger behind to make some photographs — it's not easy finding visual correlatives for what is basically a bunch of numbers on spreadsheets and deals made on the phone. A couple of Xerox Capital's senior execs catch up with me. They look pale and shaken. "How do we deal with you Canadians?" they whinge. "You're all so ruthless and aggressive." As Steve Hudson, the Newcourt founder, loved to say, "You eat what you kill."

———

The wind has shifted to the east exposing a reef to the sun. Two gulls and a crow have landed on the brand-new little island and squabble over a dead fish. All three are big talkers.

1978

Sometimes I thought that magazine editors would assign me to a story as a setup. They were amusing themselves and checking to see if I had the right stuff — like the time I was banished to Moose Jaw to fly with the Canadian aerial acrobatic team, the Snowbirds. A Vancouver magazine writer, Sean Rossiter, was to do the text and I was to provide the pictures. He flew east, I flew west and Moose Jaw was the monkey in the middle.

When we arrived in a prairie heatwave the mood of the flight team was sombre. They'd been rehearsing for an air show only a few days before when one of their crack flyers came barrel-rolling out of a dive as the small aluminum casting that held the rear stabilizer wing to the top of the tailfin disintegrated and the pilot had to eject from his little Tudor jet. As the plane was rolling out of control he'd unluckily hit EJECT when upside down. He was less than 100 feet above the prairie when the charge went off. The hole he made on impact was still fresh as was the memory of his death for his teammates. I found it hard not to stare at it. Years later I watched the CNE air show with my two young sons from the third-floor deck of my downtown Toronto house. As the Snowbirds team climbed out of one of their standard show maneuvers I realized it was fucked. I did have a little insider knowledge having been inside it once myself. I tried to quickly turn my sons around but I wasn't fast enough. They saw another team member die.

Rossiter and I were given a brief course of instruction before suiting up for the rehearsal flight. You wouldn't run a marathon in one of those flight suits. In fact you'd be lucky to stagger to the plane. The outfit included two parachutes, a tent, a PFD, a rubber raft, an axe, utensils and enough food for a week in the bush. All this was attached to your backside. Before waddling out to the planes we each signed a waiver promising not to go after the Queen if we got killed.

We did this in the base canteen where Rossiter declared he needed hydrating before going up. While he sucked down a chocolate milkshake I asked the flight captain if I could have a couple of barf bags. Sean laughed at me so hard that he sprayed a couple of us with his shake. Nevertheless, I stood my ground and slipped the bags onto the clipboard built into the thigh of my suit. We then monster-walked out to the runway.

The little Canadair Tudors are training jets configured so that student and instructor sit side by side in the cockpit. It's very cozy. Rossiter was lucky — he got to be in the middle of the formation — but I had to fly at its very edge so that I could take a photograph of the entire formation framed by the pilot beside me as we banked into a turn. When we got airborne it proved to be a very rough ride. We rattled through the columns of air rising in the prairie heat like a springless, steel-wheeled Mennonite wagon on a rutted road. It was truly a boneshaker. Not only that but those guys fly so tight that their wings overlap. The pilot had to work the stick like a game controller. Every movement by the lead aircraft had to be exaggerated by the adjacent planes and then magnified again by the plane on the outer tip where I was. As if this wasn't dizzying enough I quickly discovered that I couldn't see through my viewfinders because the oxygen hose got in the way. I tore off my facemask only to discover that I was breathing a nauseating admixture of kerosene fumes and jet exhaust generated by the plane only a few feet in front of us.

We pulled so many Gs on the turns and dive recoveries that my Nikons and arms seemed to weigh a thousand pounds. On some maneuvers I couldn't even lift them. As I knew I wasn't going to last long I quickly raced through my shot list and a couple of rolls of film. After 20 minutes I reached for both barf bags and asked the pilot to take me back to base. When I'd finished puking I began to prepare myself to face Rossiter. As we approached the runway I looked back and was surprised to see that the whole formation was coming in behind us. I'd thought I was the lone wimp.

After the team had lined up their planes in a neat row I climbed out and steeled myself to face Sean. When I asked the ground crew which plane he was in they told me to approach the one with the opaque canopy. When it opened the smell of puke was overwhelming. Both Rossiter and the pilot were covered in it as were the seats and the instrument panel: I daintily dangled my neatly closed airsickness bags. Fifteen minutes later I was leaning against a hanger with the Snowbirds and the American Golden Hawks, a cold beer in my hand. Meanwhile Rossiter was lugging pails of soapy water out to his plane where he was removing barf from the instruments with a toothbrush.

I was in my mid 30s when I did this and was already old compared with the team members who were all in their early or mid 20s. Last year when I was in my early 70s I dropped into the aircraft museum at the Hamilton airport. In among all the nifty fighters, bombers and bush planes squatted a dinky Tudor. When I mounted a stepladder to have a peek inside I was horrified. It was so small, so fragile and so primitive. I'm amazed I ever got in the damn thing to race off at 450 miles an hour.

"Beloved Vancouver writer Sean Rossiter dies at 68," *Georgia Strait*, January 8, 2015. Sean Rossiter died on Monday, January 5, at age 68 after a decade-long battle with Parkinson's disease. Tears were shed.

Canadian Pacific owned the Calgary Tower. In the 1980s, before the corporation was dismantled, it seemed that CP owned everything. They had the railway, of course, but they also had an airline, ships, trucks, office buildings, industrial parks, shopping malls, hotels, coal mines, an oil company, and at times, it seemed, various governments. It was a powerhouse.

Today I'm just trying to get a little power. One of the public relations managers wants to promote the Calgary Tower restaurant in a corporate publication. As I'm in town to glamorize various real estate holdings, the tower gets added to my list. A young couple will enjoy a romantic dinner at the top of the tower with "scenic" Calgary spread out below and beyond the restaurant window. Dinner is to be at dusk when the still visible scenery will be decorated with twinkling big city lights like Christmas. This means that I will have to light the couple and their table.

An assistant and I haul cases of studio strobe lighting up the tower and set them up as the service staff sets the table with dishes, candles and flowers. We tape down the power cords that snake down the aisle to duplex outlets in the core of the restaurant. Then the models arrive along with the evening's first dinners. Everyone takes their position and the beautifully plated meals arrive. When I'm ready to shoot the restaurant begins to rotate. My couple lift their glasses in a toast. They look longingly into each other's eyes and the lights go out.

The tower is an axle holding all the services while the restaurant is like a wheel that rotates around it. As the restaurant turns my extension cords get tighter and tighter until the turning torques my plugs from their outlets. The headwaiter shuts down the electric drive and we add several hundred feet of additional extension cords. The world begins to spin again and people lift their forks. I get in a few exposures but each one is flawed. Sauce dribbles down my guy's chin and then his date drops her knife. We make adjustments and go at it again. Just as the distant Rockies rotate into view my lights again go out. The manager stops the rotation motor and fetches additional power cords from a closet. I add the last pair I have and we wind them a couple of times around the tower, plug them in and start again. By now the restaurant has rotated past the Rockies so we'll have to do another full 360 to get back to the ideal background. We almost make it when we run out of extension cord and are once again plunged into darkness. The headwaiter turns off the rotation motor.

At this point I encounter western alienation. When I crouch down to re-power my lights a trio of late middle-aged farmers in tractor hats loom over me. They've driven hundreds of miles south to Calgary with their wives for this night of a lifetime and they'll be goddamned if some pansy photographer from Toronto is going to ruin their romantic evening spin. They bully the headwaiter and manager who rush off to turn on the motor switch. To hell with Toronto, corporate headquarters in Montreal and every bastard in the east. The farmers will dine, the world will turn and I'll hire a photo retoucher to fix the chin dribbles and gravy on the tablecloth.

I should have known better. I once had lunch with the Italian classical guitarist Oscar Ghiglia in Niagara Falls' Skylon Tower dining room. He took one sip of the soup, gagged and wrote "Don't eat the soup!" with his finger in the condensation on the window pane. All through lunch his message repeatedly circled the restaurant. We were having coffee when the waitstaff finally figured out why no one was ordering soup. And during my brief career as the glamorous woman across the table during editor Charles Oberdorf's stint as a restaurant reviewer — we shared a studio for years — I once asked him what he'd learned after eating so many restaurant meals. He adjusted his glasses, leaned toward me, cleared his throat and whispered, "Never eat at the top of anything."

2002

And never eat everything. For me it's never eat animals or birds although I do make a guilty allowance for the occasional fish.

104

So my worst meals were camped on the tundra on the Boothia Peninsula, northwest of Hudson Bay. The Bannock bread was fried in lard, huge chunks of caribou body parts were forever roiling around in a tub of boiling water and the nearest vegetable was 1,000 kilometres away. While I understood why people hunted — buying processed food in the co-op store was like shopping at Tiffany — the incessant killing really bothered me. The young boys were taught that if it moved, kill it. Every gull that landed, every siksik that ran through the camp, every narwhal that entered the harbour had to die. For the elders that was how the young would learn to be good providers. And don't believe that stuff about Inuit using every piece of the kill. There was always tons of waste. Rotting body parts lay all over Kugaaruk, the nearest hamlet. You could never forget mortality.

Some of my Canada Post assignments were a pleasure to execute. In 1980 I researched and wrote a booklet to accompany a series of stamps based on Inuit prints. *Singing Songs to the Spirit* was a beautiful little book, the first, I was told, that actually made some money for the post office. It had lots of space for me to be an anthropologist and do some justice to a complex history. I was able to background the pages that presented the actual stamps with historical photographs recording the scenes and activities that were stylized in the prints on which the stamps were based. And I managed to spread the wealth around by buying rights to Arctic photographs done by various photographic colleagues. I still like that book. I later worked on stamps and booklets about forts, historic Canadian textiles, golf and the Olympics.

Other projects were near nightmares. Try writing a history of Canadian higher education that included the story of the development of Queen's University in a tidy 350 words. Try making it more readable than a telegram or a tweet. Every *the* and *a* was a word count crisis. With no room for colourful modifiers all one could do to keep the reader awake was to maintain a prose rhythm that could propel the story forward. It was hard work.

Nevertheless, the little commissioning gang of four at Canada Post in Ottawa were an intelligent and interesting group to work with despite the very modest fees they were able to pay designers, artists and writers. Sometimes quite improbable things happened while their projects were being executed.

For several years my local letter carrier in the west end was a smart and quite sweet little guy. We'll call him Gordy. He soon noticed all the mail I was getting from his corporate headquarters and was curious about what was going on. I explained that I periodically worked on stamp designs and commemorative booklets. We began having frequent dialogues about the Corp. One day while I was walking up my street with a client we ran into Gordy doing his rounds. He loved to gossip about his bosses and on this day he was relishing the fact that he's just heard that the postal Corp. had printed an enormous run of Christmas stamps with the umlaut over the wrong vowel in Noël. Gazillions of stamps had to be destroyed and reprinted. Gordy took delight in declaring the big boys in Ottawa a bunch of assholes and I took wicked delight in introducing Gordy to my companion Georges, the "asshole" from Ottawa who'd made that mistake.

1975

I'm sitting on a Queen streetcar next to an east end punk. He's sizing me up, looking at the bulge in my jean jacket breast pocket that betrays my wallet. He's also looking at my watch. You know that at whatever stop you get off it's going to be his stop too. My problem is not my wallet or watch but the $700,000 worth of diamonds and gold in the pockets of my Levi's.

I've been doing this monthly for a year now, riding the streetcar to a hotel downtown, picking up the latest jewelry designs from a shop in the lower level arcade of a hotel, stuffing it into my pants and then taking transit back to my studio where I make the photographs. Each month the shipments get more valuable. Sometime, somewhere, this has got to go bad.

———

I arrive at the island to discover another round of asset stripping. My ex has visited the one thing we still co-own and she's been shoplifting. The heavy German chef's knife is gone as is the big Israeli manual juicer. She did buy those but not many of the others. A Chamula house cross, a memory from my work in Mexico a half century ago, has vanished and my little Japanese teapot is gone. For her it's just a pretty little blue and white teapot with deep red ring around the lid and ochre dots orbiting it like little moons. For me it's much more. When it's in my hand I remember my long, lone walk through the rainy back streets of Kyoto in the days when I would go with some regularity to Japan. I was wet and dog-tired the day that teapot called me to the window of a neighbourhood shop. It was not antique and just a few steps above the stuff in a hundred-yen shop, but it had a welcoming friendliness worth much more than the few dollars it cost. It was made for daily use. I bought it. It's true I'm not a big tea drinker but I miss it.

1972

I've been moving around Ontario for weeks now, filming and photographing in the province's prisons. There's considerable variability in the institutions, both in physical plant and philosophy. Old near-dungeons like Guelph coexist with modern institutions in Brampton that seemed based on a notion of class upgrading. If we could just instill middle-class values in all these grotty working-class criminals then everyone will be nice, life will be nice, the world will be nice. The new cells have designer fabrics and furniture. There's classical music. Inmates learn the language of sensitivity training and therapy. It's class war. It's creepy.

I'm allowed to read inmate's files. With the exception of a handful of middle-class boys who got caught dealing dope, the files are all the same — neglect, no education, family violence, alcohol, no money. No wonder.

Nevertheless it's painful to watch the process. After many days filming group therapy sessions in a women's prison I'm allowed to record visitors' day. The tough guys from outside come in to see their wives and girlfriends. The women all have the new vocabulary of therapy. Their guys don't know what they're talking about. They can't talk to each other. They're being split apart. It's a strategy; it's sad.

Those were the days before the cells became full of Black faces and a different kind of cultural war began.

I spend a lot of time in Guelph and eventually acquire a couple of inmate assistants. I get to know them well and start to appreciate the strange disfunctions they live with. The inmate I get closest to is in for robbing a country general store in southwestern Ontario. He did it in November. He spent weeks parking a concession road away, hiking through the cold wet fields to a ditch across the road from his target. He'd lie in the damp ditch for hours memorizing the farmers' movements — when people came for their mail and supplies — until he knew the few minutes when the proprietors, an old couple, would be alone. He struck after a month of research and scooped up

$85 — so much careful planning to earn a fraction of minimum wage at the cost of great discomfort. Stupid.

Yet he wasn't.

When I am about to leave Guelph after several weeks of work several inmates come to say goodbye. They tell me that they figured I was a good guy and so when they get out they want to do something for me. They usually charge $1,500 to take somebody out but for me the first death would be free.

———

My old friend Billy stands on the high bluff edge talking to me over his shoulder. He begins to descend the battered soft face of the precipice, waving his arms as he talks, not focused on where he is. I want to warn him but I'm too late. He stumbles and falls. I can clearly hear his body thumping on the clay face as he cartwheels toward the rocks below. The final lakeside impact sounds like a softball into a mitt. When I start up in my cabin bed I remember that my dream is also too late — he is already dead, the victim of a midnight car crash on a Tennessee exit ramp two years earlier. Why has my brain changed the script?

1988

Their colour goes, then weight and finally the sores appear and you know that another friend has succumbed. This mystery illness is shadowing the land like a dark nimbus driven by a hard wind. People in the way are falling like old trees.

The Ontario Ministry of Health has concluded that a major public awareness campaign is mandated. The population needs to understand how AIDS is spread and how it's not. They need to know more in order to protect themselves and slow the wildfires. There will be thousands of posters for public buildings. Illustrated brochures are to go to every home in the province. The Ministry will provide the words. I'm to make the photographs.

The shot list proves to be very long. I'll need dozens of models and numerous locations. By the time all the models are assembled, Ministry and agency reps, assistants, makeup, wardrobe and handlers we are in excess of 60 people. I hire people to load cameras, hold reflectors, corral the models and keep track of their hours. Some of the crew that I hire are fellow former students from my film school. A small fleet of vans is rented to move this little army from location to location. It's all to be done over an extended weekend of very long days.

Less than a week before the session there remain a couple of setups that still are not cast. And we are weak on diversity. One morning I'm in the agency office at reception talking to the main art director and designer when a young guy enters with a courier package. The director and I look at each other and simultaneously say, "You can't get AIDS from a drinking fountain." This handsome Black kid would be perfect for that poster. We explain the project to him. When we tell him how much he'll be paid for drinking from a public water fountain his eyes light up. Suddenly a courier's hourly rate looks stupid. As he's still in his teens he needs to run the offer past his mum. He'll get back to us.

His mother turns out to be a well-known Canadian artist who often works with photographs. His father is a well-known figure in municipal circles. The kid goes to his mum. She says no. He pleads: it will be an adventure, he could really use the money. This kitchen argument won't go away. Finally mother enquires about the photographer making all these pictures including some of her son? When he tells her she suddenly relents. "Okay, if it's Mitchell, then it will be okay." She knows of me.

We begin this intense weekend shoot at Queen's Park. Not at the legislature but in the actual park with its wonderful trees and numerous interesting nearby buildings. It's hard work but we're well organized and move through the long shot list like a guerilla force. Every few hours a catering truck arrives and refuels our little army. I finally get to the drinking fountain session. Our young courier seems to know exactly what to do. It goes well. His hours are recorded; he signs a release; the cheque will be mailed. The convoy moves on to a new location down by Cherry Beach.

During the following week the many rolls of film are processed, proofed and printed. There are no mishaps. The brochures and posters are mocked up and presented to the Ministry. Despite the scale and urgency we have pulled the whole thing off. We're pros.

Then an ominous call came from the minister's office. I was to show up immediately for a meeting. I was puzzled. All initial responses to the pictures had been enthusiastic. Government representatives had been on site to suggest any changes and approve final Polaroids. What was this all about?

I had some anxieties as the last time I'd done a big project for a provincial ministry — Corrections — there'd been a big post-project stink because after delivery and payment for the films I'd written and published an article in which I expressed my concerns about the new direction the Ministry was setting for the prison system. The minister, the former hockey player Sly Apps, had taken to phoning my wife at home demanding to know "where I was hiding out." She didn't know precisely. I was doing visuals for a museum project in Stratford at the time.

When I arrived at Queen's Park the minister was in her office surrounded by a cluster of grim staffers. Ontario has had a string of large women in various portfolios. This minister was even larger than all of them and a chain-smoker to boot. She scowled at me. How did I explain what had happened to one of my models at the hands of an assistant of mine? What was I going to do about it? I had no idea what she was talking about.

As this very awkward meeting progressed it became apparent that the woman I'd known at film school whom I'd hired to track the models' hours had seduced the boy at the drinking fountain. He'd gone home after losing his virginity and told Mummy. How could she have done this to me? And on an AIDS shoot for Christ's sake?

As we talked this thing through I discovered that the seduction had taken place some days after the shoot. My assistant had run into our handsome courier boy on the street and had invited him back to her place. He'd gone. It happened. How could I be held responsible for this post-factum event? I agreed that it was extremely unfortunate and I understood why his mum had felt betrayed by me and complained to the minister. But I wasn't an afterhours baby sitter. I didn't accept responsibility. In the end they agreed. Apologies were sent to the family and the matter dropped.

But not by me. When I later confronted my assistant she confessed and expressed regrets. She would make it up to me. Why didn't I come and stay for the night?

———

With the last days of spring the river has begun to drop and the water clear. Now that sunlight penetrates to the bottom the creepy, waving marine grasses have begun their summer growth. In a few weeks they'll be grabbing our ankles and drawing us under. A thin line of mud has appeared to mark the waterline along the banks. The season of rutting and reproduction screams its arrival all night.

It's a misty late August early morning just outside of London, Ontario. We're racing down a lake in a 14-foot aluminum skiff with a 15-horse outboard. The driver is the national rowing team's coach. He keeps the boat tucked into the narrow slot between where the cox sits in the shell and last sweep of the women's eight. These women are so strong and so fast that the coach must run the Evinrude flat-out in order to maintain position so that I can photograph. I stand astride the gunwales, just aft of the bow thwart. It's a fine balance that I can only maintain if the coach has an absolutely steady hand on the tiller and we cross no waves.

I gingerly step down to the bilge just as Silken Laumann slips magisterially out of the fog in her single shell. She was never the most beautiful woman on the team, Kathleen Heddle was, and she may not have been the strongest, I suspect that crown went to Marnie McBean, but she was definitely *the* presence. Not because of her achievements, I knew little of them at the time and certainly didn't understand her triumph over abuse. That story surfaced almost two decades later. But to see her on the water was to witness a focus and purpose that produced a union of boat, sweep, water and sculler in a fluidity of movement that was silent, self-contained and powerfully hypnotic. It drew the press to her with a force that was resented by some other women on the team who'd grumble about "that Silken shit."

She was clearly isolated so I was more than pleased when at a subsequent World Cup event in Finland she suggested a couple of times that we go for a beer. She was a compelling presence because she was a triumphal survivor — over a tough childhood, flirtations with suicide and a competition leg injury that would have ended most careers. That was the power that made her so beautiful to watch on the water. The "shit" was elsewhere. Sadly the many beautiful photographs of her and the team we made were later lost when the sponsor forgot all the slide trays of our hard-won originals in a B.C. meeting room.

My pal Dougie won't shut up. I've brought him with me to Switzerland and France to assist with an intense weeklong shoot with the Canadian freestyle ski team. There are numerous events to cover, multiple cameras to load, many rolls of film to label and keep track of as well as the sheer grunt work of lugging cases of gear up and down mountains in the snow.

And there was a great deal of snow on the mountaintops at Val d'Isère and Tigné. First day out we traverse a high ridge on foot pulling a handful of aluminum equipment cases behind us. The snow we struggle through is chest deep and the wind howls over the ridge. Our beards are frosted with ice; our faces burn in the cold.

We slide and stumble down slope to where a special mogul course has been built so the team can practise and I can photograph. After watching several women on the team ski the bumps I select a point in the course from which to shoot. We dig a pit in the snow for me to lie in with my cameras. The idea is that team members will descend the mountain, hit the mogul just above me and make a hard left turn dramatically spraying snow as they avoid me. Dougie will let the skiers know where I am from the margin of the run. He will pass me freshly loaded camera bodies as I hit the roll ends.

The first couple of runs go well; we are a team. But Dougie is relentlessly social and one of the world's great talkers. He soon gets distracted and begins to talk up the young women on the slope beside him. He forgets to indicate where I am to one of the descending skiers. She rockets off the mogul just above my spot and lands squarely on me before vanishing down-slope to the end of the run. I'm wearing so much clothing that I'm not really hurt but her ski edges have sliced through both shoulders of my snowsuit. I scream a couple of obscenities at Dougie and then feel better. We finish the rest of the day without incident.

Being in amateur sport is like being in the arts. Visual artists and most writers are expected to produce for free or pocket change. In my experience the only people in the arts who get paid for what they do are musicians, especially classical ones. They have a union. So I'm always somewhat embarrassed by the realities of the many photography sessions I have done with our Olympic and World Cup skiers and the rowers. When travelling to these events, whether in the Pacific Northwest, Ontario, Quebec or Europe, I get a nice hotel room, restaurant meals and a car or van, plus an assistant.

The athletes, however, must work at menial jobs to pay for training or transport to cup events. With each competition some of them don't attend because they just don't have the money. When they do they usually bunk up four, six or eight to a room. They eat takeout and fast food. It's all they can afford. It's shabby.

This first evening the sponsor is treating the entire team and crew to dinner at an inn. The athletes are in high spirits and ravenous. One of the male team members, a contractor in B.C. by day, does his famous "ball walk" after dinner. This involves climbing up into the beams and rafters of the dining room and stalking along them like a cat with his testicles dangling from his fly. It always gets everyone's attention. We all drink — a lot.

It's well after midnight when the party breaks up and I return to my hotel. As I drift off to sleep there's a gentle tapping at my door. I stagger over in my gotchies and open up. It's the mogul girl. She's come to make up for the disaster on the slope.

Now I'd seen her on the weight machines doing a workout earlier in the day. I'd photographed her massively muscular thighs. I was terrified. We have a little talk instead and then I offer to drive her home. We sneak out of my room and down to the lobby. Every door is locked for the night. The reception desk and office are empty. We retreat to my room.

As I'm only on the fourth floor we decide to climb out my window, sneak downwards from balcony to balcony until we can jump into the big snowdrifts piled on either side of the adjacent road. It's slippery as it's still snowing but we make it and cross the street to my rental van.

I get it started but we're stuck in the new snowfall so I begin to rock the van back on forth to get out. The wheels spin and scream in the night. Lights start to come on in the hotel. Dougie looks out from his room and sees someone trying to steal our van. He calls security and the police. Ms. Mogul and I blink in the beams of a half-dozen flashlights.

2000

My old friend and photo partner K.S. is in town from Tokyo. I'm up at the island when he calls to arrange a visit. A Japanese girl, Mizuho, whom he'd met in Kyoto is with him. She's tiny and beautiful; he's well over six foot and enormous. In Tokyo some call him Mr. Belly. He loves food and drink as well as women.

They drive north and I do a river run to meet them. Mizuho looks stunning: K. looks huge. As usual he's brought great food and excellent wine. He wants me to take them out to the coast where the smooth rocks undulate in and out of the bright water for many thousands of feet. He's in mind of a picnic. I'm in mind of staying where we are or seeking a sheltered back bay as the west wind has blown hard for three days. There'll be a lot of leaping horses on the reefs and shoals. But I can't dissuade him.

So we load the skiff with victuals. After I've made sure we have life jackets and a corkscrew we take off and head west. It gets rougher and rougher. As we reach the inlet's opening to the big water the boat leaps and plunges on the freighted waves. K. indicates that he seeks a spot a bit north up the coast. Against my better judgment I begin evasive manoeuvres through the reefs and shoals. The 16-foot boat pitches and rolls violently.

We rock and roll our way 1,000 feet up the coast and then point toward an inlet in the shore. The big rollers grab the stern and pitch us forward. And down. The giant of a wave set almost pitch-poles us into a trough. As we bottom out the outboard's lower unit cracks on a rock and whacks out of gear. I struggle hard to re-engage. As the seas begin to push us broadside, threatening a broach, I finally manage to force the shift-dog into reverse. We've missed the inlet so we're now obliged to plow astern into heavy seas if we're to avoid getting smashed on the shore rocks just ahead. As I reverse the waves repeatedly slop over the transom. Despite my repeated shouts to start bailing, my passengers remain frozen in their seats — they're stunned. I watch as the Nikons and long lenses we've both brought disappear beneath the water in the bilge. In a few minutes the boat is swamped and the engine quits.

However, the skiff does have foam flotation under the seats. The boat settles into a kind of negative buoyancy just below the surface. I discover that I can row it despite the water being up to my chest and the entire craft beneath the waves. I stroke hard — it's like paddling a sub — but we make slow progress. Looking over my shoulder I glimpse a large reef breaking the surface about a hundred feet farther out. With everything I've got I make for it and stroke the boat to its windward side. I'll let the wind and waves do the hard work of pushing a water-logged boat onto this very low small island. As we crunch onto the rocks K. rolls his bulk over the side and makes it to safety. A surprisingly fit and agile Mizuho quickly follows. She reaches out and pulls me after her saying, "My-ko, I never forget you." We're safe — sort of.

It's September. The water's cold. It's rough. We're standing on a reef hundreds of feet offshore in heavy seas with a swamped boat and motor. There's no one around. We may still be screwed.

Then I notice that despite submersion of the battery and wiring, the bilge pump is still working. Our drenched trio stand slack-jawed as the boat gradually bails itself. When it begins to float I re-board, remove the cowl to dry the plugs and drain the carburetor. A few vigorous pulls and my battered 25-horse coughs to life. We're off *across* the waves — backwards.

Despite my occasional lack of judgment, such as this junket, I'm pretty good at boat handling. We make it through several thousand feet of roiling water and aggressive rocks to the deeper water of the inlet. We slowly plow backwards in infamy to my island a mile or so away. K. and I are probably having the same fantasy — undressing with Mizuho in front of a roaring fire. Maybe there'll be candles. Our cameras are gone but we still have the wine.

———

Round and round my island a merlin harries a bald eagle — a disreputable bird and fitting symbol for our southern neighbours.

1989

I'm wrestling my equipment cases into the U.S. Customs and Immigration area of the Vancouver airport. I have a flight to San Francisco and, later, beyond. The trip has two functions, one commercial and one artistic. I'm to photograph some properties belonging to Canadian Pacific.

But it's also the sesquicentennial of Daguerre's launch of the first practical photographic process. The occasion is being marked in Houston by a show featuring three photographers, a Brit, an American and a Canadian — me. My contribution is in one of the cases.

It's a show that I had originally created to mark another

sesqui celebration, the incorporation of the city of Toronto. A number of photographers had been commissioned to execute works honouring this occasion. As none of them had taken on the city's blooming multicultural mosaic, I had been urged to do so. Like the others, I had no desire to record colourful "ethnics" shopping or "exotic" signage. I had to think of something more interesting. I chose the commercial portrait.

Decades later I still owe my two sons and their mother for that one. Every weekend for three months she'd borrow a dress from her mother and we'd deck out the boys in gray flannel pants and blue blazers. Off we'd go to several appointments at commercial portrait studios. These were always booked anonymously. We'd show up like any other family to have a group portrait taken. The studios were carefully chosen to reflect the city's new character. We went to studios that served the Chinese, Portuguese, Italian, Greek, Polish and West Indian communities. We also visited the studios of the more established. We patronized a couple of studios that served successful Jews as well as one that valorized the old WASPs. I never told them the nature of the project and always claimed that I couldn't make up my mind when viewing the proofs. I urged the photographers to select for me. I was still the objective anthropologist.

Here was another lesson learned. Make your own pictures — it's a lot less work. I had to go to each studio four times: once to book, again for the session, then to view the proofs and finally to pick up and pay. Every weekend we had to tug those clothes onto the boys and ship them off to the various studios. They got pretty sick of it. Jake was old enough to sort of understand it but Ben, the younger, became a problem. Most of the studios had a program to reward the children with a candy sucker for having endured a session. Ben soon began asking for his bribe in advance. He nearly blew our cover several times.

And once I almost blew it. We had booked into Al Gilbert's studio on a classy row of Victorian storefronts where Bay Street turns into Dupont. Gilbert mostly served the successful Jews of Forest Hill Village and beyond. As soon as we walked in Al's assistant recognized me. I had to tread on his toes and beg him to keep his mouth shut; I'd explain later. When Al came out his face gave away his thoughts. "I know this guy with his family but I can't quite place him." This mystery preoccupied him throughout the session. He got so agitated that he dropped a Hasselblad film magazine on his marble floor. Broken but not busted. We got through it with our anonymity barely intact.

We then moved a few doors down the street and became an Anglo family at Ashley and Crippen.

What did this project reveal about the culture of immigration? Most obvious was the conservatism of many of these cultures. The setups were frequently straight out of the 19th century — same props, same poses, same lighting. One of the Greek Canadian studios posed the boys on a swing hung by ivy and flower entwined ropes. Mom and Dad were placed on either side looking down adoringly. The children were the true subject. Both studios catering to the Jewish community posed the mum, who in this case actually was Jewish, in the centre of the picture with a highlight glow framing her. I was just an accessory. The portraits from Mediterranean cultures established the father as the central and most important figure. Sometimes the portraits were about arrival and success. A prominent studio in the Portuguese neighbourhood posed us on a bridge, in front of a picture window that looked out on the Rockies. Presumably the message was we've arrived in the New World (the Rockies), and we've made it (our house has a big picture window with a nice view). Sometimes the message was less clear, even weird. At one Italian studio we sat on tree stumps blocking the road in a painted set of the Appian Way. Decode that one.

At the time, 1984, I wrote this text to accompany the portraits as they travelled to various museums and galleries.

Toronto, as we all know, was once a stuffy Victorian lady. However, something happened. She has hiked up her skirts and begun to cohabit with people from all over the world. Something has happened to me too. Here I am, fifth generation Anglo-Ontarian and lapsed Anglican choirboy, married to a Parisian Jew and father of two sons who have brown eyes and speak French. I, like Toronto, am no doubt the better for it and yet, like Toronto, am no longer so sure of what I am. I do know that I'm a photographer but how could I ever show in photographs what has happened to both of us?

"Such confusion, I finally realized, required professional help. My family agreed and came along for the sessions. We went to Ashley and Crippen to see if we were WASPs and to Horvath and Gilbert to see if we were Jewish or, at the very least, successfully established.

"We consulted additional specialists — Katerina would know about the Greeks and Hilario and Ferreira were experts on the Portuguese. We were examined by Wong's and Roma Studios on the off-chance that we might have become Chinese or Italian. Russell-Carib assured us that we weren't West Indian but the diagnosis from Junak studio is ambiguous. We could possibly be Polish.

"What do we have, besides a sailor suit that was washed a dozen times, to show for all of this? Well I, standing for once on the wrong side of the camera, have a renewed respect for those who earn their living by making four human beings look presentable simultaneously. All the photographers worked hard without knowing the nature of our problem. I was glad also to see that our Victorian lady was in a sense still around. The posing tables and stools, tree stumps and armchairs, ornamental plants and ivy-twined swing are straight out of her period in portrait photography. So too are the painted backdrops that whisper of Rembrandt and Rubens in the establishment studios, while fairly shouting of a new life and a new land in the studios of those who came later. Retouching also survives. As an obliterator of the stigmata of chocolates in children and of mortgages and middle-age in adults, retouching has contributed to the true outcome of our consultations.

"It is not a diagnosis but a dream. A moment when the light is kind, children have resolved all differences and love their mother. The father is present and protective while the entire family, innocent of disease, debt and the politics of the sexes, floats in a limbo outside history and beyond all time."

I later heard that when the prints were on exhibit at Harbourfront Al Gilbert and his assistant went down to see it. I had ordered one print from each studio and had paid anywhere from $15 to many hundreds for prints of the same size on the same Kodak paper although the more expensive ones did have some retouching. I had some concerns about how the high-end photographers would feel about being exhibited alongside the humbler immigrant ones. It turned out that Al Gilbert was quite amused when he saw the finished project. I also heard that people started using the series to select their wedding photographer.

However, when I showed up at American customs in Vancouver with those portraits they were not amused — figuring I was taking away Americans' jobs. It took them only a couple of minutes to deny me entry. This banning engendered a great deal of work. A number of letters from the Canada Council, Ontario's and various important museum curators and directors eventually persuaded American officialdom that the entry of myself and the portraits was not going to drive the U.S. economy into a job-destroying recession.

During the '90s these entries into the U.S. became increasingly unpleasant. These uniformed primitives were rude and frequently shouted abusively at travellers. They seemed uninformed, uneducated and poorly trained. This tendency culminated in an episode at Toronto's Pearson. I had been pulled out of line for a random agricultural inspection. Both my and my partner Sheila's suitcases were taken into a side room and rifled through. I was not concerned as we had nothing of interest and were merely entering the U.S. briefly to change planes at Charlotte. I was cleared and shown out a door leading back to the entry line where Sheila waited. When I got there I gave back her suitcase. Immediately there was screaming and shouting while a big attack dog was set upon me. All this by Americans in my country, not theirs.

Although I had travelled or worked in almost every U.S. state and had numerous American friends and colleagues by this time I'd had enough. There are many other more interesting places to go than the United States. Americans should be ashamed that these uncivil and uncultured officers are their face to the world. They even banned the very talented and quiet Rohinton Mistry because he was brown. I haven't gone back.

2003

These children of cheap oil and world-power-by-default can be both crazy and classy, generous and absolutely lethal. America's weird tapestry of extreme individualism and excess rolls out endlessly.

It's a month after I've republished my 1979 book *Monsters* about the late 19th century studio photographer Charles Eisenmann. His specialty had been making portraits of dime museum freaks. Every giant, multi-limbed, obese, tattooed or dwarfed performer on the circuit in the 1870s and '80s had visited Eisenmann's studio on the Bowery in New York.

Descendants of the photographer have just discovered my book while trolling Amazon and have invited me down to the beach town in New Jersey where they all now live. It's barely a month since my quadruple bypass heart surgery but I elect to go. Indirectly this family has been part of my life for over two decades so I can't wait to meet the ones still living. My GP Rae and my old friend Macbeth come over to the house and work hard with little pliers for over an hour removing all the staples in my chest and down my left leg so that I can fly to Newark, rent a car and barrel down the Jersey Turnpike. It's midwinter and the season throws every move and mood it has at me. It snows, it sleets, it hails, it rains, it freezes and snows again. Just for fun some fog gets tossed at me as well.

I finally slide off the freeway in the dark and skid my way through endless sprawl toward the coast. I meet my host at his office and he immediately takes me to a local restaurant where he has generously arranged a large dinner as part of my reception. He announces to the assembled diners that I've recently had open heart surgery in Canada. In Canada? It's a miracle that I'm still alive. The table is suddenly awash with stories about the evils of socialized medicine. Up there you wait decades for surgery that's probably going to be executed with a hatchet and a can opener. Bodies pile up in emergency departments; you have to shoot and trap your own hospital food. For a while I can't get a word in edge-wise, long-wise, any-wise.

Soon the conversation shifts to the superior American system. I hear about neighbours who had to sell their house to pay for dad's bypasses. People lost their second cars, even their boats to pay for follow up. When all these keeners finally pause to catch their breath before launching more tales of terror and triumph I jump in and tell them that my surgery was booked while I was still on the table having an angiogram — I didn't wait even a day. I had four of these $70,000 bypasses they're talking about and after leaving the hospital a week later I was handed a bill for $35 because I'd had a private room. That was it. But the power of myth is greater than the power of truth. My country sinks further into the third world. Things are so bad up there that I may be the only one still alive. Maybe I should appoint myself President of Canada. That would be okay as long as I understood who the real president was.

I try a few more times to get my story across but the propaganda from their health lobby has been just too effective. My dinner mates simply cannot absorb what I have to say so I give up. I turn to the couple next to me and inquire about their lives. Turns out he drives a truck and she's a grocery store cashier. They have ordinary jobs but an interesting hobby — they collect dead bodies, well, mummies actually. Their bungalow is full of them. I have trouble following the story but it seems that their latest acquisition is the preserved body of a musician with some connection to Elvis Presley. They bought him somewhere out west, Vegas rings a bell. The tricky part was getting him home. The guy was rigid, most stiffs are I guess, so they had to wedge him between the bucket seats of their Camaro. His head was back against the hatch, his feet on the dash. But that wasn't the tricky part. Their way home was obstructed by a few states that had intrusive laws banning the ownership and transport of corpses. You had to sneak across state lines at night and drive on crummy back roads. It was all a big pain in the ass and an infringement of their liberties.

I was already feeling nostalgic for Canada. Even Don Cherry was looking pretty ordinary. I had actually once done a project with him. Cherry had contracted to do a series of ads for pink insulation. They were television ads so a big studio was booked for the film shoot. It had an adjacent smaller one on the other side of the wall where I was to shoot stills for a poster campaign. We spent hours setting up before Cherry arrived. He came in accompanied by his wife and, of course, that little boss dog. Don was already costumed in one of his neck-brace shirts and a jacket that screamed at the top of its lungs. He was taken in to meet the film crew, the client's people and the agency writers, designers, account managers, etc. There must have been close to 60 people. When that was done he was brought over and introduced to my little crew of a half-dozen assistants, hair and makeup people and loaders. It's been said that half of success is just showing up. Well, most of the other half is remembering people's names. With just one introduction Cherry got them all — all 70. It's a skill practiced by successful politicians and people in sales. Remember their names and people love you for it. Myself, I don't really have it.

Cherry would work with the film crew and then come over to my side during their teardowns and setups. He'd address each of my little gang by name and they'd do anything for him. We'd get him into position and I'd cry, "Go." He'd immediately launch into his Don Cherry schtick. I'd shoot until I was sure I had the right moment and then I tell him to stop and he'd become just an ordinary guy. All day it was like that: Okay Don, go! Okay Don, stop! His internal hard drive would spin; his internal hard drive would stop. The act was obnoxious, the opinions outrageous but he was a treat to work with — a true pro.

I'm back in the U.S. on my annual six-week photo dash documenting Canadian-owned commercial properties all over North America. Each year as I flit through dozens of cities in as many days I encounter new holdings. Among this year's acquisitions is a mall in Monroe, Louisiana. This little city in the southern portion of the state has the standard American decaying downtown with the obligatory boarded-up little art deco office tower standing in blank-eyed dominion over the ruins. The mall on the edge of town is where all the action is. I rush into the parking lot in my rental and search out the manager. As usual I have about six hours to cover the whole thing before leaving town.

The discipline that I'd have to bring to these operations became legendary among various assistants I had over the years. For a couple of seasons I had a rock and roll bassist named Crash — for good reason — who worked up an elaborate mythologizing scenario for these mall incursions. In his

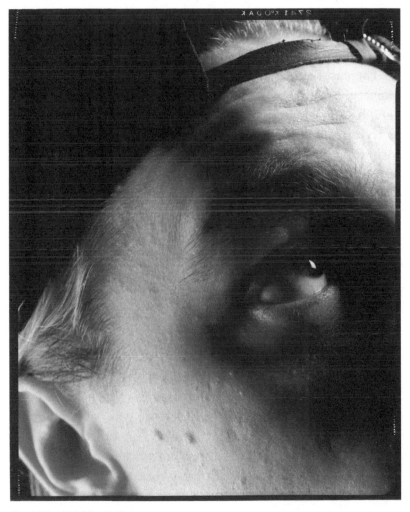

Crash Kowalski (John Bell)

version of my secret life as The Mall Master I'd appear, all in black, mysteriously at dawn, backlit with a lot of dry ice fog at the main mall entrance. With my jaw set, skinny legs akimbo and a holstered light meter on each hip, I'd pause for a few dramatic seconds while my Crash-composed theme song worked itself into a frenzy. Then I'd heroically stride in my black stretchies down the main corridor shooting every last mothering shoe store, card shop, electronics outlet and jean joint until there wasn't a single store untouched by my steaming shutter blades. At closing time I'd leave a still smouldering mall and vanish mysteriously into the suburban night.

The last year that Crash worked with me this fantasy movie got a little messy. Unbeknownst to me Crash and his band had a hit song and a video playing on MuchMusic. We'd be trying to work our way through some bleak shopping centre in Calgary or Kelowna and a bunch of teenyboppers would spot Crash and start screaming. They'd take out your tripod and trample your camera bags to death. Worst of all was that my starring role as the mysterious Mall Master was getting eclipsed by this bass-slapping upstart. We finally had to have a heart-to-heart about who was really the boss.

As my long day shooting the Monroe mall was winding up the manager offered to take me to dinner. I'm not a meat eater so dining in the land of the pork belly pig-out was always a challenge. My saviour in the South was usually the lowly catfish. So when the manager asked what I'd like to eat, I, of course, suggested that fish. Were there any good cat shacks around? Well, yes there were; he named two different ones. Which would I prefer? When I asked him what the difference was he told me that one of them was a 24-ounce drive away, the other a 48. I had no idea what he was talking about but since this was America where bigger is always better I choose the 48-ounce shack.

I soon found out how Monrovians measured distance. He drove me to a chain drive-in that looked like a Dairy Queen but was called Daiquiris Unlimited. We pulled up to the take-out window and he ordered two 48-ounce daiquiris and both promptly appeared in a pair of foot-tall Styrofoam pails. After we'd manhandled these things into the car's cup holders we pulled out into the street. Being a sucky Canadian I pointed out there was a cop car across the way. It was then pointed out to me that the officer was also enjoying a daiquiri. Apparently in this part of the state, drinking and driving was your god-given legal right. You could be charged with drunk driving but not with drinking. We wheeled off and onto the interstate.

As the mall manager drove he sipped his drink through a straw. I just had to see what a half-gallon daiquiri looked like so I pried the lid off my pail and peered in. The only other time I'd seen a liquid with that weird green glow was when photographing pools of spent fuel rods at the Chalk River reactor.

————

We've been paddling this long shallow bay for nearly an hour. Inches below the surface long emerald sea grasses roil in the wind-whipped waters, grabbing our blades and greedily fingering the bottoms of our boats. To look down is to drown.

My photographer colleague Geoffrey James and I are having dinner on the Piazza Navona. We're with Gilbert Reid who runs the Canadian Cultural Centre here in Rome. The others at the big table are various local cultural luminaries — writers, publishers, artists, journalists, cultural bureaucrats. Gradually talk turns to Canada and they start grilling Geoffrey. He demurs on the grounds that he's actually Welsh. He didn't come to Canada until well into his adult career as a writer for *Time* magazine. But they should talk to Michael. He's the real deal — born

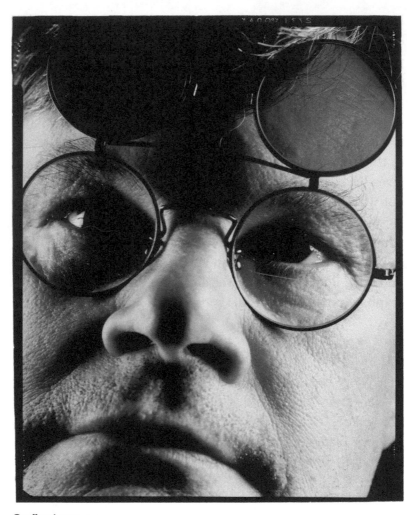

Geoffrey James

there, parents born there, grandparents and so on. My family probably cut down the first tree and cheated the first Indian. In fact, I'm so Canadian that I drink beer for breakfast.

This cultured crowd draws back in horror. They hadn't realized that they were dining with a primitive. I secretly have to confess that I have done as accused but really only occasionally and only on my northern island and only in summer and only when I was really thirsty and only for hair of the dog. I keep this to myself as all these sophisticated Italians are scrutinizing me for hairy palms, big incisors, small cranial capacity. Finally Paula, a well-known feminist journalist, stands on her chair and gives a speech about how it's only right and appropriate that a hairy-chested, bearded, plaid-clad, real Canuck guy like myself get all his B vitamins from beer. As she sings my praises my mind drifts off to an old McKenzie brothers routine. As I recall they're sitting in front of a pup tent wearing lumberjack shirts and toques. They've got a huge pile of two-fours — Molson Ex, Canadian, Labatt's Blue, 50, Mooschead. They're conducting a blind taste test; they've got slabs of Canadian bacon over their eyes so neither can cheat. They're going to find a winner but as it turns out neither of them can distinguish between any of the great Canadian brews. By the time they're finished all the cases are done and the bush is carpeted with empties. Finally Paula finishes her speech and sits down. I'm in love.

But she's a woman and — as every guy knows — they can be devious. There's often a price to be paid. Paula announces that we're all going to a Roman bar she knows to watch me drink beer. *Exeunt omnes.*

I obediently follow my new love down into this bar where she orders me a couple of beers while the crowd gathers round. The brews arrive. They're in one-litre bottles; they're fortified like sherry or port. The drink is 20% alcohol. I try to down one of them and fail utterly. I've let down Sam McGee, Grey Owl, Charlie Farquharson and Don Cherry.

After the Roman beer humiliation with Paula we all repair to her boyfriend Gianni's apartment. It's in the heart of the old city. We climb up several flights on spiral stone stairs and reach his huge dim apartment under the eaves. As I'm still conscious he pours me another drink and we all go into his bedroom and get seated on his ancient four-poster bed facing a towering armoire. He opens its antique doors to reveal a giant

TV. He then fetches a videocassette and inserts it into a VCR. Press play.

It's the most boring movie I've ever seen. A dashboard-mounted camera is recording every mile of a drive down a bleak highway. As it's now about two in the morning I start to doze off. To keep me awake Paula begins to supply voice-over. "A tree, a rock, a lake, more trees, rocks, lakes, trees and so on and on." Suddenly I wake up. It's highway 69 slicing north from Barrie toward Sudbury and my island. Soon as I announce that it's game over. Gianni fast-forwards to a section where he veers off the highway and reconnoitres a few trailer parks and garage sales in small northern towns. Everything is shot from arm's length — just above the knee. The engagingly naive Canadians proudly show off the features of their particle-board trailer interiors, the plastic fridges, the shag on the floor. The tour of garage sales is even worse — plaster statues, velvet paintings, weird lamps, sets of *Reader's Digest*s, jars of old screws and nails. My beautiful country never, ever looked so pathetic.

When I step from the cabin door there is a sudden scramble in my little herb garden in a hollow. A pair of big Canada geese chase their goslings down to the water and swim off annoyed, their plans for a salad and a shit aborted. The parents glare at me as they chug off escorted by their little tugs.

2002

I'm due at CityTV on Queen West by 6:45 a.m. to be inter-viewed on the morning show. It's a half-hour segment during which I'm to discuss my book about the 19th century New York theatrical photographer Charles Eisenmann. I've worked up a highly compressed talk on popular culture in immigrant America and the place of dime museum freak shows and photography within the frenzy of America's Gilded Age. I believe it's interesting. I think I'm media savvy.

But upon arrival I discover that I'm to share the 30 minutes with a dozen young women vacuum-packed into T-shirts, micro shorts and stilettos. This giggling pack of blondes are finalists in the Miss World Hooters competition. I'm not a finalist in anything.

One of them begins to gush about the grand prize. Soon all of them are squealing about this prize. Even I start to get excited. The prize! The prize!! Finally it comes out. The totally awesome, fabulous, panty-peeing incredible goal that all of them are clawing their fellow contestants for is . . . a weekend of free shopping in the West Edmonton Mall!

So I lose the pop culture wars by a wide margin. Who can identify with my rubber-skin men and lobster boys? Not even my pictures of Myrtle Corbin with her four legs can compete. I get out a few words of background and show a few photos before retreating to the Queen car and toast at home.

My little media tour isn't over yet. I've been booked for a segment on a morning radio show. The station's specialty focus is "talk radio for guys." After the TV disaster I've dramatically shortened my pitch. However I still naively think it germane to set the scene — late 19th century lower Manhattan and the popular dime museum — it explains why these photographs even exist. I get two sentences into my explanation before the host cuts me off.

"That's great, Mike, but let's get to what the guys are really interested in."

"What's that?"

"Ya know, that chick Myrtle with the two vaginas."

As I sit at my cabin desk I listen to birds. Every May and June there's an amazing chorus from the surrounding bush. I understand that it's basically "fuck me, fuck me," but it's still beautiful. For much of my life it was just a background — not anything I thought much about. But now that I'm moving rapidly into my last years, knowing has become more imperative. I now have more time to observe and reflect. Knowing has become urgent. There's not much time.

In an attempt to unmask these secret singers I've bought a bird program on DVD. For the uninitiated like myself, it's much better than a classic Peterson guide. You can see the birds in colour, see them fly, perch and hear them sing. Ideally I'd like a device that you can stick out the window, record the song and have it search a database for a match. Instead I have to search through hundreds of songs to uncover identities.

This weekend my elder son, Jake, is with me. He comes from a generation of button pressers. They dive right in to computers, dialing, keying, turning and tuning their way into an understanding of how a program or device works. I'm still a child of the mechanical age where if you fooled around with the wrong knobs or levers you got burned or lost an arm. Their keyboarding seldom has consequences. Losing data happens all the time. Shrug. Laptop terminally crashed? Shrug. It's already a year old so it's junk and an opportunity to buy newer and faster.

Jake and I have the wall of windows at the west end of the building wide open. As he scrolls through the entries playing bird songs I become aware that we seem to be hearing each one twice. I ask him to stop twitching through the database and carefully play a single birdcall. He does. It comes back to us. We try another. Same thing. Some little feathered friend out in the woods is toying with us. We play more songs: he mimics each and he's really good. I'm enjoying the game but Jake's generation is different, it's one nurtured on competitive video games. He quickly scrolls way ahead in the program and finds the call of a hawk. Our game is over.

1977

A mature city will have many specialized museums, some of which will be absolutely unique to that city. London has a steam pump museum upstream on the banks of the Thames. Philadelphia has the Rosenbach museum of rare books and illustrated manuscripts, and Detroit its various Ford museums. Although Toronto has lost its quirky medical museum it still has one devoted to shoes, another to postage and others to broadcasting, pioneers, Highlanders, textiles, railways and sugar. However few know that Toronto the Good has long had a museum of contraception. It displays vaginal plugs, penis protectors and pessaries of elephant and crocodile shit. It is there that you will discover that women of northern New Brunswick once drank a solution of beaver testicles soaked in alcohol in order to prevent pregnancy.

My very first assignment for a national magazine sends me to the museum's headquarters in darkest Don Mills to photograph various animal skin condoms and the many instruments of torture to which women have been subjected. A favourite is a series of loops and knots tied in monofilament by a fly-fishing doctor for an Inuk woman in our far north. It was his interpretation of the IUD and was implanted for decades until removed by astonished staffers at a Toronto hospital.

However, it was in the office of host Ortho's president that I found my favourite object. His office credenza, normally the territory of Chamber of Commerce trophies, giant ceremonial cheques and corporate golfing photos, supported what appeared to be a beige plastic filter coffee maker. This thing was designed to be a teaching tool for medical students. Where one would normally expect to slip in the filter basket hung a life size pair of soft pink plastic testicles. The device was accessorized with sets of alternate scrotums that could be locked into place like a bayonet-mount camera lens. Each pair of testicles modelled a different pathology to be diagnosed by squeezing the coffee maker's soft plastic balls.

My dreams are getting so banal — they simply take some inconsequential event from the previous day and work it endlessly, beating it to death until one is desperately sick of one's own mind. And I'm now too old to have exciting wet dreams. Sheila asks me how my dreams were the previous night and I tell her how bored I am with their small mindedness. They're starting to seem like network television.

"What are you going to do?" she asks.

"Search for a new dream provider."

"What do you think will happen next in your dreams?"

"I think they'll soon have commercials."

2015

The dreams I'm now having nightly are a subset of the basic anxiety dream. They're all about frustration. For some reason I'm driving a TTC bus in a bleak suburb of Toronto. I now marvel at the brain, my own brain, for imagining all the details of this place — the four lanes of traffic, the potholes, the median littered with garbage and its salt damaged grass. I pull the bus over to the shoulder because smoke is pouring out a hole at my feet. I dismount and open the hood at the front to investigate the source. Now that I'm awake I realize that this was stupid because the engine, like weekend drunks, is at the back of the bus. Just as I find the little levered valve that is the source of the smoke one of my sons, I can't see which one, suddenly appears and flips the lever. The bus takes off, driverless and empty.

I set off on foot in pursuit. The bus runs along ahead of me, doing the route on its own. At each stop, just as I catch up, it takes off for the next stop. The bus begins to get ahead of me. Worried that it's going to kill someone I hail a cab. The cabbie dumps his current fare with his luggage into garbage-strewn median. I catch up to him and breathlessly explain the emergency as my bus drives itself around a corner and out of sight. The cabbie agrees to accept my fare but wants to go to Tim Hortons first.

———

Four Roman Catholic priests from New York were the previous owners of my island. Their faith is a puzzle to me. They clearly didn't trust God to protect them: they had NRA stickers on all the windows. Like most Americans they didn't have a *cottage*, they had a *camp*. However, unlike good Catholics they called it Camp Kosher. Each removable round burner plate on their wood stove had a secret Star of David cast into its bottom. They entrusted God with only one job. Every liquor bottle, empty bean can or old tackle box they'd ever owned found final rest in the bushes on Crown land behind the island. It was God's job to do waste management.

A major Canadian bank has built a new training centre in the northeast part of Toronto. Branch employees from across the country come here for training sessions and upgrades. The bank was having problems launching new financial products. Information packages would be sent out from head office to local branches across the country. Many of these packages would go into a drawer — for good. Change was work. It was also scary. Small town bankers are very conservative.

Many of these sessions were conventional classroom ones but there were also exercises aimed at getting people to be more receptive to challenge and change. I photographed sessions where the many dumpy small-town women from local branches were encouraged to rappel down the tall face of the building's interior atrium under the guidance of professional climbers. Some of these women would burst into tears, trembling as they went over the wall in their harnesses. This was not like going to the mall. Their terror at the top was alarming but photographing their triumph when they got down alive was deeply moving. I never found out if this exercise actually opened any drawers.

The head of that bank also went through some changes. He got seduced by a well-known courtesan, a small-town Ontario girl who realized that she could make a career with her charms. A few physical enhancements and lots of practice in bed and she was off, sleeping her way through corporate Canada. She gave these driven men a great ride. Most of these guys were savvy enough to get the game. Not this bank president. He left his wife, married the girl and soon bored his trophy to tears. He was always on the phone — business, business, business. She cashed out in Nice and he retreated to run a bank in Ireland.

The new training centre was a handsome contemporary building with a big bleak atrium. The bank has been sold on the idea of hanging banners that will add colour, character and some history to that space. Since the bank has a small museum in its former headquarters building on Place d'Armes in Old Montreal, I'm dispatched to find suitable materials to photograph in large format for transfer to fabric. As it will be an intense week of work — lots of material to cover and film that will need constant reloading, sheet by individual sheet — I take my longtime helper Joanne with me. A side benefit for her is that her mother and sister live there. She can see them in the evenings.

The bank has a large collection of 19th century mechanical banks. However, these toys are quickly eliminated. Time and attitudes have changed. Cast iron "darkies" flipping coins into slotted watermelons are off message for a bank catering to a multicultural society. The toy banks are projected for removal from the bank's museum — into some kind of dark storage.

However they do have a collection of bank-issued notes of different denominations. Few Canadians realize that this country's various retail banks issued their own notes well into the 20th century. The familiar Bank of Canada bills debuted quite late in our history. I've seen several collections of these private banknotes. They're beautiful. Instead of dead politicians or obsolete royalty they feature engravings showing how we once earned our livings — ships lock through canals, farmers harvest wheat, we mine and make things. As these notes are stored in a room off the dome that crowns the building, Jo and I set up a studio high in the building at the base of the dome. I've brought studio lighting, a copy stand and a 4x5 Linhof with a flat-field close-up lens. We set to work copying these wonderful bills. It'll take most of the week.

Although we're working in a somewhat neglected part of the old building we are not alone. Nor is it quiet. The historic building is undergoing repairs to its upper storeys. We can hear workmen shouting, pounding and sawing. Occasionally they clomp by on the other side of the dome. We work long hours in a pool of light under the 3200° Kelvin quartz lights laboriously copying bills. Otherwise we keep the room dark to ensure colour purity on film.

Several days into the project I have an animal sense that we're being watched. I glance over to where a clutch of yellow hardhats peek in our door. Just as I do this I hear their foreman stage-whisper, "See I told you guys, this is the actual place where they print the money."

After a few days on the bank money job Joanne suggests we have lunch with her mother and sister. Jo has worked with me for years and her family is curious about this guy with whom she spends so much working time. An Old Montreal fish restaurant is selected — it's nearby. It's a place where you eat seated at a long counter. The four of us gather in a line, the mum between her daughters, me at one end. The two sisters spend the entire lunch complaining about men. I wisely keep my mouth shut except to eat or drink. Now this is a prominent Eastern Townships family, the daughters look rebellious but the mum looks Westmount. The daughters drone on; their mother is silent — I can't see her expression. Finally, at the lunch's end Mum pats both her daughters on the head. "There, there, dearies, don't get so fussed. Men are only good for two things: sex and moving furniture."

———

My Hong Kong born friend E.L., physician, musician and photographer, has once again invited herself up to my island. Remote and isolated, my small rock seems to encourage women to shed their clothes. While I write in the screen porch, she follows the light around the island, making little nests with pillows and a quilt in which she curls up. She loves the sensual heat of the sun.

Far across the inlet I hear my American neighbour start the engine of his boat. He reverses off his dock, turns and accelerates toward mine. I shout to

E.L. to get dressed. She retreats to her room wrapped in the quilt and emerges a minute or two later in a skimpy summer dress. Discretion ensured, we go down to my dock to greet the visitor. I introduce them, exchange news, then she asks him if she can see his island. They speed off together and I return to my work on the porch. Minutes later I hear a cry, look up and spot two tiny figures on his dock. I fetch my binoculars. She's already naked. America is a can-do culture.

A business consultant hired by Frank Stronach's Magna International has somehow convinced head office in Aurora that the global auto parts maker needs a documentary project — a book of photographs — celebrating Magna's production culture and success. And someone else has convinced him that my longtime photography collaborator Dougie and I are the guys for the job. Now a man like Frank who can go from being yet another immigrant tool and die maker, grinding out custom parts in a little garage downtown, to near global dominance in the business has got to be interesting. I looked forward to being a fly on the wall.

We began with a meeting at corporate headquarters where we met the senior people and are poured the corporate Kool-Aid — Frank was a patron, everyone was looked after and paid well over minimum, all production was via cutting edge technologies, etc., etc. We were shown copies of the Magna Charter that laid out these values. Then we set off on a multi-day tour of local production facilities.

At the time Magna had some 60 plants scattered around greater Toronto — we visited perhaps a dozen. All were anonymous small plants with under a hundred employees — strategically too small to unionize. None carried Magna signage on their exteriors; the only hint that they were Magna plants was the framed charter somewhere in the front office. While all local management and senior technologists were white and European, the production areas were awash with brown faces. You soon discovered that wages were not as advertised and production was not so high tech. While there were some sophisticated machines controlled by the then new technology of touch screens, most were the old familiar grimy tools — stamping machines, welders, drill presses and grinders. If you expected efficient rolling production lines you would be disappointed. Parts were wheeled by hand from station to station in old wooden bins on iron wheels. The 19th century met the 20th only to slip back to the early industrial revolution. Once again rhetoric and reality had failed to hold hands.

———

I'm on a 20-mile run up the northeast coast of the Bay when a heavy fog begins to build. Cold waters left from a harsh winter plus a warm front drifting in from the west make for a condensing environment. A Coast Guard buoy-tending ship steams a couple of miles ahead of me on a north reach. It's in sharp relief and then it vanishes; it looms as a shadow — light flashes off a bright surface — then it's gone again. I motor slowly north in a dazzling void.

A couple of hours later my main GPS becomes erratic and after some minutes finally shuts down. For once "belt and suspenders" Mitchell has no batteries for his backup portable positioning system. I know I'm getting close to where the mouth of my inlet releases river water from the interior into the Bay but from my perspective, several miles offshore in this white void, it's difficult to pinpoint where it lies. Many hard-rock reefs and shoals lurk ahead.

I boot up my depth sounder and begin to watch the read-outs — depth, bottom contour and water temperature. The bottom profile in this part of coast is so irregular that it gives few location cues but the water temperature does — it's beginning to rise. It peaks and then falls off. I tack back to the warmest water and swing east toward the coast, a plume of warm water from my river begins to guide me in. Every minute or so the temperature rises by a degree. I motor cautiously at a few hundred rpm, the diesel settling into an easy rhythm. The temp numbers continue to rise. Finally a white pine's top emerges to starboard before vanishing into a void but I have recognized its wind-sculpted shape. I know that tree. I'm going to make it in.

One brilliant sunny day in the early 1980s I set up a heavy tripod on the sidewalk crossing the Bathurst Street bridge. Using my 4x5-inch view camera and a panoramic film back I made several exposures of the view looking east through the big-shouldered girders of the bridge. The view encompassed the towers of the financial core, the yet-to-be transformed railway lands and the Gardiner and Lakeshore expressways. The large format film comprehended enormous detail. I liked this photograph so much that I made it a habit to return every couple of years for a remake. Each new take was positioned a little differently in order to accommodate the ever-changing skyline and produce a structurally balanced image. These photographs tell the city's story.

If you look carefully at a small section of one of the early ones you can see graffitied across a pedestrian bridge in the far distance the message "Homes not Domes." In a subsequent exposure in the series the lumpen form of what had just been named the SkyDome obscures that bridge. A year or two earlier when I'd been sent to make a portrait of Don Smith, president of EllisDon, the general contractor that was to build that stadium, I remember him bragging that it was going to be so huge that it would be visible across Lake Ontario from Brock's Monument at Queenston Heights. I later checked that out. Not only was he right but you didn't even need to ascend the monument to see that aesthetic monstrosity. From atop the Niagara escarpment it looked like a huge toad squatting on the far shore.

Occasionally I'd exhibit very large prints from the series in public galleries. Eventually they caught the eye of one of the Reichmanns who were busy not only building Canary Wharf but also further transforming Toronto's downtown. They liked my most recent photograph from the bridge but since I'd made it they had completed another office tower or two. Would I make a more current version of the photograph so they could hang in their offices?

The commission fee that they offered, which included one-time reproduction rights only as well as a large colour print, wasn't exactly generous. However, any amount that contributed to the furthering of the project was useful to me so I reluctantly agreed. I eventually executed the picture on a brilliant but ferociously bitter day in the middle of February. I got so cold waiting for the right light and a gap in the bridge traffic that I actually thought I was going to die.

I delivered a print that they did subsequently publish on the cover of one of their glossy print pieces. It was later framed and hung on an office wall. Everybody was happy. But about a year later one of the Reichmanns called me at the studio. He told me that they had finished looking at the photograph and wished to return it to me, minus the frame, so they could get their money back. This is how they'd become rich and I didn't.

Erect a cabin in this landscape and you build not only for yourself but also shelter for your neighbours in the bush. Birds soon nest under the eaves, bats sleep under cedar shakes, red squirrels hide in the attic, mice and wasps retreat inside come fall and a hare trembles under the floor. Everywhere there are insects — spiders, carpenter ants, wood roaches and flies. The crickets move in as do late summer wasps. Soon there's gnawing at night and sawdust in the morning. You have become a landlord.

Photographers don't often get titles but on this job I have one — principal photographer, BCE Place. For the next couple of years I will provide a variety of photographic services to this project — hanging off the top of the TD Centre, flying to Milan for a one-day shoot, photographing the Chrysler building from the roof of the Empire State Building. All this as BCE Place stealthily climbed into the Toronto skyline. I started before there is even a hole in the ground.

Much of it is about marketing. There will be a great deal of space to lease and finding suitable corporate tenants is vital. Square footage charges will, of necessity, be high. Over the next few years I will see considerable waste and dubious ethics.

Like all big architectural projects it begins with an expensive model. In the past when doing architectural shoots I'd begun to wonder if some of the big developers could even read drawings. A couple of times I'd been present when the model for some future project was delivered and you'd seeing a light bulb suddenly illuminate in the client's eyes. Some may call these big developers "visionaries" but often they weren't very visual. When my ex was working on lobby designs for the Bank of Montreal tower at Bay and King she'd show up for a meeting with the Reichmanns with a series of presentation boards presenting colour schedules and material samples. They'd be glanced at quickly and then she'd be told to take a good sized area of the lobby under construction, have the finishes installed — marble walls, brass, flooring, etc. — and call the client in when it was complete. A Reichmann would show up, dismiss the program and ask for a new design. A whole new set of boards would be made up and met with the same instructions. The marble would be torn out and new stuff installed, presented and rejected. These sample spaces were larger than the average Woodbridge monster house. And they were rebuilt several times. Undoubtedly the computer programs that now allow architects to take clients on virtual reality tours of proposed projects have saved a lot of money, time and grief. However, BCE Place, now Brookfield Place, was before all that.

A huge mockup of the block-square project was constructed inside a suite of offices located high up in the adjacent TD Bank towers. I did a number of all-night shoots there, a spooky experience as the HVAC systems would shut down after midnight. In the absence of the white noise they generated all one could hear at two in the morning was the grinding and groaning of the tall structure as it swayed in the wind. It could be quite alarming. One night I did my own groaning when the nine-foot-wide blue paper sky I'd hung above a large model of the whole complex collapsed on it, destroying part of the intricate model of Santiago Calatrava's steel and glass atrium.

At one point it got decided that a large hardcover picture book would be a lease deal clincher for the project. It would feature historical photographs of the site, my model photographs and some new ones that I was to take of the historic facades along Yonge Street and Wellington that were to be preserved. The ground floors of most of these 19th century buildings had been extensively modified and butchered over the decades but the upper floors were relatively intact. I was to record those, square-on, for the book. How?

I soon discovered that getting access to them from facing buildings across the street was impossible. Windows were sealed, landlords hostile and many wires were in the way. I tried to get city permission to run a cherry-picker bucket lift up and down those streets but it proved to be a massive challenge. Some of them were Toronto streets, others under Metro and one was a provincial highway — too many jurisdictions, too many bureaucrats and rules. It's always easier to say no and go to lunch.

Finally I booked a truck driver and his 53-foot tractor-trailer. We'd pretend to be making a site delivery. I climbed up with an assistant onto the trailer roof and set up a tripod and large format camera. We drove majestically up Yonge Street while cops innocently directed traffic down below. None of them ever looked up and uncovered our scam. As I frantically shot I congratulated myself on having dreamed up such a brilliant solution — until we turned onto Wellington Street. I'd forgotten about the high voltage trolley lines that hung just above trailer height. Down went my tripod while I dove for the deck.

We crawled over to Bay Street, then down to Front and back up Yonge to face the same cops who once again failed to look up. This time I lay on the trailer roof like a sniper and got the pictures. They're handsome but don't look at all death-defying.

That wasn't the first time I'd cheated the Guy with the Scythe on that job. One afternoon when I was working with a client in my Queen Street East studio the phone rang. The BCE gang wanted me to immediately rush down to the TD Centre with a camera, go to the roof, lean over and make photograph of their site, just a block-sized hole across the street at that point. The picture was for a leasing meeting the next morning. I said I couldn't: I was working with a client. They reminded me that my title, Principal Photographer, came with an obligation. My studio client was now looking anxious so I demurred once again.

The voice on the phone said, "It will only take you 45 minutes."

"I can't."

"We'll give you $500."

"No!"

"$1,000."

"I'm really sorry."

"$1,500."

"I can't leave in the middle of a shoot."

"$2,000."

"Regrets."

"$3,000."

"Apologies."

Twenty-five years ago I discovered that I had my price. For four grand in 45 minutes, I could be bought. I gave my client a cold beer, grabbed a camera and a cab, met security at reception, walked out on the roof, crawled out over the edge with two big guys sitting on my legs. I hung over the granite plaza spinning 700 feet below and squeezed the shutter. On the way back to the studio I had the cab stop at the lab. They'd courier the results to BCE at eight the next morning. I was back in the studio in 50 minutes. I knew that as a photographer with two boys to support I'd peaked financially. But the experience was awful. Selling out wasn't worth it.

1978

I'm working on a magazine story about secret rooms. In each one I'm to do a portrait of someone whose life depends on that room. So I photographed actor Barbara Hamilton in the green room at the Royal Alex down on King Street and the province's chief justice in the judges' anteroom at Osgoode Hall up on Queen. I travelled to Smiths Falls to photograph Hershey's head chocolate maker in the conching room where huge granite rollers slopped back and forth in giant tanks of chocolate. The smell there was so strong I couldn't eat Hershey's Kisses for years. That space is now a legal marijuana grow-op.

But the best room of all housed the reactor at Chalk River. It was a big spooky-looking *2001* monolith surrounded by swimming pools that held spent fuel rods. You could look down through weird water to where those things seemed to glow on the bottom. We still haven't figured out what to do with those rods. It feels like we'll be arguing about them for another 10,000 years while they lie about quietly giving us all cancer or kids with six fingers.

I've always felt like the perfect child of the nuclear age. I'd lived through fallout shelters with boxes of beans and macaroni stored in the basement should rockets and bombers fly in over cottage country. But my closest link of all was the fact the initial full day of my life, November 4, 1943, the graphite reactor at Oak Ridges, Tennessee, went critical for the first time allowing scientists to make plutonium from uranium, a crucial step in the creation of the bomb. Just three months before my second birthday nearly 130,000 people got incinerated in Hiroshima and Nagasaki — all this and that other huge Holocaust nestled inside my lifetime.

I was charged with solving a puzzle. A well-known but anonymous donor had given the Art Gallery of Ontario a collection of negatives and prints made in the Lodz ghetto during the Second World War. They were the work of Henryk Ross, a 1930s Polish photojournalist who freely plied his trade until the Nazis goose-steeped their way across Poland on their march to world domination. Ross and several hundred thousand fellow Jews were subsequently penned into the Lodz ghetto for the duration of the war. There the Jewish inmates self-managed the internal affairs of the ghetto while German peasants dressed as soldiers patrolled the periphery.

Ross became the ghetto administration's official photographer. By day he recorded the scenes the Germans wanted to preserve and promote; by night he recorded the events they didn't — the casual violence and the concentration camp cattle-car rides to industrialized executions. He got those photographs by hiding in sheds and poking his Leica lens between the buttons of his overcoat. He had vision and guts as did his wife, Stephania, who assisted.

In 1944 Ross, sensing that the Thousand Year Reich was ending somewhat early, buried his photographic evidence in a corner of the ghetto. After liberation he returned and dug it up. The negatives, prints and posters were water-damaged but had, by and large, survived. He took them on his postwar exodus to Israel and there tried to organize his material. One of the things he did was contact print his 35mm negatives, cut them up into tiny individual frames and paste them, about 40 images to a page, in a sequence to make a book. It was a huge amount of work — he fiddled with the sequence for years. The result makes no sense.

My writer's and photographer's job was to interpret this broken narrative of weird juxtapositions and random repetitions. I had a headache for days. The most frustrating part of the process was my own mind. I kept recognizing something in Ross's sequence but I couldn't articulate it. It was only after the AGO/Yale University Press published my attempt in the book *Memory Unearthed* that I began to understand what I'd been looking at.

A quarter century earlier I'd returned from the perilous process of photographing the Sandinista's revolution in Nicaragua and experienced the strange and powerful dislocations that we now call PTSD. Ross's scrapbook of images was an unconscious graphic representation of his emotional and intellectual trauma. It wasn't his intent but it proved to be the only way he could cope.

The exhibition *Memory Unearthed* at the Art Gallery of Ontario had its costs. The Jewish community of Toronto gave generously. It wasn't just part of the history of a people; it was an intimate part of many Toronto Jewish families' lives. Among the big supporters was Barry Sherman, the founder and CEO of Apotex, the generic drug giant. At the exhibition opening I watched Barry corner Matthew Teitelbaum, then the AGO's director. After their animated conversation Matthew wandered toward me. When I asked about the subject of their exchange Matthew said it had been about the high prices charged for original works of art. Barry couldn't understand them. He thought paying so much was crazy when you could buy a reproduction in the gallery shop for a few bucks.

"Did you convince him otherwise?" I asked

"No. How can you argue with a guy who makes copy drugs for cheap?"

One of my obligations was to join the project's curator and the other three writers for two nights of public readings and dialogue focused on the exhibition. The first evening, attended largely by members of the photography community, went well. The audience was alert, interested and vocal. It put those of us on the stage at our best. However, the following evening, a private function for the financial supporters of the exhibition, was dismal.

The hundred or so invitees were a good cross-section of the country's richest Jews. They represented many millions made in finance, retailing, real estate as well as generic drugs. Many of them had roots in the ghettos and historical connections to the Holocaust. The room seemed redolent of gloom. And very still. Despite all of us having laboured to reduce our months of work to individual five-minute presentations, the attendees couldn't stay with us. While we raced through our slides and expositions much of the audience was lit by the glow of their smart phone screens. We talk, they check their emails. We debate, they text. A 70-year-old shadow darkened the room. This shadow will darken yet another century.

And another trauma. Barry Sherman claimed to have an IQ of 180 but he spent much of his career suing his competitors in patent wars as well as his family members and friends to whom he'd lent money. He'd become worth some four or five billion over the years, but this way of life didn't seem all that smart to me. As it turned out the Shermans had their own terrors. In December 2017 he and his wife, Honey, were found hanging above their basement swimming pool.

A long dark shadow stalked the Jews that shared my generation. Born during or just after the Second World War, many had had parents or close relatives in the camps. The stressed environment they grew up in was manifested in many strange behaviours. The hands of these 20-year-old university students would shake while doing the simplest tasks. They had a wry humour that combined some sense of superiority with self-loathing and deprecation. Many had eating disorders. They were a little bit crazy. My own difficult mother-in-law — she had spent four years in the camps as young woman — told me that she had never met Jews in Europe like the ones she encountered daily in Toronto.

For one raised as a meat and potatoes WASP the food obsessions were immediately most noticeable. Food, food, food. Eat and eat. Before one meal was finished they were talking about the next. One year in the early '70s I drove from Toronto to southern Mexico with a Jewish friend who eventually became a political economy professor. For me it was a voyage through ever-evolving landscapes and cultures; for him it was a perilous expedition from meal to meal. Everything was anxious appetite. He'd awake talking about what we'd have for breakfast. Soon as we got rolling on the road each day the talk would immediately turn to lunch. The pitch of his voice would rise ever higher as noon approached. There would be long speculations about menus. I'd pull off the road and he'd rush into a diner where he could barely read the menu for the shaking of his hands. After ordering he'd break into a sweat in anticipation of the delivery of food. When it arrived he'd be unable to hold a knife and fork. He'd have seconds and thirds. It was nuts.

Another food-obsessed North End Winnipegger lived in a world where in a prelapsarian past the restaurant food had always been better, tastier, cheaper. He lived in a present of precipitous and perilous decline. I once took him with me on an assignment to Washington because I knew he wanted to experience its new Holocaust museum. I paid for his transportation, accommodations and all meals save one. The morning we planned to return I suggested we have breakfast in the hotel in order to save time. When he was presented with a $12 bill for his meal he raged out of his seat. I'd ruined his day, even his entire life by forcing him to eat a hotel breakfast instead of driving all over D.C. looking for a cheap diner. The entire breakfast room looked on in slack-jawed horror as he crashed his plate on our table scattering cutlery across the floor. He looked insane. By the way, we did get to the Holocaust museum. He lasted less than 20 minutes before skulking out to the forecourt of the building. He said not a word for the rest of the day.

In the early '70s I decided to take a gap year from graduate school and left Mexico for Toronto. To support myself during that break I took what I assumed would be a simple, relaxing job doing maintenance at the 22-storey "free university" called

Rochdale College. Within months I was one of the managers of the building with an extremely stressful job. I did it for a year and then returned to graduate school to study film and photography. I gradually lost touch with the Rochdale crowd.

Years later I ran into my Rochdale co-manager on an east end street. A prairie WASP, he'd converted to Judaism and married the daughter of a rich Jewish scrap metal dealer. He invited me to have a beer and catch up at the large house they'd bought together. As we hadn't seen each other for decades I went. We sat at the big eat-in kitchen island with our beers. His wife stood between us with a J-cloth in her hand. Every time one of us lifted our glass she'd dart in and wipe the imaginary ring from the granite countertop. Gulp, wipe, gulp, wipe, gulp, wipe. It was the most stressful drink of my life.

The shadow. I still struggle to comprehend the experience of my late mother-in-law who, captured in Paris at age 19 by the Nazis, was locked up in a concentration camp for four years to daily experience unimaginable horrors. She talked little of it but at one point told me that after days of screaming hunger they were served soup with human body parts floating in it. She worked as a nurse so she knew.

Many of them spent years in psychotherapy, going twice a week for decade after decade. This became an integral part of the culture. There'd be periodic announcements: "I've graduated!" Then the sessions would begin again. I could never see signs of much improvement from all this talk therapy but perhaps it allowed them to function out there in the world at all. The costs to the health care system of this postwar immigration must have been enormous but by later in the century they were giving back. The old WASP donor families sitting on the charitable boards of hospitals, orchestras and museums were gradually replaced by generous Jewish ones. And they, in turn, are now moving aside for Italian, Chinese and South Asian generosity.

Living in a city as culturally mixed as Toronto is an enriching experience but not always easy. Those of us who have been in Canada for generations — those that our former leader, Jurassic Steve, crudely called "Old Stock Canadians" — are too polite to talk about the sometimes difficult accommodations required. I will.

It took me a long time to make peace with Portuguese neighbours from the Azores. They always seemed primitive, dour and uncommunicative. In my part of town the fathers often beat their sons who would then hit the streets in a vengeful rage, stealing and vandalizing. Those kids smashed into our cars at night so often that the Anglo professionals on the street took to leaving their cars unlocked with windows down in order to minimize the nightly destruction. Let them have the parking change in the ashtray. Forget owning a car radio or a GPS.

At the time, in addition to a van, I owned a late '60s black Ford fastback with the Mustang V8 and a manual tranny — three-on-a-tree as we then called it. The girls I knew in the photo world named it the Black Beauty and asked for rides, but to those sons of the Azores it was the devil. They'd come at night, climb onto the garage roof next door and jump onto the car's. Day by day the profile of that car got thinner until eventually you had to slouch in the seat to clear the head liner. While those guys were at it they'd steal whatever photo gear I'd left locked in my van, itself locked in my garage. Usually it would be my lighting kits that were too bulky and heavy to lug into the house at day's end. Those thieves were never very smart about it, often dragging the big cases into the Silver Dollar Room a few blocks away in order to fence the stuff to lounge lizards. It never seemed to occur to them that it would be a good idea to remove my shipping labels, Air Canada baggage tags and other ID. Sometimes a sober Samaritan would surreptitiously tear off a tag and phone me.

I'd trot over, with or without the cops, reclaim my gear and buy the caller some drinks.

At that time my sister lived in a small industrial building situated on one of the very few designated laneways with full services — water, sewers, power. They were on their roof deck one day when police arrived in full force, cordoned off both ends of the block and began breaking into the garages lining the lane. Most of them contained a brand-new Mercedes and a shipping container full of appliances. Each local family had a family business. The wives worked as night cleaners at the big department stores downtown. They'd stuff goods into garbage bags, put them out on Queen and Yonge for their husbands to pick up and store before the big move back to southern Europe. All these old ladies in black were cuffed and stuffed into paddy wagons. Canada was just a short-stop free shop.

Integration and acceptance takes time. I'm now on another old downtown street and once again have Portuguese Canadian neighbours. The retired dad often secretly shovels my walk. His son supplies me with exotic tomato seedlings every spring. They take in and feed my cat when I'm late getting home. In short, they're perfect Canadian neighbours.

I think in some way the issue is peasant culture. They've left their country of origin where they had little and encounter here a world of plenty that seems inaccessible. They're in a hurry to join the party. Here I'm also trying to understand the behaviour of the many immigrants from China — not the educated and assimilated from Hong Kong who become doctors, architects and engineers here, but the destitute immigrants from the hinterland. When Sheila and I were making a film about the last year of photographer Mary Pocock's life I filmed her several times in the palliative ward at Princess Margaret Hospital. It was a very beautiful new facility that featured interior room windows filled with huge colour transparencies based on photographs that Mary had made in Italy.

Everything in that ward was designed to give extremely ill people some peace and comfort. Mary loved it.

Across the hall from her was a room occupied by an ancient Chinese grandmother. Once a week her extended family would come and visit her for an hour and every week they'd exit carrying off everything in the room that wasn't screwed down. The grandmother would be left on a bare mattress with no sheets, no covers, no bedside lamp, no water jug or glass, no cushions, food tray, nothing. It took the "nice" Canadian nursing staff weeks to get up the courage to confront the family and demand that they bring everything back. It was a strange way to thank their newly adopted country for giving the family matriarch such tender care.

We'd also done a free fundraiser film for a downtown special needs school with a playground that was just a barren muddy yard behind a chain-link fence. Our short film encouraged people to donate monies to buy playground furniture and plantings. Money was indeed raised, furniture installed and shrubs, trees and flowers planted. The next day the stuff was gone. The very committed principal wouldn't discuss the security videos that revealed that old Asian grannies from the neighbourhood had come after dark to liberate the hard-won goods.

Nobody wanted to deal with them or knew how. The thinking behind it was literally so foreign and we're so constrained by ideas and ideals of political correctness. My way of dealing with this kind of stuff has been to go and visit the country of origin of people who were driving me crazy. When I got to experience first-hand the very overcrowded, unequal and uncivil society that was the legacy of Mao's Cultural Revolution then I had some compassion for those who behaved badly here. I knew I had to go there when after several years of trying to live beside an utterly irresponsible and indifferent Chinese neighbour — garbage everywhere, no house maintenance and numerous illegal units — I retreated one summer to my Canadian-spoiled-brat private island in Georgian Bay. En route I stopped at a marina in Parry Sound to pick up some boat parts. When I saw that a group of giggling Chinese guys there had just rented an outboard and were heading out into Georgian Bay, *my* Georgian Bay, I suddenly felt sick to my stomach, I was so upset. Then I was upset with myself having such a racist reaction. I'd had numerous close Chinese Canadian friends, including some great girlfriends. It was a strange and unsettling emotional schizophrenia. I was dealing poorly with the experience of the Other and I was supposedly once an anthropologist.

———

I created much of this building with my own hands. Its cupola leaks, a few doors stick, and various animals and bugs sneak in through unintentional gaps, but I did get a few things right. When I sit in the reading chair in the main room I can see through the washroom door to a tall, narrow window placed next to the glass shower stall. It gives out to a view of the island close behind where white pines crown a beautiful rock face rising out of a slim channel graced with water lilies and wild rice.

This building has taught me many things — not just the role of architecture as shelter but also a damper of the world. In its back bedrooms the world is low-level white noise — a faint song of surf, a hiss of wind in the pines and the sirens of insects. Yet in the big front porch, a room of slim columns and floor to ceiling screens, the world roars. Waves break a dozen feet away, air bullies through the screens and the whole world stomps about. I now realize how a building can impoverish the senses and put distance between the self and the environment. It protects but also diminishes.

A light bulb swings over a small table in a log cabin on an island where two photographers duel at the midnight hour. Outside, on all sides, the black Ottawa River is a night train racing for the St. Lawrence, the Gulf and a dark cold sea.

Photographer Geoffrey James and I are playing Scrabble . . . to the death. We've been burning up the board on the same game for hours, neck and neck, tooth and nail, drink for drink. James is being so competitive that I'm determined not to let him win.

Somewhere around midnight Geoffrey suddenly inflates and with great pretension lays down a word exactly in the middle of the board and stentoriously declares himself the winner. I look down at his victory word . . . "*yeg.*"

"Geoffrey! What the fuck is that? That's not a word. That's bullshit."

Jowls shaking like Diefenbaker, Geoffrey declares that it's a perfectly good word — Philadelphia slang for safecracker. I, the little guy from small-town southern Ontario, glare across the table at this Oxford-educated, former *Time* magazine writer and now instant Brit Twit. Of course there's no dictionary in the cabin and the roiling river is indifferent to my tragic loss.

The next day my first wife, Annick, and I begin the long retreat to Toronto. When I reach the beginning of my half-block-long downtown driveway she orders me to stop the car. I do and she jumps out, mounts the front steps and vanishes into the house. By the time I've parked my car at the back and dragged our bags to the front she's back outside with a dictionary in hand. She confirms that there is indeed a Webster's word for safecracker. Triumphantly she announces that *yeg* has two gs — *yegg*! Now that's loyalty. I'm not a loser.

When I was starting a family my wife worked for a large commercial architectural firm. It was one of those business-oriented partnerships designed to cover all the essential bases. One partner was a WASP, the other Jewish. One was in the old Granite Club, the other joined the Jewish Primrose Club. It worked well for years: commissions came from the old establishment and also from the ambitious, parvenu developers who were transforming skylines not just in Toronto but New York and London. This firm still exists today although the partners' names have been reduced to initials. It's a formula that's still used although today's most successful firms have taken on greater partnership ethnic diversity in order to reflect the multicultural makeup of Toronto and court global business. Nowadays you've got to add an Asian partner — a Chinese or Japanese Canadian — and perhaps a South Asian or an Arab. The main thing is to make money and get mentioned regularly in the papers.

Anyway, my then wife who is Jewish but very secular had to take a lot of shit from the Jewish partner. He hated the striped socks she wore to work. He thought the colours she wore too bright and the interiors she designed too playful. When I went to University College in the 1960s all the Jewish girls wore maroon and black. That was it — a very somber palette that must have informed his sense of proper dress. It was a culture still in mourning.

The partners had a kind of good cop/bad cop routine. The Jew would give her hell and then the WASP would invite her to dinner at a hotel he owned. The buildings this cultural marriage produced were staggeringly mediocre but the firm made pots of money because they kept their eye on the bottom line and were tough. Photographs of the firm's offices in the 1960s showed all workers in white shirts, ties and business jackets when the world outside was rebelling in bell-bottoms and tie-dyes. Things hadn't progressed much when my wife worked there a decade later.

Despite her perceived solecisms she soon graduated to running a department of interior designers. She had many buddies among the architects who actually did the grunt work of getting detailed designs finished and the buildings up. Their projects could be huge. I remember her doing floor and reflected ceiling plans plus colour and finish schedules for a building of a million square feet. No mean feat.

She continued working into the early months of her first pregnancy without complaint.

Then one morning I got a tearful phone call. Would I come and pick her and several colleagues up immediately. Puzzled, I jumped in the car and headed up the parkway. When I pulled into the office parking lot I was greeted by a huddle of crying women. They were all pregnant. All had been fired by the Jewish bad cop. Now no benefits would have to be paid. It was creepy to go in and collect their stuff. All their architect buddies scurried for cover or kept their heads down on their drafting boards. They all knew it was wrong. In fact it was totally illegal. But they all wanted to save their own skinny asses. It showed the depth of workplace friendships — not very. It was shameful.

In the car I urged the women to file a labour complaint and sue. But they were all now too preoccupied with their pregnancies to start a war. They let the bad cop get away with it.

Years later when I served on the curatorial and acquisitions committee of a major museum I sometimes had to share a board table with this man. He had no memory of who I was and had probably treated so many people badly that most were erased by utility. He'd been a collector all his life and when he made some little donation to the museum I had to witness a lot of sycophancy on the part of curators and the director. When you knew the backstory of the money it was painful to watch. One longed for justice.

I run the river with a friend, bankside cedars browning, pines fading, but waters sparkling with the crystal light of fall and its breezes. A few days later I'm taking in the same light on the Seine. However the thickets of Paris, that city of foolishly self-important buildings, are composed of selfie sticks. Every tourist under 35 has one. Dead selfie sticks litter the sidewalks where poor African immigrants hawk replacements. Everywhere in the Pompidou, the Musée D'Orsay and the Louvre, one's view of the paintings is blocked by young tourists taking selfies. They even take them during videos at the Louis Vuitton Foundation, entering the darkened screening rooms just long enough to capture themselves with a frame from videos like Christian Marklay's *Crossfire*. They're all young people struggling to be individuals in a world of seven billion. Who could have ever guessed that the true democratization of photography would be brought about by the telephone? We fly home.

Sheila and Michael at Les Deux Magots, Paris

A few years later I had a more extreme selfie experience back in Toronto. My younger son, Ben, had leapt into the lineup for Kusama tickets at the Art Gallery of Ontario. He must have started at dawn because by the time he scored tickets for himself, his girl, as well as Sheila and me, there were 45,000 people on hold. The big draw in this fun house carnival by Japanese pop artist Yayoi Kusama was the six mirrored "Infinity" rooms. The capacity audience on the Thursday evening we went had a median age under 30. All the young women teetered from room to room in stagger-steep heels and clothes so tight and skimpy that bared body parts squeezed out like toothpaste. This vain and horny crowd shrieked from mirrored room to room taking infinite selfies inside each before rushing off to the next, totally oblivious of Kusama's paintings and sculptures. Their gallery visit had nothing to do with art.

We quickly discovered a workaround the lineups for each room. Spectators were being admitted for 20 seconds at a time in trios. As most of the shallow screamers were couples one could join a second line, much shorter, as a single in waiting to be paired with a couple. So we did. I seemed to inevitably end up doing my 20 seconds of vanity time with pairs of shrink-wrapped young women. Later when we left the gallery I puzzled over what all these fashion girls were doing with the balance of the evening. Sheila had the answer. "Oh, they're back in their tiny rented condos trying to figure how to Photoshop the grizzled old lurker-guy, you, out of their Infinity photos."

2006

We are five, seated at one end of the boardroom table in New York's Museum of Modern Art. Our job is to interview roughly 40 candidates for the position of photography curator at the Art Gallery of Ontario. One by one the impressive c.v.s enter one end of the room, spot the tiny cluster of interrogators at the far end of a table like a runway at LaGuardia and quickly shrink. The discrepancy between the paper and the person is frequently huge.

Of the small handful of applicants that are of interest it soon becomes apparent that they see Toronto through an old lens: as a tryout town where one polishes a few skills and contacts before moving on after a couple of years to somewhere more important. Others clearly have no interest in doing the grunt work. The AGO's photography department has been on a donor-driven acquisition binge that parallels the classic donor edifice complex. The rich love to get their names on cornerstones and carved granite door arches but seldom have any interest in backing up their building donations with operating funds. Utility bills and replacement roofs aren't sexy. The thousands of recently donated photographs in the collections have yet to be properly catalogued and conserved. Most male applicants for the job clearly see that part of the job as toil beneath them and best dumped into the laps of worker-drone grad students. The gallery needs a curator who will prioritize that unglamorous task.

The other scarce commodity is an individual not only intimate with the medium's complex history but also sympathetic to the concerns and production of contemporary practitioners, especially domestic ones. Americans have been steamrolling over the medium for much of the past century. It's time to recognize and nurture the many talents at home. This position will be a very large house with many rooms.

After doing more interviews and hosting finalist presentations to staff back in Toronto we five announce our decision. This results in me, and I'm sure some of the others, being pulled into corners and grilled by senior staff. Why were we proposing the selection of the "junior candidate"? What was unsaid but suspected was why were we not only supporting someone who was recently out of graduate school but also female and gay. But we collectively stood our ground; the committee's choice was honored in the end. We got a classy woman with one foot in the past and another firmly planted in the present who knows her stuff and, best of all, is not an import but a deeply established Canadian with roots in both Anglo and Francophone culture. May the era of hiring Brits and Americans to run our cultural institutions soon end.

So what about photography? Can a photograph make a difference? Do pictures matter? Have all of us who take this so seriously been wasting our time? Do they do anything useful beyond greasing the wheels of commerce in advertisements and packaging?

Unquestionably they can and do.

Roger Fenton's 1854 photograph of the so-called Valley of the Shadow of Death in Crimea was a progenitor of millions of war photographs that were to shape and change public attitudes to all future conflicts. No one can forget their first viewing of Nick Ut's *Napalm Girl* and the outcry it generated. The photograph of drowned three-year-old Alan Kurdi on a Turkish beach changed attitudes toward refugees and influenced Canadian immigration policy. And when I was an undergraduate at University of Toronto I had a friend there who was a medical student. He always carried a crumpled copy of Steichen's *Family of Man* in his bag to remind him why he was studying to be a doctor. For him that book's photographs had healing power.

Finally, everyone on the planet was affected by the 1972 Apollo 17 crew's photograph of the entire Earth as a vulnerable little blue and brown ball lost in a vast black limbo. It energized the environmental movement and made us feel like rats clinging to a shipwreck in a dark, disturbed and hostile sea.

It's the second of September and I'm alone on the island. The heartbreaker crystalline autumn light has arrived, allowing every rock, tree and living thing to strut its stuff.

FIVE

A TARNISHED
LITTLE REVOLUTION

"We struggle against the Yankee,
enemy of humanity."
HIMNO DE LA FRENTE SANDINISTA

"You can always rely on America to
do the right thing. Once it has
exhausted the alternatives."
WINSTON CHURCHILL

1984

The room is pin drop silent. After being marched into Comandante Olga's office at gunpoint I am ordered to sit in a low chair facing her desk ten paces away. She's a big woman in a fighter's uniform with a practised scowl. Two soldiers cradling automatic weapons stand on either side of her. The pair of soldiers who'd escorted me in fidget with their weapons somewhere behind me. She glares with displeasure.

After travelling around Nicaragua for 10 days photographing the ongoing revolution I've been ordered into the Comandante's headquarters. Her people had designed a program for me — places to go, situations to photograph, people to interview. Word had gotten back to her office: there had been deviations and digressions. I had been caught asking my Jeep driver to suddenly stop en route. I had chosen houses at random and knocked on doors, gotten myself invited in, had asked questions. I had taken unauthorized photographs of ordinary people who hadn't always understood what was correct. I had gotten too close to Presidente Daniel Ortega at a rally. All this was treasonous.

Finally she spoke. From now on a soldier would travel with me everywhere. And there would also be a handler to take notes and report on everything I said and did. I made no reply — I had no power to stop this. A stiff silence returned to the room. After some minutes she lifted a sheaf of papers off her desk and tossed it toward me. It fell short on the floor. "Pick it up!" she snapped. I leaned forward and retrieved the papers. "Read!"

The 10-page, single-spaced document was written in somewhat imperative legalese Spanish. I began skimming through the typewritten pages. I was to express my solidarity with the Nicaraguan people and the goals of their revolution. I was to do the same for the Cubans. I could do that — what the Sandinistas professed to be attempting was certainly an improvement over the regime of Samoza and his American backers. Ditto for Fidel and Batista. After some time in Mexico and Peru I was all for reform. The document droned on and on about imperialism, colonialism and exploitation. Buried just before the florid ending was a paragraph in which I agreed to surrender all my film and notes to the Comandante for editing and correction before leaving the country. They would make all choices. They would write the captions. There was a space on the last page for me to sign and date the agreement.

I dropped the document back on the floor, leaned back in my little wooden chair and crossed my arms. Our eyes met.

"Sign it!"

"I can't."

"Sign it or there'll be no more travel and no more pictures."

"If I sign this thing and people in Canada and the U.S. find out that you edited the work and wrote all the captions this project will have no credibility. The whole effort will be useless. The National Film Board will toss it in a can."

"Sign it or leave the country!"

"Como usted guste. I'll go home tomorrow and there will be no show, no essays, no travelling exhibition."

Comandante Olga stood up.

The tension set the soldiers to fiddling with their guns.

She sat down.

I stood.

Finally Comandante Olga rose to her feet and made for a back door. Just before exiting she turned to me and barked.

"You have until Friday to sign. In the meantime, there will be no more travel or pictures."

She exited slamming the door.

If I didn't get shot in daylight the night would bring adventures. My home base in Managua was a garden shed with a bed and washstand, camp stove and a hook on the door. I'd dump my camera bags there after a long dusty day in a Jeep, pump water in a pail, strip and start to wash off the day. This was usually when the tapping began. Finally I'd answer in the nude, peeking around the door, my bath water dripping on the bare board floor. They seemed to have worked out a schedule, those women, for they never doubled up. There was a beautiful Colombian whose Nica husband had died in the fighting. A skinny Ecuadorian with a baby would try to work my heartstrings. There were young Nicaraguan women as well. There was nothing there for any of them — not much for anybody. You couldn't buy the simplest staples — bread, flour, toilet paper or toothpaste. Soap was a luxury. Those were heady times for the people but it was hard for them to have hope. At forty I was still a passable contender. I represented two car garages, TVs, thick towels and a soft life. They all wanted out and knew well their only capital. I just wanted to eat and sleep. I'd gotten through another day and survived.

Many nights now I feel close to not. I'm now in my late 60s and, aside from the usual handicaps of being no longer young, I have a heart that has been repaired three times. Mostly it seems to work fine and then suddenly it will wake me, pounding hard and fast in the dark. Sometimes I can't get up the stairs — all this despite my having been so good. I drink several medicinal glasses of wine each day and haven't eaten dead animals for decades. I walk everywhere, brush my teeth and eventually pay my bills. Like Woody Allen, I eat my broccoli. Yet, I suppose I take chances — like going alone north to my cabin or sailing my little catboat to where water meets sky. One day my family will find me sprawled slack-mouthed in the screen porch or the bilge of my boat. In either case I will smell bad.

Comandante Olga has been forced into an uneasy truce. After leaving her office I'd managed to find a phone and following several hours of failed attempts had finally gotten through to Ottawa and described the wall I was up against. The museum and the film board moved quickly. Soon the Canadian ambassador in Costa Rica — we didn't have one in Nicaragua — was on the phone to Managua and the pressure was on. Canada had not endorsed Reagan's position on the Sandinistas and was in fact a supplier of some aid and political support. We had a little push and shove. The Comandante grumpily backed off and I was back on the road.

After a couple of weeks in one sad hamlet after another it was a pleasure to drive into Granada, a charming small city at the north end of Lake Nicaragua. As we were in transit to the south this was just a lunch break. A rude little café was found and we settled in for the inevitable plate of bland rice. This country was like its capital, Managua — a city with no centre. The 1972 earthquake had leveled its core leaving a city like a donut — a huge hole of rubble in the middle surrounded by a suburban fringe of modest buildings.

In many ways the country felt the same. I'd done enough travelling and working in Latin America to appreciate cultural differences. You knew you were in Mexico because you could see, hear, smell and taste the country. In fact you could feel and taste each state. And Peru was Peru, not Bolivia. But Nicaragua had been so badly abused — the Americans had been raising hell here since the early 19th century and the Spanish before — that the country didn't seem to have its own culture. There was little evidence of any national dress or dishes or drink. It was a hollowed-out state trying to reconstruct itself.

In Granada I met the bird of hope. Slipping through the kitchen to find a washroom I encountered the cook's parrot. I've always enjoyed those birds, even when they're mischievous. And they often are. One bird that I got to know well on the coast of Oaxaca used to fly into the beach palapa where I ate every day after work. Long beams supported the thatched roof that sheltered a half-dozen rough picnic tables. I'd fetch my plate of rice and fish and sit down. The bird would position himself on the beam above, aim with a beady eye and shit on my lunch. I'd slide down the table and he'd follow and aim. He was fast — and very accurate. Ha ha.

And there were others with various impressive skills but the Granada parrot topped them all with his ardor and patriotism. With the cook's encouragement it sang all the many rousing verses of the Sandinista hymn. Perfectly. True revolutionary triumph is a big green parrot staring you hard in the eye while it repeatedly choruses, "We struggle against the Yankee, enemy of humanity."

The forest is very quiet this morning — no wind rustle or sighs, no birdsong, no cries. The command is to walk silently, stepping from moss hummock to bare stone. A few minutes on I hear a whirling, then a metallic clatter as a hundred dark small shapes are thrown toward me. A flock of polished grackles is on the move, streaming through the understorey and parting around me as they rattle by as if I were a rock in a stream. Just as abruptly they are gone and the woods fall back into the silence of the north.

I've been back from Nicaragua for seven weeks now. The first week I'd spent in Ottawa doing a rough picture edit with staff from what used to be known as the Still Photography Division of the National Film Board. A few days into the session I fainted dead away in their offices. An hour later I was on an evening flight to Toronto and feeling like death. I went straight from the airport to emergency at Toronto General where a nurse took my temperature and rushed out of the room. When the doctors discovered where I'd been for weeks they began a frantic series of blood workups. For several hours various hospital staffers rushed in and out of the examining room in a state of excitement that I was feeling too awful to participate in. Then the room went quiet — for hours, for almost four hours. Finally around 3:30 a.m. an intern entered the room with a scrap of paper in his hand. "We thought you had a new strain of malaria that's just emerged in Central America as you have a temperature of 106. We had lab people come in and got a couple of pathologists out of bed because it was our first case. But everybody went home hours ago as it turns out you just have pneumonia. Here's a script for an antibiotic. Put your coat on and turn left out the door. The all-night pharmacy is only five blocks away."

So there I was, soaked in sweat from the fever, facing a long walk in the dark in minus 25 degree weather, because I was just a disappointing loser with a banal disease. I reeled off to the drugstore and then staggered the 20 blocks home because I couldn't find a cab.

When I got over all of this I went to work researching and writing captions for the 50 photographs we'd finally selected. A revolution is an immensely complex social, cultural, economic and strategic political process. I had done all of the work with a trio of Hasselblads because I felt it required the greater descriptive powers of a format larger than newsy 35mm. I made large colour prints full of beautiful detail. They told you that many of the Sandinista soldiers were just scared kids, that the uniforms were cheap and inadequate and much of their equipment just Soviet junk. The prints described the destruction in loving detail — the medium has no morals. Yet the prints remained mute. They needed words to give context and explain what you couldn't see. This was supposed to be a visual exhibition for display in museums. What I began to create was a book to be screwed to the wall. It was an immense amount of work.

Spring gradually pushed winter aside while I wrote and researched and revised. Soon it was early May and the leaves snapped out — spring in Toronto lasts 15 minutes. I continued working in my cluttered office at the back of my little Victorian house a block from the university. The deadline was fast approaching.

One day I heard an explosion, then another one and another. They continued with terrifying regularity like a doomsday drumbeat. My office began spinning and I forgot where I was, who I was and what I was doing. The keyboard I worked turned

Greek, the books lining the walls threatened to bury me. I was in a sweaty panic.

Slowly, gradually, painfully, I pulled myself back together over the course of a couple of hours. Eventually it dawned on me that it was Victoria Day and there'd been the traditional 21-gun salute a few blocks over at Queen's Park. Everything was going to be fine.

All those days watching the contras creeping through the bushes, the nights sleeping on the ground with rats scampering over me, the destruction and the deprivations had caught up with me. I'd been surprised at how calmly I'd been able to carry on with photography while shit was erupting all around me. At those times the world became very bright and intense, all my movements slowed, but I never felt afraid. I was to discover later that I'd just buried it.

This all happened more than a quarter century ago. I'd never heard of post-traumatic stress disorder. The Second World War had receded into Roman times and Canada had yet to go into Afghanistan. There were no glib correspondents chatting on the radio about PTSD: it just didn't exist.

A couple of months later it happened again. It was Hiroshima Day and commemorative sirens went off. This time I knew what was happening. I was experienced. I got it all back together in a couple of minutes.

The Nicaragua show went on the road. Over the course of the next five years it seemed to go everywhere. There were some awful installations of it and some very good ones. The tour of B.C. encapsulated both. I was sent out to Kamloops to talk. Nobody in town knew where Nicaragua was; nobody had ever heard of the Sandinistas. The cruel and paranoid foreign policy of our neighbour was of no interest. It was depressing.

In those days I was constantly flying across the country executing assignments in disparate western communities. As a photographer I always found that the most curious and alert people in the country seemed to be in Saskatoon. The doziest were in Vernon. They'd trip over your tripod, had zero interest in what you were doing and seemed to be stumbling through life in a terminal mall coma.

But B.C. redeemed itself. The Vancouver Art Gallery paired my show, *After the Triumph: Nicaragua*, with Goya's *Disasters of War* and gave both a whole floor. It was just brilliant and beautiful.

The exhibition also went into enemy territory. Part of it went to the New Museum in Manhattan. I took it across the border myself. American customs agents broke open the crate and looked at the photographs.

"What's he got there, Bob?"

"Just a bunch of pichurs of spooks someplace in Africa."

And Reagan was spending millions on the counterrevolution.

———

The bald eagles have returned. Last year I discovered them nesting high atop a white pine that towered over a small island in a hidden inland beaver lake. They had three of the biggest, ugliest bird babies I'd ever seen. Benjamin Franklin had thought the bald eagle a bird of such disreputable behaviour — it's a carrion bird — that it was an inappropriate choice as a national symbol for America. Nevertheless the States went ahead and stole the image of an eagle holding five arrows in his claws from the confederacy of the Iroquois. The colonists' only creative contribution was to up the number of arrows to 13, the number of colonies. Today it would appear that Ben Franklin was prescient. The large juvenile eagle commandeering a treetop over my harbour is having trouble looking large and in charge. A dozen crows are baiting and shit-bombing it mercilessly. It finally retreats to the beaver bog. May its emblematic country do the same.

SIX

FILTH

*"Each American generation passes the torch of truth,
liberty and justice in an unbroken chain all the way
down to the present. That torch is now in our hands.
And we will use it to light up the world."*

DONALD TRUMP
CONGRESSIONAL ADDRESS 2017

1979

I'm on a magazine photo assignment to cover a hobo convention in Iowa. After flying into Mason City at midnight
— there'd been a connection delay — I discover that the basic
car I'd booked for the drive to Britt has been rented to someone
else. Only thing they have left is a full-sized Cadillac Eldorado.
We go into the parking lot where several tons of steel iced in
white enamel with gold trim are simmering under a lamppost.
I take it. The car and I levitate off through cornfields and small
towns, windows down, the sweet smells of a country summer
pillowing through the interior. Perfect.

Britt is just a small town but I still can't locate writer Jim
Christy who's supposed to have come in from Alaska. Without
knowing his angle on the story I start shooting to illustrate it.
After a couple of days of this I have a bunch of new hobo friends
but still no writer. The guys are getting sick of Mulligatawny
soup cooked in an oil drum so we decide to crash a big church
picnic somebody has heard about. Seven hobos cram into the
Caddy and we set off for the Baptist lunch. My passengers
demand I roll up the tinted windows and crank up the AC.

Soon as I comply I regret it. None of these guys has washed for weeks. The car smells like a plugged toilet. My eyes run.

When we glide into a churchyard of sunhats and high heels some 30 minutes later all eyes are on the fancy car and its VIPs. I park dead centre in the garden party and release my seven buddies. You could see every church picnicker's dental work and tonsils. They all vanish into the church leaving us alone to enjoy their Lord's bounty spread out on the picnic tables.

Later back in Toronto the staff at *Weekend* magazine spent days trying to screw Jim's text to my pictures — we'd missed each other completely. From that point on I always wrote my own text and captions.

1970

It's the start of a new decade and I'm trying to move back north after several years in Mexico. My girl and I have made our way up to San Antonio by bus where I've located a driveaway company. They have a big Buick station wagon that needs delivery to the Bay Area. California sounds good so I book it. When I go to the office the next day the boss takes me out back to see the car. It's an enormous Detroit boat with lithoed wood grain on the quarter panels and a hood large enough to accommodate patio chairs and a barbeque. He drops the tailgate and demonstrates the bouncy suspension. "You just take that girl you had with you yesterday and give her a good pounding in the back here. You'll love it."

I sign the papers, get a map and pull out of the lot to return to the six-dollar-a-night motel and retrieve my girl and our stuff. We head out for the freeway and freedom. As we clear the last overpass the transmission begins to thump and after a mile or two goes into full cardiac arrest. I hike back into town under a blazing sun and phone the car guy. A tow truck picks me up an hour later and by afternoon we're back where we started in the six-dollar motel.

Three days later the same car guy calls the motel office with a message — this time he's got a good car. I catch a bus across town to see it. It's an immaculate but tiny pale green Ford Falcon that belonged to an old lady who only drove it to church. In fact she died in it on the way to church and she's left it to her stepdaughter who's awaiting delivery. The only problem is that the recipient lives in South Carolina, not exactly a shortcut to my new life in San Francisco. We have a conference and decide that the prudent thing would be to retreat to Toronto. I still have some cash in a local North Carolina bank near the university where I'd worked. It could get us home if we got to it. We take the car.

We have no money but I've kept a Texaco credit card that was mailed to me upon first graduating from university several years before. Turns out it still works so it buys the gas for the trip. We also find a motel chain will accept it so we've got sleep and one meal a day covered. The world is once again ours.

We set off eastward across the U.S. It's a route I already know well — beignets and chicory coffee in New Orleans, Georgia truck stops stocked with Jesus trinkets and weapons where the big rigs pull in with TVs flickering on their dashboards. A half-day from our small town destination I phone in to time our arrival. It's the poorest white town I've ever seen. When we finally locate the street it's like the second coming. Everybody is out in their front yards to witness the arrival of the neighbourhood's only car. The family comes out of their ramshackle frame house in tears. We're heroes.

I like this job. It's another one of my cross Canada trudges but this is different and a bit crazy. I'm to photograph explosions. The first one is near home. If you drive west from Toronto on the big Highway 401 there's a point where the Niagara

Escarpment stands proud on the south side near Milton. Until recently this raw reminder of old seas was a somewhat wild place. There are tiny wizened cypresses on the limestone cliff faces that are thousands of years old. The mesa-like plateau above suggests a hidden world.

When I drive up the escarpment road and crest the top I do encounter the unexpected — much of that enormous promontory is hollow. A huge open pit quarry has removed its belly. From its rim the trucks and trailers below on its bottom look like Tonka Toys. This is no small operation and today it's about to get bigger. A whole grid of long slender holes has been drilled deep into the west rim. Tanker trucks have come in and pumped millions of ammonium nitrate prills, like little white fertilizer beads, into these tiny tunnels. By themselves the prills are stable and harmless. You could spread them on your garden and eat what they make grow. But mixed with kerosene or diesel fuel and a blasting cap they become deadly. Think the Oklahoma bombing.

All these drill holes have been linked with little plastic tubes that lead to a single detonator. Once activated the entire grid will go off in a millisecond. We discuss where I should establish my cameras. I set up tripods on the south rim and screw motor drives on several camera bodies. A warning horn will tell me when to hit the button. The long rolls of film will rattle through in seconds. I've only got one chance.

The wait in the summer heat is electric. I feel a slight breeze as heated air rises from the bottom of the quarry. Several tiny figures in safety vests and hard hats move slowly on the far rim. I'm sweating under mine. Waiting, counting, breathing, tensing — what's taking so long? The horn suddenly barks, I squeeze my remotes, and one whole side of the quarry ripples like a flipped blanket. Then the big boom comes as powdered rock dust rises and a second report as a huge chunk of escarpment lands on a pickup parked on the far side of the quarry bottom. My first shoot on this job is witness to a major miscalculation. Soon a circle of tiny quarrymen are way down below me staring at a one-foot-high truck. It looks like a yellow waffle. This job will be interesting.

Later I go to western Quebec and the Eastern Townships where I'll see them make this stuff. It's the hailstones on a summer day principle. A continuous spray of liquid ammonium nitrate is shot into tall steel cylinders a handful of feet in diameter. Fans at the bottom keep the droplets cycling up and down inside these towers. Like drops of water freezing into hail on updrafts, these droplets coalesce and with each cycle get bigger. As optimum size is reached the air jets die and the prills of AN fall to the bottom. They are sorted and graded. Those of optimum size for explosive use are culled. The irregulars are bagged and sold as fertilizer. Simple.

Explosive plants are interesting. Each step takes place in a different building. The buildings have blow-out walls and are separated from their neighbours in the production process by high earth berms to prevent disaster spread. At one complex in Quebec stands an industrial cluster that looks part refinery, part futuristic city and part spaceship. It's an abandoned nitroglycerine factory, the process that made Nobel rich. Dynamite is now considered too expensive, too volatile and dangerous for regular use but the prize it funded lives on.

I go back to recording explosions. Here in the townships they're testing underwater explosives. There's a large pond in a field with a sod and concrete bunker on one side. A cable arrangement like a large clothesline stretches from it to the far side of the pond. The explosive package is hung from it like a pair of socks and it's run out to the middle of the pond where it's lowered beneath the surface. The testers retreat to the safety of the bunker, the only person left outside is me. Once again my tripods are set up on the rim, I have long rolls and motor drives. They signal, I press; with a big burp the whole landscape rises a few inches before settling comfortably back to its favoured place. This becomes part of the job — being temporarily levitated and then slumped down. I'm always amazed that my shots are sharp when my tripods are so rocked and rolled but they always are. It's because everything is being uplifted in unison — my tripods and cameras, the explosion, the landscape and me.

I go into northern Ontario in the fall. Around Timmins the trees have gone gold and the black ruins of old mining head-frames advance across the landscape like giant mantises.

The fabled Dome mine is now an open pit but its original drift tunnels still penetrate the walls. They're like hanging valleys, suspended hundreds of feet above the bottom, seeming so inadequate to the quest for precious metals when compared with the great greedy maw of the pit. I shoot great carpet explosions here too but do my best work sneaking off to photograph the theme and variations of spray-painted stakes and fuses for myself. I also photograph in a mine run by a woman who'd inherited it from her father. She's desperate as the returns have been low and she's nearly bankrupt. She's tough but her panic is palpable.

The miners have a checklist before going underground — *spectacles, testicles, wallet and watch*. It's meant to be a small funny and it is the first time you hear it but on a day when I'm down a few thousand feet I run through the list and realize my wallet is gone. Rerunning the morning through my mind I realize that the only place I could have lost it was when I slipped during the early morning snowfall at a Timmins Tim Hortons parking lot. A message goes up to the surface and men are dispatched to the donut shop. They arrive to discover that the lot has since been plowed with snow piled in a single pyramid rivaling Giza. They are joined by other coffee drinkers who dismantle the tower of tons of snow by hand until they find the wallet of a total stranger — me. This can make you love the people of small northern towns.

Deep underground at Timmins

I soon get even more reason. This is the kind of assignment on which I would normally take a guy assistant. However, this time I had taken Anna, a sweet-faced woman in her 20s, along to schlep cases and load cameras. One morning, moments before we were to go underground she picked up her cell messages and discovered she was pregnant. I reluctantly let her work that day but when the miners in the drifts down thousands of feet found out they wouldn't let her do anything. They taught her how to operate one of the ore trains so she could majestically follow me around in her personal locomotive towing my equipment cases behind her. Whenever she stopped some miners would leap out of the shadows and carry cases for her. Those grimy, sweat-stained miners were far more gentlemanly than many Toronto toffs.

There is more. I slowly work my way across the top of the province toward Quebec, following that secret, unseen subterranean belt of metals that slither eastward through the rocks. At Val-d'Or and Cadillac I go deep underground, more than a mile down, where the mantle's heat makes you sweat and the rock walls are hot to the touch. Set charges, retreat, photograph the smoky aftermath, the machines rushing in, the darting outlines of men. It's a bit like combat — the heat, the stabs of light, the shadows and the brutal noise.

The landscape above is broken, scarred, raped. Rock piles, tailings, raw roads, slashed trees and here and there the great black maws of old mines waiting for you to walk in and fall through dark space. This is the brute, impolite side of Canada. The rude part with a long history, the part hidden away behind remote stands of spruce where we bang away at rocks with big crude tools and sell the results to the rest of the world where refined things are made. We're just the choppers, the crushers, the lifters. These are the skills we export around the world, dragging abuse and exploitation in their wake. It's a hard industry. It makes a mess.

My last stop is far to the west near the B.C.-Alberta border. The scale dwarfs everything I've ever seen. The trucks here are the size of buildings. And so are the buckets of the giant shovels. You could live in them. And because they need real power, lots of torque, they're electric — like streetcars and locomotives. These huge machines are actually plugged in and crawl about dragging huge power cords behind them like your vacuum crossing a rug. The last rolls finally exposed I fly home. My next assignment was photographing hats.

———

It's been a week of island silence. No people, no wind, no boats. No singing insects, no birds. I'm alone on my point under the pines when from the south a strange rumbling sweeps up from the forests across the inlet and roars toward me. Its pitch rises and an enormous low-flying aircraft emerges just over the treetops and makes straight for the island. A massive swept back shadow daggers over the water as a B52 bomber, its eight engines thundering, threatens past. What war game are the Americans playing now?

1989

I'm back in San Francisco again to photograph a couple of buildings. This assignment includes getting a dramatic late afternoon view of a modern office building downtown. When I scout the location I realize that the best view of the structure will be from a late 1920s art deco skyscraper at the head of Market Street. This is always tough — cold calling the property management and convincing them that they should give a stranger, a photo lowlife and, what's more, a foreigner, access to their roof or a high window so that the required image can be made.

I once had to persuade an intimidating owner — I was later told he was an international arms dealer — to allow me access to the roof of his Manhattan tower so that I could photograph the Chrysler Building. He was skeptical and abusive but relented in the end. I was escorted to the building's roof by a pair of guards carrying automatic weapons. The building was a sleek silver erection with tinted windows but its roof was a shantytown of weird plywood shacks. Every move I made was minutely scrutinized. Security called me "the photo fucker." I got the picture.

My cold call at the vintage office tower in San Francisco eventually yields permission. I am escorted up a dozen floors and taken into a small empty office lit with a single sash window. The building is a classic of its period — clad with ceramic tiles and designed with a series of step-backs that create numerous little rooftops as it rises. It had been a Manhattan idea: one that allowed light to reach the streets far below. I raise the sash and squeeze myself, a case of gear and a tripod out onto a two-metre-square roof more than a hundred feet above the sidewalk. Once I have my tripod set my escort leaves. That tripod is jammed against the low parapet on the Market Street side and I am jammed against the parapet behind. As I make my exposures the building begins to shake. I am told later that the 6.9 Loma Prieta earthquake had lasted only fifteen seconds but as I clung to my tiny heaving roof raft being showered by tile shards it registered as many lifetimes.

———

A sudden wind howls around the cabin. Panes rattle in their sashes, a big branch rubs the roof, the porch screens hiss and cry. As the gale intensifies the big wooden cabin shutters and groans. These northern buildings have no real foundations: they merely squat on little piles of stone and cedar shims, ready to levitate. I stand alone in the middle of the 40-foot main room in the sepulchral light. Dark trees dance in every window. I become very small.

A design studio I often work with has called and booked a studio session for the Senior "A" Hockey League and the Allan Cup. The league plans to publish a glossy commemorative book for the season. The publication needs a cover. Over the next few days various objects to be included in this still life begin to arrive at my studio. The selection eventually includes the Allan Cup itself.

We spend a long day setting up and lighting this tableau. Once the photograph has been approved we return all the props except the cup — it's to go somewhere else. So the cup sits for a week or so on a table beside the seamless backdrop awaiting pickup. The week passes and I haven't yet heard anything so I move it to a shelf and get on with other projects. After a few weeks I need the shelf space so the cup is moved offside in the studio. Still no word. Eventually my assistants get tired of tripping over the thing so it gets stuffed into a far back corner of the building. Out of sight is out of mind. The weeks come and go. I come and go.

Many months later I get a call toward day's end from some guy connected with the league. He sounds frantic. He's almost incoherent. I have to ask him to repeat his message. It seems that the Allan Cup is to be presented that night in Sault Ste. Marie and nobody could remember where it was. I don't tell him that even I don't remember where it is. There're many miles and only a few hours separating the cup from its big moment.

As I dig through storage in back of the studio I try not to get frantic. Finally I find the cup behind the studio fridge just as someone pounds on the studio door. It's the incoherent guy. We jam the cup in the trunk of his Honda and I watch the taillights vanish into the night. So let me see. It's a bit over 700 kilometres to Sault Ste. Marie. That's gotta be at least seven hours of driving time. How's this ever gonna work? Did some guy in a cold arena have to tell lost trophy jokes to restless players and the crowd while a small Japanese car hurtles along the Trans-Canada Highway through a dark, empty northern Ontario night?

2014

It's like hockey cards. I've always wanted to have the full set — of pine trees. My tiny island has 26 white pines and a lone Jack but no reds. The secondary road to the reserve where I leave my van in a clearing and load my skiff takes you through several zones on the way to the river. There are spruce swamps, tamaracks and lots of majestic white pines. However, around certain corners are magnificent stands of red pine with their distinctive pompom-like clusters of needles — always in pairs rather than the white's clusters of five that the Iroquois thought represented the original five nations of their confederacy. They seem to prefer the sandy shelter of the interior rather than the wind-ravaged granitic shores where white pines thrive. Several times I've waded into the bug-infested interior to search beneath the giant reds for a baby that I can dig up and transplant. None. Nothing. Never.

Finally one realizes that the reds must, like the jack pine, be a species that requires a forest fire to encourage reproduction. Mercifully forest fires are in short supply around here so there are no young trees. After a fleeting fantasy of becoming a secret firebug I get real and start making inquiries at nurseries. Nobody stocks red pines anywhere in Ontario that I find. However, a garden centre in the Sound agrees to try and source some. I request four to accommodate an inevitable mortality rate. Some weeks later the trees arrive but my ex-wife beats me to it. She spirits all four trees off to her new place on a Lake Ontario island. Skunked. Winter comes.

The following spring I skulk into the same garden centre and ask if they can source a further pair of reds. They will call me when they arrive but never do. I have this kind of trouble with pretty much everybody north of Barrie. On a pass-by in mid-June I drop by and enquire. They haven't gotten around to phoning but a pair of red pines in the backlot has my name on them. With full knowledge that I'm cheating I slap down a credit card and squeeze the pair of meter-tall trees between the seats of my van. At least I'm not introducing an invasive species.

Those trees now stand some 50 feet apart on the sheltered back side of my island.

So far so good. However I feel only semi-fulfilled. After some 200 years these trees can reach a commanding height of 30 meters. Mine have 29 meters to go. I'm only 71.

Trees teach us to slow down. Of course, when you're going to live for a hundred years or, even several thousands, you have the luxury of taking it slow and easy, an inch or two of height and girth a year, a few more twigs and then a long sleep with the bears during winter. And trees long ago decided to communicate quietly underground through their interlocked root systems. No hot-blooded arguments, no idle cell phone chatter, just stately patience.

SEVEN

A BESTIARY

*"That it's rough out there and chancy is no surprise.
Every live thing is a survivor on a
kind of extended emergency bivouac."*

ANNIE DILLARD
PILGRIM AT TINKER CREEK

———

Another spring. We've made it! The sky is velvet gray, it's cool, a light west wind drifts a fog like puffs of smoke down the inlet. High above a merlin harries a turkey vulture that languidly cruises off to the west. Canada geese hector in my harbour while cranes gronk in the next inlet. My birches and alders have just leafed out and my little orphan red pine is radiant with survival. Once again there is hope.

She's flown in from Tokyo with her lanky teenaged son and pretty daughter who's just on the sweet side of 12. I picked them up at Pearson and we began the long drive north. Harumi and I had sampled many Tokyo bars together and now the turn was mine. What was really Canadian — in Barrie, Waubaushene or Parry Sound? I decided on lunch in a Barrie Swiss Chalet. The service was glacial, the chicken dry and salty, the fries soggy — disastrous. In Parry Sound we bought the week's supplies at a No Frills grocery outlet. No one was impressed there either. Then we hit the river.

It was a stunning day. A soft wind dashed sparkles on the

waters while small clouds scudded across a sky of blue perfection. The river run was a song of swallows, swifts and herons. Its backwaters were dressed in white water lilies and blooming pickerel weed. Where the river surrendered to the Bay a warm and gentle wind tossed tiny whitecaps into the acres of wild rice and rushes. And the land everywhere was green, green, green.

After mooring and emptying the skiff I filled the cupboards and the fridge while Harumi organized her children. My chores finished I went to find them. They were huddling together under the pines on my little point watching a pair of loons treading water in the inlet. Harumi who'd been here twice before was clearly laying out guidelines for her kids — life jackets, fish hooks, rattler avoidance and care around the many oil lamps. As I drew up behind the trio I heard her stage-whisper one last instruction, "And most important of all is that whenever Michael is around never, ever say the word *beaver*."

1981

Small animals. I flew on assignment to London with an executive of a big Canadian life insurer. I'd been working with this manager on the company's annual report for some time. He was always impeccable — perfect haircuts, neatly trimmed mustache, elegant ties and bespoke three-piece suits. He was the master of the two-martini lunch.

I usually travelled on his assignments alone but for this one he had decided to accompany me to ensure that all went well with the senior management of the British subsidiary. A waiting limo at Heathrow swished us through rainy streets to the Four Seasons Park Lane where we'd booked rooms for the week. Except they hadn't quite. As their records showed us arriving two days later we would be forced to share a suite for the first nights. Our luggage — my road-battered camera cases and his suite of five impeccably crafted, matching leather travel trunks that diminished in size like Russian dolls — was loaded onto a brass cart and slinked into the elevator. We hissed up to our floor and were ushered unctuously into our rooms. In addition to a sitting room and office there was a large bedroom with twin queens. We began to unpack. My clothes were simple — photographers have to look neat but dress durably for case lifting and lighting setups. He had more suits and tailored shirts than I'd seen in a shop window. He carefully bedded his shirts in the dresser drawers while his suits were marched into the closets and his shoes paraded down below. This sartorial sorting took in excess of an hour. Another fifteen minutes were devoted to arranging soaps and crèmes on the shelves of the bathroom. Finally he was down to a single unopened valise.

What could possibly remain? I busied myself loading cameras while he opened the locks of this final suitcase. He carefully folded back its lid and began unrolling the tiny blankets protecting the contents. One by one he withdrew a half-dozen Steiff teddy bears dressed in suits that mimicked his own. Once each tiny toff was comfortably cushioned on his bed pillows he began the introductions. Each had a name and each a history.

———

Every year has its resident bear. This season is owned by a gangly male with a strange blond blaze between his shoulders. Come mornings he's shambling along the crescent shore that cups my little harbour. Occasionally he retires behind a shoreline thicket and spies on me through the underbrush. As spring sags into a torpid summer he's emboldened to wade over to my little island and vandalize my buried gray-water tank. A generous seeding of cheap

Chinese mothballs over it soon discourages any further treasure digging by this biker bear. By solstice we've gotten so used to each other that I let the gap between us begin to close. Soon he's sniffing around bushes not a dozen feet from where I work on a laptop under some pines on the point. The following day when I'm working in the same spot I look up and see him cruising the shore of a neighbouring island several hundred feet to the west. I watch him approach the sturdy trunk of a giant pine that's fallen across his path along the shore. Will he slide under it or elect to clamber over it? Neither can be done with dignity. I hold my breath as he closes on the trunk that's thick as an oil drum. Upon contact he casually flips it out of his way. Our days of hanging out at the point as a gang of two are over. This bear works out with logs.

1975

The small grassy pen at the Toronto Zoo has three occupants — me and two black bear cubs. They are having a giggle. In order to photograph them I must crouch on the grass, camera before me on the ground while I try to capture them playing with my childhood teddy bear. One cub will playfully perform for the camera, scooting and tumbling about before me. As soon as I get my eye down to viewfinder level and frame a cute cub photograph, the other bear scoots around behind me and bites my backside. I shout at the little bugger who then rewards me by scrambling around in front of my lens while my previous model scoots around to the bite-the-bum position for a nip. These bright little animals clearly enjoy the teamwork of this game. I get sorer and sorer until I'm driven to retreat to their keeper and the gate. Ha, ha.

A new bear stalks the perimeter of the island. A late adolescent, he is so black that his profile looks like a paper cutout. When he turns away he becomes a hole in the landscape — an egg-shaped portal to another world.

1969

One midnight 40 years ago I faced a pack of wild dogs howling down the cobbled street of a small Mexican pueblo. I knew the wild dogs of Mexico well. Individually they were scrawny, sulking curs; collectively they were brutal and brave — canine killers. And this pack had sensed a prey — the terrified 60-pound jaguar that had just leaped to my shoulders. *Madre de Dios!* The *tigre* and I were in trouble once again.

I had spent several years working on an archaeological survey crew exploring the Pacific coast of Oaxaca. We were quite a mix — a bitter Cuban, a La Jolla millionaire, an aging surfer, a Carolina professor, their families and me, the solitary Canadian. We'd roll into the isolated settlements along the coastal plain, park our Jeeps, show our papers to the *mayores* and inquire about artifacts. The villagers would show us the pre-Columbian potsherds and plates they'd ploughed up in their fields or stumbled on in caves. Occasionally a *campesino* would show up carrying a magnificent burial urn. These always bore a carefully sculpted effigy — of a god, a bird or beast. Country people always named these urns for the creature they depicted.

In one tiny hamlet fronting an enormous brackish lagoon the news of our purpose had arrived ahead of us. The locals were waiting with their string bags bulging with the handwork of history. We carefully inspected everything, identified the owners and made appointments to visit the region's tombs and ruins that had given up the treasures. When we'd finished interviewing everyone only a small boy and his baby sister remained. He approached me shyly and whispered, "My father has a *tigre*."

Now, an Oaxacan jaguar effigy urn is among the most magnificent of all pre-Columbian artifacts — and among the scarcest. This was a pot I had to see. I arranged to visit the boy's father, a butcher, the following day.

We made many site visits after the next day's sunrise, driving deep into the thorn forest and hiking high into the hills. It was dusk when we finally returned to our camp outside the village. While my colleagues prepared supper I set off to find the butcher and his boy. Their shop fronted a cart-track that was the hamlet's only street. I was led behind the building to a hardpan courtyard where the tiger pot was kept. A little kitten on a rope cowered in a corner. It turned out to be the tiger.

As I crouched down to inspect that animal I realized it was no ordinary kitten. It had very heavy legs, large feet and enormous eyes set in a big square head. Much of its coat had fallen out but where it hadn't I could see that it was spotted like a leopard. Its very long tail was ringed with stripes of gold and jet. It was potentially a spectacular little beast but clearly one that was very ill.

The butcher had recently shot its mother in the mountains. Her pelt had fetched a peso bonanza that encouraged him to return for her kits with the intention of raising them to adulthood for slaughter and sale as well. However, his shop meat was far too precious to share with small wild things so he'd fed them only water and stale tortillas. One by one the little carnivores had died of malnutrition. I was looking at the sole survivor and it was truly a mangy little tragedy.

Sometimes we put our hearts before our heads and do dumb things. I began to negotiate for that little cat and so three mescals and 20 dollars later I was the owner of a baby wild cat. And a lot of trouble.

The lagoon had been the last stop of our field season. We were soon packed and on our way up the coastal sierra and on to distant Oaxaca where we'd have real beds after months of hammocks, and beer with real dinners instead of water and endless beans with rice. As I drove our Jeep through hours of mountain switchbacks toward the city the little *tigre* yowled in a crate at my feet.

In town we began a season of lab work on regular office hours. At day's end I'd walk down to Oaxaca's enormous market and negotiate for offal and leftovers to feed my little cat. He grew quickly. His eyes brightened and his coat began to grow in. Soon I had a magnificent animal with long strong legs, a sturdy square chest and a most handsome face. And his huge dark eyes got bigger and bigger. In no time he had grown to the size of a large dog and was ready for walks with a collar and chain. If we went down into the city centre the pedestrian traffic on the wide walkways of the *Zócalo* would part like the Red Sea. The locals found him absolutely terrifying. "*Tigre*, jaguar, margay, ocelot," they'd whisper. I never did figure out which of a half-dozen possible species he was.

Tigre lived in my apartment on a hundred feet of chain. He'd wander around the furniture, weaving in and out until he was finally jerked to a stop by the end of his tether. At this point a dog would have sat there and whimpered until its owner obligingly untangled the mess and the cycle could begin again. *Tigre* would simply turn around, retrace his steps and liberate the hundred feet. He was a very, very intelligent animal.

He was also still a kitten. Sometimes I'd be walking through my living room and a yard-long furry arm would sweep out from beneath a chair and down me on the flagstone floor — playful kitty. He also enjoyed leaping onto the kitchen counters so he could plow through the piles of dishes, cups and glasses until everything lay shattered on the floor. I bought replacements in bulk. But whenever I got so desperate that I was ready to release him in the mountains he'd crawl into bed with me, cozy up and begin a purr that came from that place way down where the daily earthquakes that shook the valley of Oaxaca were born. This was a pet with a woofer.

He was also a wild animal. He loved being outside and so when I was home I'd tie him to a tree in my courtyard so that he could explore the garden. *Tigre* eventually grew strong enough to sever his chain. He made a few breaks for the mountains and more than once was gone for several days. But he always returned. At night you'd hear him on the roof or calling from a tree. He was proud — he never came when you called him home but he made sure that you could see him and reach the short length of chain that remained hooked to his collar. I'd gently pull him down and he'd slip through the door ahead of me. In no time he'd join me in bed with his earthquake 20-cycle-rumble. Once again we'd have forgiven each other.

However as *Tigre* got bigger life with him got harder. One day a visit to the market had yielded a whole heart from a bull. I carried it home, a heavy brown-paper-wrapped bundle the size of a volley ball. Upon entering the apartment I set it on the counter of the kitchen just outside my bedroom that had a bathroom at the back. I rushed in there to pee. When I tried to reenter the kitchen I was confronted by a jaguar, a lion and a sabre-toothed tiger. The *Tigre* had a kill and until it was consumed no creature was going to pass. A bull has a very large heart. The *Tigre* kept me prisoner in my bedroom for 24 hours. When he finally finished and fell asleep I slipped out and shortened his chain. We were finished. That midnight I led him up the cobbled road to San Felipe and freedom in the mountains. But first those wild dogs came and came and came.

As *Tigre* trembled on my shoulders I began pulling

cut-stones from the road. When the wild dogs leapt at me I'd split their skulls to save us both. Yet even with their brains spilling from their cranial cups and eyeballs dangling those dogs kept coming, growling, leaping, tearing. However, finally their losses were greater than ours and *Tigre* and I were able to beat a bloodied retreat for home. Our time together was not yet over.

Some months later I returned permanently to Canada without the tiger. But cats remained central to my life. My partner loved them. At what was the nadir for me there were 18 cats sharing our apartment. The place stank. It was insane but despite the undifferentiated kitten chaos I still managed to find some favourites. Max, a pearl gray long-hair, often kept me company. He was always dirty and disheveled but one day he begged to be admitted to my darkroom where he began to clean himself up for the very first time. As I worked a long shift making production prints Max sat under the yellow safe-light washing and grooming for at least a dozen hours. Then he jumped down, nuzzled my legs and cried at the darkroom's back door that gave out to a fire escape. He'd always been an indoor cat so I endured more than an hour of his insistence before opening the door. Max strutted out into the world in his fancy new suit. I never saw him again. I still miss him.

And *Tigre*? Well, some months after that encounter with the dogs I met an American artist travelling Mexico on a Guggenheim. He'd done some drawings in Chiapas that I loved. He in turn loved *Tigre* and often drew him. We finally affected a trade. I got a handful of pictures and *Tigre* retired to Florida, a location that I'm confident pleased him more than the icy streets of Toronto could have. When I look back I realize that *Tigre* taught me an important life lesson — a wild animal is a wild animal is a wild animal.

Sculptors John McEwen and Dennis Gill and I are running a small skiff down a wilderness river to Georgian Bay. It's a peaceful late September afternoon but I know that we're being watched by moose, deer, birds and beaver. And while there could well be bears out there too, for sure we've got one in the boat. McEwen had welded up *Ragged Ass Bear* from a box of steel stars several years earlier just for the pleasure of it. Now after a few seasons standing in tall grass behind his studio, that bear is finally on the move.

At the mouth of the river sits my small island with a high domed hump of the Canadian Shield at one end that's come to be known as Sulkers' Rock. What better place to put a bear in charge? When we arrive I call a friend up the coast for help and a half hour later three guys drinking beer turn up in a canoe. They get out and John gets in. Five of us grunt the heavy bear back and forth on the rock while McEwen directs placement from out on the water. Finally we secure *Ragged Ass Bear* in four holes drilled deep into the Canadian Shield and John drinks a toast with Ziggy, my cat.

For an artist this was a dream installation. Makers of public sculpture spend much of their time negotiating with developers, architects, planners, unions and tradesmen. They have many masters to please and many compromises to endure. The works have to be bulletproof, safe, inoffensive and able to compete with power poles, traffic signs and all other cacophonies of modern life. This installation was almost perfect for McEwen. Only money was missing.

Watching McEwen's bear guard my rock took me back some half-dozen years to a visit I made to the Midi in France. On a gray winter day I crossed the Dordogne and drove north in a steep valley. Despite most things being shuttered for the season I spied a sign for a painted cave and went in. We've all

My cat Ziggy and McEwen's ragged-ass bear

seen photos and film of drawings in Paleolithic caves. What they don't tell you is that the animals in those paintings are not flat. The hunters of 12,000 years ago sought out bulges in the rocks that could become bodies, cracks that could be limbs and tails and holes that would become eyes. The animal images they created are staged along the courses of the caves so as to become encounters. Exploring the surviving paintings today one is acutely conscious of keen intelligences speaking across the millennia.

McEwen is an admirer of the late ecologist Paul Shepard. It was Shepard's contention that the painted cave is an externalization of our heads. The images within the caves may be of animals but are not about them. Rather they are fossil thoughts — the animal images represent human fears and triumphs, life and death — the encounters with great mysteries. These fundamentals are still part of our mammalian brain. It is this dark, non-verbal part of our consciousness that

McEwen is trying to understand when he makes sculpture. He has produced numerous life-sized silhouettes of animals such as wolves and dangerous dogs. When these are encountered end-on, all one sees is a two-and-a-half-inch-thick slab of steel. As one moves, the profile of a predator appears. It can stir the hairs on the back of the neck, like rounding a path in a forest and suddenly coming face to face with a big wild cat or a bear. Over the millennia such experiences have profoundly shaped human intelligence.

We have always modelled the world in order to comprehend and control it. A doll begins the experience of motherhood; lead soldiers emulate warriors. And teddy bears? We all know that the bear is a shamanic animal. While much art is beautiful or exciting, art that addresses the ancient and archetypal dance of predator and prey is rare. It seems to me, however, that when sited well McEwen's works can take on that challenge. He has caught a corner of human experience that is deep and essential.

As I write, it's midwinter in Toronto. Up north, the cabin shutters are up, the boats pulled in and an unsafe rim of ice grows out from the riverbanks so I can't now visit *Ragged Ass Bear*. But I know that he's guarding my little harbour and cabin as the winter sun goes down. During the night he's at his post but not alone. Ursa Major, the Great Bear, and its minor namesake wheel through the black sky keeping him company until I can return and see the stars of his coat flash brightly in the sun of a new spring.

It's Harumi's second visit to the island and she's a woman taking possession and a position. My bush cabin has failed to meet Japanese standards of order or cleanliness. It's got spiderwebs in the corners, dead flies on the sills and pine needles accumulating where the floors meet the walls. She knows what a Canadian wilderness cabin looks like — her family owns one — in Japan.

I've seen it. It's got central vac.

After her brothers took over their father's pharmaceutical business and bolstered its success they rewarded themselves by importing a wilderness experience from the wilds of Canada. The monstrous log cabin ordered from British Columbia came loaded. In addition to sporting assorted rustic gables, balconies and tall stone hearths suitable for rock climbing, it arrived equipped with a full complement of trophy heads — angry bears, rampant bucks and ducks as well as schools of shiny dead fish stuck on little varnished escutcheons. All this game was elegantly misidentified by little brass plaques.

The furniture squatting beneath the 30-foot ceilings was either twiggy or modelled on those log bridges you find in Jasper or Banff. Try to imagine them with upholstery. The Hudson's Bay salesman who filled the family's order of HBC blankets, parkas and toques must have promptly retired. It was only on the second floor that the cabin's true location was revealed. Each enormous bedroom contained only tatami mats and a futon. But every time I sat in the cavernous living room below I expected a CP locomotive pulling dome cars to arrive at the front door.

The biggest offenders in my cabin back in Canada are a series of animal hides. I'm no hunter but I had connections with a local auction house that often sold these things to Americans. They'd invariably be rejected at the border. Even caribou antlers, which lie all over the tundra and regrow annually, would be sent back by U.S. border officials as endangered ivory. Some of this orphaned stuff would get passed on to me.

One morning as I paddle back from the open Bay I hear a series of percussive reports. It sounds like someone is being spanked or shot. When my little island came into view it all proved to be true. Harumi has hung a polar bear rug from a pine branch and is beating it with a broom. By the time I get to shore the hide has been through a shredder. When she sees me she storms into the cabin shouting over her shoulder, "It's just an old stupid dead thing." She slams the door. A wolverine and a musk ox had already been disciplined.

During the great party of the '80s I would annually contrive a Christmas poster to send to all the people who commissioned my photography. My assistants and I usually had fun cooking these things up. We always tried to connect them to events of the passing year. We often made use of leftover props and supplies from the year's assignments.

When a friend closed his studio he left a dozen rolls of nine-foot-wide seamless paper backdrops in mine. The neutrals were soon consumed but for years we were never able to repurpose several huge rolls of bright crimson paper. We became determined to use at least one in the course of creating our newest poster.

My assistant, Crash Kowalski, and I were in the habit of closing a long day in the studio with a beer. During one of these sessions we decided to hang one of the red rolls from the ceiling and photograph the whole setup from the rear of the studio so all the lights, cables, stands — the entire contrivance — would be revealed. The centrepiece would be a reindeer with a big rack leaping toward the viewer through a tear in the red backdrop. Merry Christmas!

The next day I assigned Crash the job of phoning taxidermists all over southern Ontario to try to locate a rental ruminant. It took two long days. Eventually Crash was dispatched with a van to bring our model from a suburb to the city while back at the studio I prepped the lighting and background. I carefully cut the huge tears in the seamless for the head and neck to burst through. Two lower gashes would accommodate the forelegs.

The buck arrived icy cold — it was early December — accompanied with a note demanding its return in a few hours. We'd have to work fast. We got the head placed in less than an hour but the legs proved to be tricky — every placement looked awkward. Eventually I had an epiphany. We'd been rented legs from the wrong end of the deer. The setup would have to be adjusted to reveal only hooves and ankles.

When finally all was convincingly in place we had less than an hour to make photographs with a big view camera. As the whole tableaux was essentially a *nature morte* I'd elected to use studio hot lights instead of flash. The deep setup dictated a small aperture that in turn necessitated long exposures. Tests with a Polaroid back on the camera revealed a reindeer on the move. The head and hooves were blurred in every exposure despite my careful focusing on the ground glass.

As the clock closed on our final hour the studio began to smell. The hooves visibly drooped and trickles of blood stained the paper at the animal's throat. The deer's mouth slowly opened and drooled. Our taxidermal trophy was actually a freshly frozen carcass.

Merry Happy Merry

Christmas reindeer

2002

The wind has shifted on Barrow Lake out on the tundra behind Kugaaruk in Nunavut. It sends the millions of ice crystals floating on the lake down to the end where Sheila and I camp to make a film about traditional kayak building with a trio of Netsilik Inuit elders. The breeze and moving ice have created the biggest wind chime in the world. The sound is as ethereal and magical for the ear as northern lights are for the eye.

———

Five turkey vultures ride the end of day thermals across the inlet. The light is like butter. Something has died.

I've been slowly climbing the red sandstone cliffs of Badami in southern India since just after dawn. The carved cave temples devoted to Vishnu and Shiva are now far below and the clifftop not 20 feet above. My climbing rule is never look down. Upon glancing up I glimpse a small dark face awaiting my arrival. As I finally pulled myself over the lip a tiny goat stands above me. This kid is so black, and so glossy, it appears to be an absence in the sky. When I lie down on the warming rocks to catch my breath it curls up at my side. Refreshed a half hour later we set off together on a long journey across a barren rocky plain. For many hours its shiny coal hooves make the rocks ring like bells. This is our day music as side by side we explore the vast sandstone plateau. Whenever I stop to rest the kid lies beside me. We drink water from the same spring, we share the same breeze and the heat of the same sun. Come day's end my descent is secured by the sweet spirit of a very small black goat. I can see his small dark face watch me all the way to the bottom.

Risk. How do you make that concept, that idea, vivid and fresh again? Walking a tightrope, the apple and arrow, crevasse jumping and knife play are all tired ideas. We are to visually evoke the idea of risk for a software company specializing in financial risk management.

It's fun to spin concepts; it's the execution that's difficult. Take this idea of risk. How does one make it urgent and real? The agency's creative team has conceived an elaborate tableau. In the middle ground a pit bull tethered to a metal ring by a leather leash strains to get at a cat sauntering across the background. However, the cat is unknowingly at risk because a small mouse behind the dog is chewing through the leash. I was to cast and execute this idea in my studio. My cat Hero was a master of feline cool so I hired him for a couple of tins of Fancy Feast. A pit bull rescue organization agreed to bring several ferocious dogs in return for a donation. I then rented a couple of mice from a pet store that often supplied animals to the movies. With the casting complete we began to build the simple set.

I wasn't worried about the dogs; they'd just do their dog thing and lunge at their mortal enemy, the cat. And I knew Hero was smart enough not to get into trouble. It was the mice I worried about. How was I going to get them to chew on a leash with two of their main predators in the same room?

When cast and crew assembled there was great excitement and anticipation. Could we pull this off? After blocking out the actors' positions we all retreated back to the camera.

What happened? Well, Hero performed repeatedly as anticipated — the essence of cat cool. And the mice unconcernedly chewed away at the leash that had been smeared with peanut butter and cheese. And the ferocious pit bulls? We had a principal and two understudies. We tried all three and each of them broke down completely into cowardly curs. The setup required that they face away from the camera and crew while fixating on the cat. These alpha dogs couldn't bear putting their backs to the crowd behind the camera. It made them feel vulnerable. They were so upset that they never even noticed the snacking mice behind them or my Siamese tom cocking a snook. They just slobbered and whimpered.

Kayaking through a series of small islands along the foreshore of the big Bay I slip through numerous narrow and shallow channels. A scruffy coyote appears over a rise — silhouette against the sky — trots down to the shore and begins to lope along beside me, not a paddle length away. I can't read it. It's neither afraid nor aggressive. It doesn't seem especially curious. It just is. We're simply being together.

I'm completing my first summer as an archaeologist. It's September and the grad student workers have all returned to school. Only I remain on this Cape Breton peninsula, wrapping up my excavation so I can submit a report and return to school myself. Nova Scotia autumns are often heart wrenchingly beautiful and this one is exemplary. Every morning I drive down to the site in the polished brightness of the fall and begin the day's work — alone. By mid-afternoon the light has warmed and begins to rake across this small barren peninsula that jabs into the North Atlantic, surrounding me on three sides with the sounds and smells of the sea. A scrubby forest of conifers advances on the fourth. The rhythm of these days is pacific and comforting.

With each day as the first sharp shadows begin to draw my excavations a visitor arrives. He trots out of the woods and paces circles between my works and the declining sun. Backlit, this elegant fox, in full enjoyment of his prime, has a coat that glows like fire. He advances on a secret labyrinth, cautiously cycling closer until finally achieving my excavations. By five each day he's a fire fox, head on his paws, coat flaming and flickering in the late light and sea breeze, eyes assured but powerfully alert, resting barely two yards from where I work. We are cautious neighbours, provisional friends, a pair of fellow mammals secretly sharing a small private moment in the history of the world.

In my senescent 70s I've become a cat lady. I have two. Long-limbed and fit, Ziggy is white with two black circles on his haunches that from behind look like panda eyes when he sits down. He's had a long and distinguished career in property management — he operates two entire blocks of downtown Toronto and has imperial ambitions in others. At nine years old he's approaching our 60 and now faces a rival. He arrives home nightly with new scratches and scars on his face. The real estate business is very competitive.

Once home he has to deal with Billy Bonkers, a rescue who arrived several years after Ziggy. Billy looks like one of Toronto's Ford brothers, short limbed and stocky, except that he dresses better. Morning, noon or night, weekday or weekend, summer or winter, Bill is always in a tux. While Ziggy is out visiting the various beds and bowls he has up and down the street, Billy stays home guarding his food dish. Both cats get fed first thing in the morning and then again when CBC Radio's *World Report* comes on at six. By nine a.m. every morning Bill is back on duty at his bowl. "Hey Bonks," I caution, "nine hours to go until supper." Billy is undeterred, he stays on station like a doorman until the light fails and I get the food out. By the time I fetch his bag of overweight management pellets he is losing consciousness from neglect. Every night is a close call.

I don't want to make him sound like a slacker: Ziggy is not the only one with a profession. Billy has a career as a big-box greeter. When either of his human serving staff comes home Billy rushes to the door and begins a series of roll-overs. His roundness helps him be very good at it. I always see this as enthusiastic hello acrobatics, but for Billy the start of a roll is a consequence of malnutrition collapse. It is only the momentum generated by his fall that carries him through the manoeuvre and back onto his feet.

Billy stays home because the world is just too big for him — not the other way around. He was brought to my doorstep after his owner, an old friend, died in a lonely, midnight car crash on the Tennessee interstate. Bill, Billy's owner (did he really name his cat after himself?), had family way out west in country too tough for mere house cats. They dumped Billy on me and caught the plane back to Calgary after the funeral. When Billy was let out of the carrier he took one look at Ziggy, who was looking quite buff and Siamese, and bolted up the stairs and into the back bathroom. For weeks he was just a pair of eyes under the claw-foot iron bathtub. That was his first posting.

To be honest, I probably wrote him off as a sharp-dressing loser but Sheila was more understanding. Everyday she'd find time to sit by the tub and talk to him. For days and days he was just a pair of glowing eyes in the sub-tub gloom — remember, tuxes are black. When he finally emerged he staggered downstairs, found his bowl and settled in. He still has little truck with me but he adores Sheila. During the last hour of the day they drink tea together and watch *Coronation Street*. Sheila is still nostalgic for England where she was born. Billy doesn't remember.

Cats are basically solitary animals. These guys don't need each other. Ziggy's coping strategy is based on aloofness — he tries to ignore the guy in the headwaiter's outfit. Billy has developed his own version of Whac-A-Mole to deal with the white senior with the panda spots, ringed tail and a black bat on his head. Since Ziggy appears to be assembled from a box of parts Billy figures the best strategy is to deconstruct him. When Ziggy comes in from outside Billy clobbers him. Ignored, Billy whacks again. Whac-A-Cat, Whac-A-Cat. Ziggy does a flying flip onto his back to present all his electro-razor claws and titanium teeth. Score: 0–0. No giant stuffed mouse-toy in purple plush for either of them.

What has all this got to do with anything? It's relevant because I finally stopped calling cat-sitter friends and tricked both cats into carriers and drove them north to the island. Ziggy stepped out of his cage on the dock and immediately went into forest management. At first I worried about him because there are lots of predators in the woods — minks, fishers, coyotes and wolves. However he seems able to survive the backcountry. I suspect that it's because he looks too weird to be prey. What's this funny white thing with eyes at both ends?

The big transformation came with Billy. He finally discovered the out-of-doors. He'd sit for hours near the water's edge watching butterflies like Ferdinand the bull. As you know, the water's edge is only a dozen feet from the house. But Billy quickly got braver and has gone at least twice that distance from home base. I'm thinking of getting him a plaid flannel blanket and a black leather collar. I'll find an old hubcap he can use as a food bowl. He can then move up from being a member of the big downtown elite to good old boy. He's got the build for it.

When Ziggy comes back to the cabin after a day's work in the bush he repairs to his fort in the crawl space above the indoor washroom. I like to watch him planning his assault on his lofty retreat. He easily leaps onto the set of drawers against the washroom wall but from there to the top is a good six feet straight up. Ziggy analyses this distance with his X-ray vision, does his trigonometry and statics as well as ballistic analysis. They say that dogs are two and a half times more intelligent than cats but I've never seen a dog that could do this. That IQ stuff is just bullshit. When his computations are complete Ziggy takes an all-mighty leap straight up, grabs a building collar tie with one paw and heaves the rest of his body onto it and casually strides onto the bathroom roof and vanishes. He could easily work out the trajectory of the space shuttle.

2014

My oldest friend Macbeth and I head upstream after four days of work opening the cabin. It's been a brutal winter so we're more than a month late — on our usual date this year the ice was still a metre thick. This ice had snapped one of the dock's heavy steel rings I had drilled a half foot into the hard rock of the Shield.

The sky is largely clear, just a few horse tails, as I swing the skiff on the final turn from the inlet and up into the river's mouth. The west wind is at our backs but it's still cold as I accelerate into the current. One can feel the aluminum hull twisting as we cut through eddies and upwellings. A third of the way upriver I spot a large dark shape high in a tree by the south bank. I cut the throttle and we glide up under a large bear some 40 feet up the trunk. He skillfully pulls in small branches and chews on the new buds and young leaves all the while balancing in a tree clearly stressed by so much weight so high up. Large branches snap and fall into the boat. Occasionally he glances down at us without interest and continues lunch.

I had heard that the tough winter had taken out many animals but this first trip in had given us many visitors. A ruby throated hummingbird had buzzed in through an open door, realized its mistake and spiraled up into the cupola in an escape attempt. There it went into auto flight, endlessly repeated the same escape strategy under the tiny roof, round and round, rattling off the little windows above the main roof line. Finally

Macbeth brought in a ladder and climbed into the cupola with a landing net. He quickly caught the exhausted bird. Taking the net outside and opening it on the ground exposed its very small occupant who panted in shock.

A few minutes later it was off. Then I spotted a half-grown hare crouched immobile between the back of the cabin and a yard-high white pine. It watched me but failed to bolt. After a few hours I offered it half a carrot — I've seen the cartoons — which it took and devoured. It then hopped into its new home under my house. Then I looked up and saw a particularly handsome raccoon working my shoreline, scooping up clams. Two geese came in low overhead like fighter jets. Sandhills called from the back bay and a merlin gave me cheek when I got too close to its private tree on my island. Or so I mistakenly think. I return to the front and a beaver swims by. Everyone's back at work.

Almost two weeks later I'm back up. The small hare crouches in the same place, nose twitching, eyes darkly alert. It's early June. Despite a very harsh winter plants are beginning to bloom on my little world. In tiny pockets of soil on the granitic bedrock a new life cycle has begun. Photography can be a meditation. Looking through the viewfinder makes the world go quiet and bright. I twist a macro lens on a new body and set out to discover what flowers sing on my third of an acre. It's already too late for trilliums and wakerobins; besides, they prefer the sheltered woods back up the river. It's too harsh down here where the west winds leave the white and jack pine in charge. As I slowly work my way around this tiny island I encounter a total of 10 different flowers, all coexisting with the dandelion, always a brazen trumpeter of spring. The sky is uninflected today, the offshore wind is warm, birds sing, I feel at peace. My body, noisy and demanding for the past several days is finally quiet. I've bought a little more time.

EIGHT

DREAMING

" . . . an' me a writer and poet who should be havin'
adventures an' experiencing all the diversities and
paradoxes and ironies of life and passin' over all the
roads of the world and digging all the
cities and towns and rivers and oceans and
making all the chicks . . . by God!"

ROBERT CRUMB

FRITZ BUGS OUT

The 1980s were good to picture makers. Corporations spent
freely on printers, designers, illustrators, writers and photographers. Hundreds of thousands were lavished on annual
reports that were as much vanity projects as financial statements. One insurer that sent me overseas several times had
only a handful of shareholders, most of whom had inherited
their positions and didn't bother to even open the document.
The rationale for the spending was that the glossy books we
produced would serve as ambassadors for the companies and
be key marketing tools. In practice people in sales seldom
wanted to change the way they did things. The annual reports
languished in boxes and drawers.

As money began to flow freely into the pockets of photographers there were some unanticipated consequences. Several
years into the decade a magazine editor got interested in work
I was doing with a computer graphics group. We decided to do
a men's fashion spread set in a computer-rendered virtual environment. While this concept is commonplace now, over three
decades ago it was uncharted territory. We had no precedents

to work with and we'd be pushing the rendering capacities of then current computers to their limits.

We booked a large studio, as the concept for the double-page spread would involve nearly a dozen models in the picture. We were a good-sized crowd as all the computer people were in attendance as were the publisher, the clothing designers and the usual makeup and hair people. We were trying to make some mini-history. This would be an expensive session that had serious potential to fail. The room was tense.

I glued transparent templates onto the ground glass of my viewfinders. They would give me both the perspective and placement of the figures. As soon as I was ready to go the art director arrived. He barked a series of rapid-fire instructions and then disappeared. A few minutes later he was back shouting incomprehensible orders like a Gatling gun before vanishing once again. So the day went.

As these were early days in the '80s money party it took me perhaps an hour to understand what was going on. The guy was scooting into the studio washroom every quarter of an hour to do lines of coke. Each time he'd emerge turbo-charged for a quarter of an hour and then collapse into silence and retreat.

It made for a horrible working environment, one that for the next half-dozen years became all too ubiquitous. Work pressure drove many photographers into the washrooms. They blew much of their inflated fees into their noses. I watched a number of very talented people age a quarter century in a handful of years. Some lost their studios, houses, even their families. Friendships were destroyed and the users looked like death. They became zombies.

It was in this environment that I learned how to coordinate designers and printers, negotiate endless meetings, even write corporate-speak and do a good president's letter to shareholders. It was interesting to learn how corporations made their money, what holdings they had and get familiar with the people who ran them. I developed an understanding of business and a respect for what some could achieve. Although many managers were essentially private sector civil servants, a few took risks that were major creative acts. I enjoyed talking with them; they, in return, treated me well. I enjoyed being a fly on the wall.

As that decade boomed Toronto real estate got very expensive and studios became unaffordable. I had been renting for a couple of decades and as prices got higher I began to look for alternatives. Then I got an idea. I knew that the stock of Great Lakes bulk carriers was aging. There were vessels on the lakes that were a hundred years old. There were still dozens of steamers. I had some knowledge of the fleets and had favourites. As I write this in 2015 one of the handsomest classic lakers, the *Montrealais*, is being broken. I've watched her climb the flight locks on the Welland, I've kayaked into her enormous bow thruster and run my hands over her big bronze prop. She was the very last steamer built in Canada. Now she's gone.

When these ships are retired they are sold for their value as scrap — not much. Knowing this I began searching for vessels suitable for conversion into floating studios. I concentrated on locating the gearless vessels that Great Lakes sailors call flatbacks. I understood that self-unloaders with their enormous above-deck booms and complex conveyor and tunnel systems below were too expensive and time-consuming to convert. But the fates threw me another hand. I found the *Grand Rapids* and the *Madison*.

Sister ships, these 330-foot vessels were railcar ferries that had carried entire trains across the top of Lake Michigan since the 1920s. They had a quadruple attraction for me: they had enormous, completely clear interiors on the main decks; they were cheap; they were historic vessels and they were steamers. Each had a pair of magnificent triple expansion steam engines down in their bellies. As they had been commissioned for year-round service their bottoms were very heavily built so they could ice break. In the non-corrosive waters of the Great Lakes they would float for hundreds of years. They were the perfect ships for the job. I set about assembling a team — money people, a developer, a designer, a real estate professional and so on. It was a solid group. We began having meetings using Captain John's floating restaurant in what had been Marshall Tito's personal yacht, the *Jadran*, as our boardroom. It was exciting — until the bureaucrats got involved.

The staff at the Toronto Harbour Commission were terrific. They understood the project immediately and loved the idea of assembling a historic ships collection in the harbour and reinvigorating the decaying and underutilized Cherry Street industrial area. I soon had assurances that we could negotiate for a 1,000-foot section of Polson Quay, just above the bottom of Cherry Street. Now I had the ships, the team and a place to moor them. However, all of this was attached to a big city that moved like frozen bunker oil, had little imagination and seemed professionally negative.

I was told that a project on this scale would have to include parkland. This sounds impossible when you're dealing with ships but when I offered the top deck as a public lounge area and the wheelhouse and enclosed passenger seating cabin for conversion to a coffee shop, restaurant or, even better, a bar, that objection subsided. When I was asked in one meeting to explain how the engine rooms would be used I, without even thinking, blurted out "gay bar." That image of sweaty young men partying between five-foot diameter pistons, enormous connecting rods and gigantic propeller shafts was too much for the municipal mind. I was never asked again.

To make the project viable I needed "live/work" zoning. Our plan was to have the units constructed by a prefab home-builder and trucked to the site. The units would be loaded on the stern of the ships, skidded down the rails on the main deck toward the bows until each vessel was full. Every unit would be two storeys high and run from one side of the ship to the other, a distance of about 65 feet. Openings cut into the topsides of the hull on the quay-side would serve as entrances, the ones on the water-side would give access to individual private docks. Every tenant could have a canoe at their doorstep. Not permissible. Dangerous — like steps with no handrails.

The generation of urban planners working at City Hall had all gone to school in an era when they were taught that different areas of a city should be devoted to discreet functions. This was partly a reaction to the bad old days of the industrialization when workers lived on grimy streets in the shadow of smokestacks. Toronto had had many examples of this. The Massey works were in the middle of town, as were the Inglis plant, CCM, the CP rail yards and various meat-packing plants — hence Hog Town. The scions of these families, the Masseys, McLeans and Allans, were among my oldest friends.

So the current dogma was that people couldn't live and work in the same space. The city had enforcers to make sure that this didn't happen. A writer was allowed to pound keys at home but otherwise, a separate, appropriately zoned space was required. Even artists had to commute to work. This showed a total lack of understanding of the economics of creative production. It was destructive. It was stupid.

Why couldn't I construct live/work studios for photographers, filmmakers, designers, painters and dancers inside ships? Aside from it being slightly unorthodox there were many other objections. I remember some little person from the city triumphantly declaring that my scheme was unworkable because housing could only be built in areas that were served by public transit and there was none on Cherry Street. I never got an answer when I inquired why not dedicate a bus to a Cherry Street route. It could serve not only my project but also the club-goers on Polson Quay, the shoppers at the huge discount food store down there but also, in summer, the beach strollers, swimmers and sailors using the outer harbour. No!

As these and other issues dragged on month after month something else happened — a recession. As the months, and then years, ground by the price of commercial real estate began to decline and, eventually, collapse. My project, which came in at $14 a square foot, was very cheap when I started but looked insane when the market bottomed out and you could rent downtown warehouse space for four dollars a square foot. I knew that the market would come back but meanwhile I was carrying the costs of a pair of huge ships moored on Lake Erie, plus design fees, etc., etc. As the costs mounted I finally realized that I had to pull the plug. My beautiful ships were towed to breaking yards in India. The losers had won.

———

They believe they're invisible, the many fishermen who troll back and forth in front of my place staring dully. Despite miles of empty shore to either side they're convinced that all pike, pickerel and bass are hanging out within 10 feet of my short shoreline. Sometimes these guys will idle several yards off my porch and sit for hours staring slack-mouthed at me as I work on my laptop. They'll discuss my place, shouting like sports announcers over their motors.

"He's got them solar panels."

"Had 'em for years."

"I figure that's how he charges up the computer."

"Guess so."

"I seen him with a power tool last week — one of them battery ones. Must charge 'em on the panels too."

"Ya do what ya gotta do."

"Just got a nibble."

"Uh huh."

"Strike!"

"Could be."

"Shit, it's just a rock bass."

"Again, eh?"

"He should get himself a new roof, them shingles are start'n to curl."

"Yup."

It's a job this fishing. They start work early, grinding back and forth before my place laying down a two-cycle smokescreen. By noon the morning shift is over, lures are retrieved and the boats race off for lunch. By one or so they're back at work, coughing their way up and down the inlet, passing and shouting to each other in their battered metal skiffs or glitter bass boats.

"Ya got any Charlie?"

"Dick all."

"What lure ya using?"

"Give up on 'em all. On bait. Gone to worms."

"Ya should be ashamed!"

"Couldn't give a flying fuck. I just want a pike for supper. Otherwise the old lady'll give me shit for wasting time."

Their afternoon shift ends around five. Some do overtime after supper.

I carry one of my kayaks down to the water. I usually use a wooden one I built myself but today I'm trying out a nifty little number with a clear polycarbonate window between my knees. I paddle across the inlet, cut around a point and slip into a large hidden bay full of lily pads and wild rice. The water is less than a foot deep.

I feel a bump and the boat humps up slightly. As I look down a large pike squeezes under my boat, briefly rolling so that I can see its glassy eye staring up through the boat bottom. A couple of minutes later another passes under the clear window. As I slip over a small rocky section a crayfish scuttles away. A splash makes me look up in time to see a bear and two cubs exit the water and retreat into the bush. Another big fish roils the water just ahead. It's another workday in the woods — rush hour in the wetlands.

And it's a secure one because all those outdoors guys perched on pedestal seats in their hundred-horse-power bass boats with stereos, layer-cake tackle boxes and fish finders can't get in here on account of the muddy shallows and the weeds. They don't even know about it. While they execute their sub-chaser search patterns on the open waters the fish all hang out here with me, safe from sonar, noisy motors and fuel film on the water. I recall that people once fished from canoes — clean, quiet and fish-friendly. The problem with that is there's just not enough to buy. Without noise, smoke and fossil fuels the economy suffers. You need 40 grand in gear to catch the free fish.

That wasn't the only time that the city defeated me. Another was the legacy of late 19th century deal-making. In return for a transcontinental railway the Macdonald government had handed vast portions of the downtown cores of various major Canadian cities — Vancouver, Calgary, Winnipeg, Toronto and Montreal — to the CPR. My years of photographing and writing for the land division of the hydra-headed Canadian Pacific eventually led to consultancy work on a proposal to convert portions of the Toronto railway lands into a public park. In return for commercial development permits the corporation proposed to create a 13-acre public park on some of the lands. The portion chosen included some switching structures, water and coaling towers and a roundhouse. Nobody told me what to do — just think of something interesting. It was an exciting assignment.

One of my challenges was to repurpose the huge brick engine roundhouse near the base of the CN Tower. A bizarre aspect of this was that the railyard tracks had been torn up before the roundhouse was emptied. Several big locomotives were left stranded inside the boarded-up, trackless roundhouse.

However, it was the big bays that remained empty that most got my attention. What could one do with these enormous pie-shaped spaces that were essentially one-car garages for locomotives? Predictably I thought like a photographer: I began to imagine one of those rooms as a giant *camera* — the Latin word for room, of course. With all their grime and boarded-up windows, each was a very dark room — a *camera obscura*. This was an ancient device, a room illuminated only by one tiny aperture, like a pinhole. Such an arrangement will produce on the facing wall a large, inverted, very soft and dim image of the view beyond the opening. It's a well-known and simple optical effect that is both amazing and magical. Whenever I taught photography I always got my students to build one so that they would understand the basic principle behind the modern camera that simply replaced the viewing wall with film or, these days, a light sensitive array. The result always excited them.

If you add a lens to a pinhole camera the image quality improves by many orders of magnitude. A lens designed for such a large camera was going to be quite a construction. I wanted to put it on the roof of the building in a rotating cupola-like housing with a right-angle mirror or prism. The lens would scan the city, the traffic on the Lakeshore and Gardiner Expressway and the ever-changing lake itself. The image would be projected on the floor of the building. It would be enormous. School kids could walk through it or put large sheets of paper on the floor and trace it. It would be amazing.

My client thought so too, and so did Eastman Kodak in Rochester as well as the president of Kodak Canada. Rochester agreed to supply the engineering and design talent and their Canadian arm, the money. Initially luck was on my side — my timing was perfect. Eastman Kodak had just lost the bid to design the Hubble telescope to the company that eventually screwed it up. The damn thing got up into space and wouldn't focus. It was like a bad pinhole. While the contractor and NASA were busy screaming at each other, a bunch of very experienced optical people in Rochester were making paper airplanes. They needed a new project and threw themselves into mine.

Several engineers came up from head office, toured the site and got excited. The designs began to pour in. My favourite was like a fly's eye. Its many clustered lenses would be so efficient at transmitting light that the whole contraption would even work at night. The circular image it would throw on the floor would exceed 10 metres in diameter. We even built a working model of it for presentations. It worked.

But negotiations with the city didn't go well. The landlord would give the developed park to the city for free in return for permission to develop the balance of the railway lands into a whole new "neighbourhood" of office towers and condominiums. Their proposal was predictable and so was the response. "Saint" Jack Layton, whose positions I would normally support, went after the scheme like a Rottweiler — it didn't provide enough low-income housing, etc., etc. There were many other objections. People got worked up and eventually my sponsors threw up their hands and my rotating camera spun down the drain of dreams like so many others. It happened very quickly. The president of Kodak Canada was on his way down from Eglinton to University Avenue to sign the final agreement when the whole thing fell apart. I had to call his cell and tell him to turn around. The huge bay I was going to create magic in became, after many more years of negotiations, a discount furniture outlet. O Canada!

———

As I sit under the pines on my little sun-powered, off-the-grid island, my laptop cooks away on radio telescope data from the University of California, Berkeley. I've been assigned my own little section of sky and when I'm not working on my computer it searches for unusual signals from the universe. The SETI project harnesses the computing power of over 9 million personal computers like mine to form a volunteer supercomputer that crunches data in search of any sign that in the enormity of space we are not alone.

1989–90

During the course of working with various Eastman Kodak engineers and managers on the roundhouse project I got to know one of the senior ones quite well. One day he invited me to his very beautiful early 19th century upstate New York country house for a drink. As we sipped beer on his big veranda he told me that Kodak had been working on a filmless still camera for a number of years. Their first patent on this technology dated back to the early 1970s but after well over a decade of fitful work they finally had a good working prototype. It had been difficult for a company devoted to producing consumables like film, chemistry and photo paper to commit to a product that required none of them. Would I be interested in testing this Nikon camera that Kodak had spent over $2.5 million modifying? I jumped at the chance.

Some weeks later I was high in Kodak's Rochester head office building getting a training course in how to use the camera and its user-hostile software. Like all engineers' working prototypes it was a rather clumsy contraption. The interior pressure plate on the film plane had been replaced by a light sensitive digital array. A thick cable snaked from a blob of black adhesive on the camera body back and led to a long, thick metal box that housed a Winchester disc pack of hard drives on a carrying strap. After a few months working out in a gym a photographer could easily walk around with that monster box dangling from his shoulder.

The engineers also had an infrared prototype based on the same technology. It was even clumsier. The whole apparatus was enclosed in housing filled with liquid nitrogen — the colder the camera was, the more sensitive the device would be to heat radiation. With the device tethered to a computer and monitor across the room I initially photographed cars far below in Kodak's parking lot. The images were like x-rays, the engines and exhaust systems of recently driven cars glowed eerily through the autos' sheet metal. Even spookier were pictures I made of intercity passenger jets approaching the Rochester airport. Fuel stored in their wings showed as a dark shadow and in most there wasn't very much. Those cost-conscious flights operated with very little margin. Finally I focused on the trees in full fall splendor at the bottom of the Genesee River gorge right beside the building. Guffaws broke out by the monitors across the room. A hidden couple on lunch break were in full *flagrante delicto* in the bushes by the river. Truly hot sex.

Much later I smuggled that first camera into Canada and gradually got familiar with it in my studio. The afternoon that I'd made a date to demonstrate it to the Ryerson photo arts faculty my colleague Dougie appeared at my door. Before leaving I made a head and shoulders portrait of him. Later at Ryerson we hooked the system up to a large screen black-and-white monitor. The assembled faculty sat stiffly with their arms crossed before the monitor. They weren't going to buy into any weird shit. My much enlarged, razor-sharp portrait of Dougie materialized on the screen. Silence. Then I began to zoom into the file. I got all the way into one of Dougie's eyes before any pixels became visible. It was only then did former department chair Darryl Williams catch his breath.

"Wow, that's pretty good!"

It was still only black and white but it was amazing.

The opinion of the rest of the room?

"It will never replace film."

As we all know Kodak repeatedly failed to truly commit to their amazing creation; that was left to the Japanese. However, on my training visit I had also been shown the very large new building in which they planned to manufacture the new technology. When I visited it the production area was confined to a tiny corner of the vast building. While Kodak has never really committed to designing and manufacturing digital cameras, they have remained a premier producer of the light-sensitive arrays used by other digital camera makers.

They were all very nice people but many seemed hopelessly parochial to me. It was as if they graduated from high school, walked across the street to attend R.I.T. and then crossed the street again to work at Kodak for the rest of their lives. The ones I knew had never been to New York City and those who came up to assess my project in Toronto seemed surprised that there was such a large city in the Canadian wilderness. They were too provincial to be full visionaries.

My days working with that revolutionary and disruptive prototype ended with a knock on my studio door. Several RCMP officers and a manager from Kodak Canada showed me their cards and a letter giving them permission to borrow the camera for a week or so. The Mounties had a project they wanted to test it on. I surrendered the gear. A couple of weeks later it was returned to me. What had they done with it?

It was a long shot but I booted up the drives. Yes, there were files. Men with handkerchiefs covering their faces crouched in the bushes. There were rifles and baseball bats. There were barricades and fires. My photographers' pictorial fantasies evaporated. Of course, the technology was perfect for surveillance. I'd shown the borrowers how to take pictures but had neglected to teach them how to delete. I erased every image of Oka's Mohawk defenders.

NINE

FACING THE LIGHT

"The evidence is in, and you are the verdict."
ANNE LAMOTT

*"Art is a sort of experimental station
in which one tries out living."*
JOHN CAGE

1978

It's night and raining, I'm waiting for *Go Boy* Roger Caron
outside his publisher's office beside the big expressway. His
train from Toronto's Union Station back home to the pen in
Collins Bay leaves in less than an hour and I must both do his
portrait and get him on it. Finally the doors at McGraw-Hill
Ryerson open and Caron hunches out chained to his guard,
Ricky. The backlit pair shamble toward me with a foot of steel
links between them. I slide open the side door of my little VW
van and we're off onto the 401 headed for the Don Valley
Parkway in a downpour. Ricky is huge.

Caron has just turned 40. His achievements so far include
75 bank robberies, some hostage-takings and assorted assaults.
His hobbies include concealing knives, clubs and loaded guns.
So far all these enterprises have earned him 24 years in jail but
he's busted out over a dozen times. Go Boy.

The Don Valley Parkway has long been an expressway in
name only. We splash slowly southward toward the towers of
downtown with the clock hands spinning toward train time. I've
got to get the picture. Finally we climb the ramp to Richmond
Street and clatter onto Front. With ten minutes to go I pull into

the cab stand at Union Station. I grab my Nikons and flash and run through the rain with Ricky and Roger. I shove Ricky behind a column and stick Caron in front. When I step back and turn he hunches his shoulders and pulls up his collar against the hard rain. I make two exposures before the flash shorts out. Both photographs are haunting, strange, threatening, perfect.

Roger Caron at Union Station in the rain as originally published in *Weekend Magazine*, January 25, 1978

2012

It's late April and raining. I turn a page in the *Globe and Mail* and discover that Caron is lying in a Cornwall funeral home — dead at 73. His life since we briefly collaborated in a downpour has included writing four books, a rampage in the Brockville Psychiatric Hospital and robbing a discount store. In 2004 he was caught in an Ottawa shopping centre carrying a wig, a change of clothes, surgical gloves, duct tape, a knife and a loaded .32-calibre in a gym bag.

A handful of years after I met him he discovered he had Parkinson's disease. He'd become a prisoner of his own body.

1977

After driving up Bayview Avenue I wheel into the Sunnybrook Hospital parking lot and locate the new addition designed and executed by my architectural client. They want portfolio photographs of the building. When I step inside this veterans' wing I suddenly confront scores of people, both men and women, who have fought for this country, suffered an injury and spent the balance of their lives in hospital. There are veterans of our peace-keeping efforts of the '60s and '70s but also of the Korean War, Second World War, the First World War, even the Boer War. This is their life — white rooms, beige corridors, shiny floors, hospital routine and pain — for weeks, months, years and decade after decade. I'm stunned.

I execute my architectural assignment, process and print the film and deliver the pictures, but for days after I can't get the residents of the building out of my mind. I want to talk to them and make their portraits. I want Canadians to see what I have and comprehend these lives. I negotiate with Sunnybrook and present the idea to the editors of *Weekend* magazine. Both buy in. I spend days on these encounters, making notes and photographing these men and women with my Hasselblads, framed by white walls and institutional furniture. The black-and-white pictures are stark because the lives are stark.

When *Weekend* decides to run them for early November my pictures are sent to the Montreal printing plant. When the pressmen on the night shift see them they decide to shut down the colour gravure presses and clean all the rollers in order to reproduce the originals on newsprint as faithfully as possible. The result appears in 40 newspapers, *Globe and Mail* included, across Canada. Many letters thump in. As this was before we'd seen Richard Avedon's portraits against white seamless, many readers found the pictures harsh and upsetting. This was, of course, part of my point, but the many abusive letters to *Weekend* remain disturbing.

1978

I slammed down the phone and stared out my studio window at the gathering winter gloom. I'd been packing my gear for a morning flight to the Bahamas to photograph the bestseller novelist Arthur Hailey. The magazine's art director had just called me with good news — I wouldn't have to go to Lyford Cay: Hailey was coming to Toronto later in the week for a publisher's meeting. I glumly unpacked my sunscreen, snorkelling gear and bathing suit.

I was now scheduled to meet Hailey at his hotel up on Bloor next to the Hudson Bay Centre. I reread the magazine profile of him that I was to illustrate. It was a bit frightening to a free-wheeling photographer. Hailey gets up every morning precisely at six. By 6:05 he's in his bathroom shaving. He's dressed and having coffee by 6:25. He's at his desk by seven, pounding out the next bestseller — one year of research, six months reviewing his notes following by 18 months of writing. *Airport, Hotel, The Money-changers, In High Places, The*

Aubrey Winch, 61, 419 Squadron of the RCAF in WWI.
Ditched in the North Sea.

(Left) Leslie Miller, 88, 4th Canadian Mountain Regiment in Flanders, WWI.
(Right) William Caswell, 90, army machine gunner in France, WWI.

Sunnybrook Veterans Hospital (*Weekend Magazine*, November 12th, 1977)

231

Final Diagnosis, and so on, for a total of 47 books and 170 million sales in 40 languages. This kind of industrial production requires serious time management and discipline. Here's a guy who schedules every minute of his day. I better not be late.

A few mornings later I lug my gear into the lobby of his hotel and ask the desk clerk to call up to Hailey's room. The call is brief. I'm told I'll have to wait. Mr. Hailey will call down when he's ready. An hour later I'm still sitting in the lobby — the clerk has heard nothing. I request a second call — Mr. Hailey says he needs a little more time. I wish I knew how you *cool your heels.*

Three-quarters of an hour later I request another call. I can go up to his suite in 15 minutes. I give him 20 then get on the elevator and knock on his door. It's answered by an unshaven, middle-aged, little man still in his underpants.

1979

I have been tricked. Somehow I have promised to do a glamour portrait of a woman I do not know. A stretch limo stops in front of my studio and a black dress and large black hat emerge as do a couple of sinister-looking men. We mount the stairs to my studio. When my sitter removes her hat and steps onto the brightly lit set I know I'm in trouble. She's no longer young and has spent too much time beside the pool in summer and on small southern islands in winter. When the men introduce themselves I recognize familiar Mafia names. They've caught my reaction to my subject's face and stare at me hard. "You better make her look good! Capisce? We'll be back in an hour." The big car slithers off into the afternoon traffic.

1999

Another little assignment has come in from Canada Post. They're launching a new stamp series celebrating hockey. I take a cab down to the SkyDome to meet my client in the lobby. It's the standard media event setup, a podium, a mic-encrusted lectern behind a low barrier and a rabble of reporters, videographers and photojournalists. As I jockey for position I realize how much I resent the hierarchical foundation of these events. I'm not a news guy. I began to set up beside someone I'd taught camerawork to many years earlier. Acknowledging our situation, he ruefully refers to himself as a "picture peon." He too feels diminished. At that moment my contact from the post office taps my shoulder. "Ottawa doesn't want you in this scrum. Take that elevator to the top and photograph the people in the room up there."

Relieved, I grab my camera bag and retreat to the elevator. It stops at a large gray room with only three occupants. Each wears a tie, a blue blazer and gray flannels. They are sitting together under flickering fluorescents on a row of plastic chairs with their trousers rolled above their knees. All three guys are comparing scars on their shins. Bobby Hull looks up at me and elbows the other Bobby sitting beside him. "See this son-of-a-bitch Orr? I gave him my autograph at a show in Parry Sound. He was just a kid. Next time I saw him he slammed me into the boards in Boston. Big thanks." All three laugh hard, the two Bobbys and the little guy beside them, Rocket Richard. Maurice is dead a few months later.

1980

The first time I met billionaire Ken Thomson was at his office across from Toronto's new City Hall on Queen Street. I'd been trying to clean up my east end studio after a particularly messy shoot when I got a breathless call from the art director of *Toronto Life*, an ambitious Brit who later went on to art direct big American magazines like *Rolling Stone* and *Esquire*.

They'd commissioned a cover story on Thomson but had no photograph to illustrate it. And the subject was flatly refusing to be photographed. As the press deadline approached they had, after many telephone entreaties, finally gotten Mr. Thomson to agree to a brief audience with a photographer who they felt he would like. If he didn't there would be no session and the matter would be dropped. I was the photographer they had in mind. The time set for this critical meeting was in half an hour.

"Keep it simple," I told myself. I rushed out of my studio carrying only a Nikon F, a single prime lens and a roll of Kodachrome. I jumped on a westbound Queen streetcar and began scanning the story which had just been faxed to me. Twenty minutes later I was in the building's lobby telling security I had an appointment with Ken. After a few phone calls I was told to take the elevator to the top where I would find his office.

When the doors opened I discovered that his office *was* the top floor. A beige carpet prairie stretched out before my feet. Some acres off to the west a small dark rectangle broke the horizon. A tiny man stood behind it.

We all know how to greet someone for the first time. The door opens, you smile and extend your hand — simple, basic, even natural. But it doesn't work so well when the distance from the door to the desk is several hundred featureless feet. As I hiked across the broadloom the desk grew to the size of a small building. After several minutes Ken was towering over me. I'm barely five ten.

In no time we were talking about art. I come from a family of painters. An ancestor taught a member of the Group of Seven how to paint and that member in turn later taught my mother and aunt at the Ontario College of Art during the 1930s. My grandfather had briefly employed a couple of Group members. I grew up surrounded by people who made art. Ken didn't but he collected it. We hit it off. He had little time so I quickly made several photographs — they were not brilliant but they were decent and did the job. While packing up my gear I asked him why he'd been so reluctant to sit for a portrait. He had two reasons. One was that he felt he had a funny chin — it looked very standard to me. The other I'll tell you about a little later on.

The next time I ran into him he was having an argument with his wife, Marilyn, in the cosmetics department of The Bay's flagship store at Yonge and Bloor. He wanted to go home and she wanted to do more shopping. Not one of the dim dollies in the makeup department seemed to have the faintest idea that the couple of seniors bickering before their counters owned the place. Ken and I had a brief exchange as he stomped out of the store.

Fast-forward almost two decades. The Art Gallery of Ontario, newly renovated and expanded by Frank Gehry, was having a pre-public opening party for patrons and various dignitaries. As a sitting member of one of the board's acquisition and curatorial committees I had been invited. As I picked my way through the amazing Thomson collection of ivories on the ground floor I ran into Marilyn who was there on her own — Ken had recently died. As we examined his tiny treasures together I began to tell her how I'd first met him years before. When I told her that he hadn't wanted to be photographed she asked me if he'd explained why. I said he'd told me that he liked to cross Bay Street to the big Simpsons department store during his lunch hour and not be recognized when he bought socks on sale. "But you own that store!" I'd spluttered out.

When she stopped belly laughing I began to rave about the collection of antique ship builders' models that he'd presented to the AGO. Artists can be surprisingly conservative and territorial about their beloved museums they love to hate. In 1995 when the Musée des beaux-arts in Montreal mounted a stunning exhibition of classic cars it seemed that every regional painter and sculptor in the country screamed solecism! As far as I was concerned anyone who could design something as beautiful as a 1929 Auburn 8-120 Boattail, a 1932 Mercedes-Benz SSK Trossi, a '34 Chrysler Airflow CU or a '35 Voisin C25 Aérodyne was a serious sculptor. Nevertheless, many little artists in Toronto decried the ships.

I told her how glad I was that Ken and the gallery had ignored them and facilitated the gift. When I told her how delighted I was that they were here she said that she was happy too. For years she'd nagged her husband to get his toy boats out of their basement.

My assignment this week is doing editorial portraits of IBM executives. All have large offices and imposing desks. It's the very early days of desktop computer production and each of these men has the latest model squatting like a bust on the credenza behind his desk. To a man they want me to include their enormous monitors as a prop and signifier in their portrait but not a single one of them knows how to boot their big clunkers up. After bumbling around for a few minutes each calls a secretary in to animate their show-machines and call up an impressive spreadsheet or graph. The women comply with efficient resignation.

Today my former student at OCA is my boss. We've been thrown together to work gratis on the annual report of a large Canadian health charity. In his role as art director he has conceived an elaborate, theatrical approach to the portraits that I'm to execute for the annual book. Imagery relating to the condition the charity supports will be projected onto the bodies and backgrounds of the individuals featured in the report. As it's still an analogue age the images will be thrown onto the set and sitter by a powerful projector. I will then photograph the subject and superimposition. It will take a lot of gear and patience to pull this one off but since I don't want to rain on a former student's concept I'm determined to pull it off. After some experimentation I assemble a system that will realize his vision.

We set up on the auditorium stage at the charity's national headquarters up on Toronto's Bayview Avenue. A half-dozen head-office women are charged with guiding the subjects to our photo shoot. Most sitters are patient beneficiaries but a handful are executives involved in managing the charity. All eventually deal with the darkened set and the discomfort generated by the glaring projections and make the photographs. It proves to be a long, difficult day.

By late afternoon the stage has gotten crowded. The staff wish to make sure that the final sitting, featuring the organization's new chief executive, goes well. Soon the boss, a recently retired president of a large Canadian oil and gas resources company, marches into the auditorium. I ask him to take up position on a stool, the lights are dimmed and the projector lit. Just as I prepare to make the first exposure my very important sitter announces that he thinks the whole setup is stupid and he doesn't want to sit for the portrait. As his session is the only thing standing between me and the completion of the assignment I try to gently persuade him to change his mind. When he retorts that the photo session is a waste of his time I remind him that we're all donating our time and resources to this project. If he gives me 10 more minutes then our part of the project will be finished and we can all go home.

"I've given away far more of my valuable time than you ever have!" he thunders back. At that moment I realized that I was dealing with a two-year-old. "Go! Go! Get out!" I shouted back, kicking the senior toddler off the set. He stomped out of the auditorium, the slamming door echoing in the big room. As soon as they were sure he was gone his support staff burst into applause.

J.J. Barnicke died today. For most Torontonians he was just a name on a commercial real estate sign — one you saw everywhere for decades. However for me he came to represent something else. A couple of decades ago when he was at the peak of his powers I was assigned to do his portrait for a business publication. I lugged my gear up to his downtown office and began to set up my lights. He turned up about 10 minutes later and we set to work grinding out a standard corporate portrait. He was all business. When we had finished he told me to lock his office door. I did. Then he gruffly asked me to fetch a low stool from a corner. I did. Next an overcoat from a closet. What?

Then this short round man ordered me to take his portrait again. He tossed the overcoat over his shoulder, put a foot on the stumpy stool and raised his double chins. Next he pulled off his tie and slipped his right hand between the buttons of his shirt. I finally got it. He was no longer a short, chubby, former E.P. Taylor beer salesman, he was the conqueror from Corsica — the Napoleon of office leasing. And I was his David.

———

A great blue heron stands in six inches of water a yard off my shoreline. He's as still as a lawn flamingo. When I step outside for a closer look he remains immobile. Same when I approach. As I sit on the shore beside him to no effect I realize that this spectacular bird is very ill. He waits quietly for nature to take its course.

It's one of those assignments that's humiliating for all parties. I'm to do a "day in the life" of Ed Broadbent, leader of the federal NDP. It will take a week.

Not all politicians enjoy these journalistic spreads. Some are very selective — St. Pierre, father of our current PM, was notorious for refusing to do sessions with Canadian photographers while being, at the same time, almost slavishly willing to perform for the British, French or American press. Being number three, Broadbent doesn't have much choice. He's got to embrace the exposure. And as a newly minted father I have little choice either: I gotta earn a living.

So we both have to endure my recording his breakfast bowl of cereal for posterity, his meetings, his hair appointment, supper and bedtime stories for the kiddies, all the banalities of his regular Canadian guy routine.

We spend a lot of time in cabs together; the days are long. Whenever I make a remark or ask a question Ed becomes the jukebox in your 1950s diner. The selector grinds across the file of 45s, selects the appropriate one and presses play. His every response is a packaged sound bite or speech. The guy is just not present. Fearing that this will show in the photographs I finally, after several of these prerecorded days, remind him that I'm only doing pictures, not sound or words. Since we're stuck with each other for the week can we not converse like neighbours? He assents but it turns out that he can't stop. After years in politics his default setting is auto response. So we stumble through the remainder of the week.

When the piece is published word comes down from Ottawa. Ed didn't like it. Having made his displeasure known the matter is dropped. However, some weeks later, after completing an assignment in Vancouver, I cab out to the airport for a red-eye home to Toronto. As soon as I enter the departure lounge my stomach knots. Ed Broadbent is on the same flight. When he looks up it's not hard to know what he's thinking as he glares at me — "I can't place him but I know that S.O.B. and I don't like him." So I retreat to a far corner of the lounge.

At boarding I'm relieved to discover that we're on a huge

747 jumbo. There'll be space. But there isn't. My seat assignment is in the same section as Broadbent and his gang. I'm in the window row, he's in the centre line of five seats. His staff sit in the row behind. Trouble begins immediately. Our democratic socialist leader is exhausted so he lies across the five seats, neglecting to fasten his seat belt. The flight attendants ask him to buckle up. No response. They plead. He refuses. The big plane squats like a huge toad at the end of the runway. We're stuck. Finally the captain comes back, there are high level negotiations and Broadbent finally sits up and buckles up. The toad takes off.

But the shit-disturber isn't finished. A couple of rows ahead of him sit several prairie farmers. Their heads block the view of the bulkhead screen before them. These guys have scrawny chicken necks and nerdy haircuts half-obscured by those ventilated tractor caps given out by feed stores and manure spreader makers. Ed begins to make fun of them for the benefit of his companions in the row behind. Once again the attendants are summoned.

———

When I was 15 I used to run these waters in an eight-foot planning hull that I'd built myself in our city backyard. The forward half of the hull was decked over with bright finished mahogany, creating a private space perfect for storing the booze I delivered in the evenings after work. I'd pick up the two-fours of Blue and Canadian along with mickeys of rye or gin at a tarpapered hovel hiding in the pines on the north side of the station channel at Pointe au Baril. That same family now runs a large and respectable marina that sells luxury runabouts to the establishment. Like the Bronfmans they're not keen on talk about the origins of their grubstake.

1994

During the 1980s I had organized a public self-portrait project for the Art Gallery at Harbourfront. A fully equipped professional studio with flash power packs and umbrellas, seamless backdrop, a large format camera and print processor was established in the north end of the gallery building, a former trucking warehouse. The medium would be 8x10 Polaroid colour film. This allowed users to see their results immediately, a novelty then, a commonplace now.

During the week established artists could book in for a day and, with the help of an assistant, execute a project of their choice at no cost. As such large format instant print materials were extremely expensive, the opportunity was quickly fully subscribed. The artists got to keep what they produced, their only obligation was to participate later in a group exhibition of the completed works.

On weekends the public participated in a similar deal. Anyone interested could book the studio for 15 minutes or so and, in complete privacy, execute a self-portrait. Again the portraits were theirs to keep but each came with an obligation to allow it to be exhibited in the public gallery for a week prior to them taking it home. As the project ran for several weeks the self-portrait exhibition was constantly evolving. Every Monday morning I'd go through the weekend's production and select pieces to hang that week. While many people used it as an opportunity to create a conventional family portrait, an astonishing number did quite unexpected things, some of them quite naughty. Another surprise was discovering just who had taken advantage of that opportunity over each weekend. More than a few famous faces showed up — entertainers, sports heroes, politicians. The project was a hit.

At the end of its three-week run I packed up the studio along with the remaining materials and shipped everything to my Queen Street studio. As the equipment was on loan for a full month and there were still several boxes of unconsumed Polaroid I decided to reward myself for having pulled the whole thing off. I would take the remaining week and do my own project. I reestablished the studio.

Although I had several competing ideas of how to use this opportunity, fate threw something else my way. That first evening back at the studio my old friend Macbeth dropped by on his way home to the Beaches. I asked him to sit for a portrait. He sat on a stool before the seamless backdrop while I set up the 8x10 view camera. It's always a magical moment when you throw the dark cloth over your head and open up the lens. The world is suddenly made strange. It floats upside down and backwards on the ground glass of the big bellows camera. A combination of optical fall off and viewing angle seems to pool the light in the centre of the frame, the edges and corners descend into mysterious shadows.

I've always found that moment hypnotic and entrancing but on this evening the image on the glass seemed lifeless. It was just a skinny guy sitting on a stool. Anxious to make an image that spoke to me I began to move the camera toward him. As I wheeled the heavy stand and camera forward the image on the ground glass became more and more interesting. I didn't stop closing in until the lens was only a handful of inches from his face which had now become a landscape on the big groundglass. An eye, a nose, a bit of lip and a partial ear had been transformed into giant landforms. I exposed several of the precious sheets, we drank a beer and then Macbeth went home. I was left alone staring at a handful of photographs.

They gave me lots to think about. Imagine a photograph by a classicist like Yousuf Karsh. His Hemingway or Churchill portraits don't really tell you anything you didn't already know about their famous subjects. Rather, Karsh's talent lay in summarizing the public image of his sitters in a single photograph.

Macbeth

This is accomplished by carefully selecting a setting, the clothing, the pose and the attitude of the subject. All these elements, augmented by strategic lighting and composition, become signifiers. They tell you who the sitter is. This often becomes a game of pretend. Churchill is a bulldog warrior; Hemingway, a rugged but sensitive artist. It's a simple message and the message is rigged.

But if you come in so close that most of the signifiers are eliminated the viewer is left with a challenge. Do you know who you're looking at? The face remains recognizable but the person becomes more an object of interpretation. Photography is put to the test. What can it actually show when the props are kicked out? Here was something to work on.

As I quickly exhausted the supply of Polaroid and had to return the big camera, I switched to my own 4x5 camera and colour negative sheet film. In exchange for nightly beers Macbeth became my lab rat as I worked out how to execute these portraits. The closer one goes to the subject, the more one must extend the bellows in order to achieve focus. The more the bellows is extended, the more the light reaching the ground glass is reduced. It diminishes with the square of the distance. Whereas a few hundred watt seconds of strobe light were enough to expose a conventional portrait, in excess of 5,000 were needed for these close-ups. The use of flash was essential, not only to fix the sitter's movement that got exaggerated at such distances, but also to avoid cooking the sitter's skin with hot quartz light. Moreover, squeezing all of this gear on stands into a few square feet required ingenuity. I employed a number of booms.

Another hazard of close-up photography is reduced depth of field — shallow focus to the layperson. I used a powerful magnifying loupe to focus. With the lens wide open the depth of field was less than a quarter of an inch. Everything else was an out-of-focus blur. If the subject moved even slightly all focus was lost. View cameras have movements. If one tilts the lens board slightly forward when making a landscape then everything from immediately in front of the camera to infinity will be sharp. Swinging the lens on its vertical axis can do the same on the other plane. The lens can be raised and lowered within the circle of light it throws to change what one sees. Analogous movements can be executed by moving the ground glass and the film plane at the rear of the camera. These must be done carefully and accurately to achieve the desired results. And some movements distort shapes. While one has leisure when making a landscape or still life, one must move exceedingly quickly when making a close-up portrait. Macbeth allowed me to practise. Each session was, of necessity, several hours long.

With practice I made portraits of my sons, Ben and Jake, and a few friends and colleagues. When the editor of *Canadian Art* magazine, Sarah Milroy, saw the results she commissioned a portrait series for the publication's 10th anniversary in 1994. The list of subjects included artists, critics, curators and collectors with a couple of museum directors thrown in for variety. I set to work.

The art world is small so we all knew, or knew of, each other. This didn't necessarily make things easier. A couple of the critics had savaged my work in the press. Now we were obliged to engage in this extremely intimate exercise. They each handled it differently. The *Globe*'s critic insisted that I carefully light his face in order to highlight the large scar/depression disfiguring one side of his forehead. I did, with pleasure. The *Star*'s critic was somewhat ingratiating, telling me that every time he passed my big house with its separate studio building on the backlot he thought of me as someone with a perfect life.

Explain each of these for me.

The project was even more uncomfortable for the women. In a world where you're supposed to have perfect skin and never age how are you going to feel about being under a microscope and having the image enlarged to two and a half feet especially when one of the sitters was close to 80? It took guts and maybe a perverse kind of vanity to participate. But they did — on their own terms. Ydessa Hendeles, once an art dealer and by then a major global collector of contemporary art with her own museum/foundation, insisted on negotiating for a couple of hours the night she arrived at the studio. This

The late John Bentley Mays, the *Globe*'s former art critic, and his scar

was difficult and frustrating. It got later and later. I thought the whole session was going to go pear-shaped but we finally reached an agreement on usage of the photograph and set to work. The image turned out to be one of the highlights of the whole series. It was stunning.

However, she later decided I had broken our agreement (I hadn't) and cold-shouldered me for several years despite importuning by mutual friends. Eventually she came around and released the picture for public viewing and sale. Subsequently a large print went into the collection of Canada's National Portrait Gallery, a vital institution later destroyed by Stephen Harper. My print is now in some basement in Quebec with many other fine portraits and its building across from Parliament Hill has been allowed to rot. Both are crimes. At one point Ydessa had an assistant order a print of the image from me. I thought that this might mean that she was not displeased with it. However, when she received the print her response was relief because the jewelry she had worn for the session had been stolen. My highly detailed portrait that I'd so sweated to get was merely ID of stolen goods.

Another subject was a woman who'd been a rival dealer in Toronto. Not only were they art competitors but also said to be competitive over which one of them had inherited the most money. Word on the street was $80 million for one, $250 million for the other. I know that more is never enough but when you get to those sorts of numbers, personally I lose focus after the first 10 million. I have other problems, like the grocery bill. This session with S. was also strange and strained. She was in the middle of a divorce and her ex-to-be kept calling her cell. After a number of these interruptions she seemed to have dealt with him. But no. He began pounding on the studio door. He'd been phoning all this time from his big dark car in my driveway. She looks gently vulnerable in the final photograph. Both women looked quite beautiful.

My next sitter was Matthew Teitelbaum, the director of the Art Gallery of Ontario. As he sat down in the cluster of light and camera stands he reached into the cast aluminum shelf attached to the camera stand and picked up a short black pencil. As he rotated it between his fingers the word *noir* rolled up in gold. "Ah," he said, "I see Ydessa has been here."

Quite a few of my favourite artists sat for these portraits — Michael Snow, Robert Fones, Geoffrey James — but oddly there has never been an exhibition of the series. A few were shown in Av Issacs's gallery during a fundraiser. One was enormously enlarged for an outdoor installation alongside the Rideau by the once and future National Portrait Gallery, and a handful have appeared at the Art Gallery of Ontario in various exhibitions but never the larger group. As my friends in Jamaica say, "Maybe soon come."

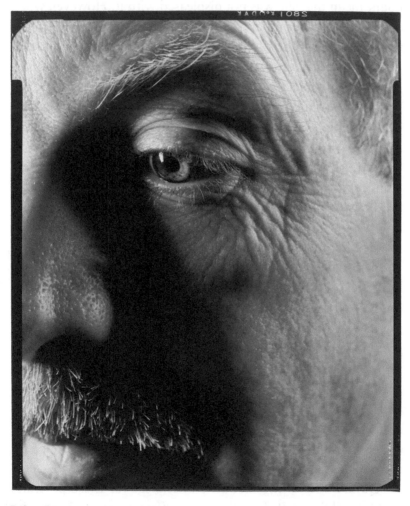

Robert Fones

Environmental photographer Edward Burtynsky has been working on a book about oil. I'm to write one of the book's essays. As part of the research we take off in Ed's Volvo for Detroit. It's winter and the season's gods throw everything they have at us as we sluice down Highway 401 toward Windsor. It snows, it sleets, it rains, it freezes. Eighteen-wheelers hurl slush balls as the car's wipers try to defend us. For once the Americans at the border find us of no interest and we are soon dodging craters on downtown Detroit streets. Bombed-out blocks crumble in the shadow of boarded-up towers. It's hard to believe that the once shining industrial capital of the planet has been so diminished. A day into the trip Ed has to replace the tires on his car — they've been shredded by all the broken glass and metal shards littering the roads. It's like one of the sad cities of Syria.

A couple of days later, accompanied by an armed guard, we pull up to the former Packard car plant on Detroit's East Side. Enormous — seven storeys high and covering 40 acres — it's darkly empty and spooky. However the dead hulk is not silent. Retching screeches and crashes leak through broken windows and smashed doors. These are the sounds of scavengers picking the bones of the century-old complex. After a few hours of exploration I get into conversation with a middle-aged Black couple as they emerge from the dark interior. Early every day they come to pull, pry and cut wires, rails and plumbing from the building's gut. By five their tired pickup is full and off to a scrap dealer. The haul will pay for the family's supper and breakfast. Then it's repeat. They've been reduced to *dalits* on a Mumbai dump.

Here is a rich country that doesn't care to share. The big auto companies have simply walked away from huge complexes when the facilities no longer meet their needs. Ford had abandoned the 1908 birthplace of the Model T on Piquette Avenue and later the Highland Park plant, home of the T's first true mass-market, moving assembly line. These hulks, and others, were left to crumble in the wan light of the industrial north. So too were the people who once worked in them. The factories, the neighbourhoods and the workers were all disposable.

West Germany

We entered a sprawling two-storey brick plant in Rüsselsheim by a back door. I dragged my camera bag up steel stairs to a catwalk high above the factory floor. The beginnings of an Opel sedan inched forward beneath my feet. I followed the line below me, taking pictures. Over thousands of feet I watched robots seize components, passing them to other robots that placed them, so that more robots could dart in and spot-weld the pieces. As the line crept forward hundreds of additional robots fetched, placed and fastened. This mechanical ballet assembled a slithering train of small sedans with neither a soul in sight nor a sound. Only at the line's end did a handful of small men appear to peer under hoods, adjust a hinge and test components before the autos slipped out of the plant like a train of shiny ants on a forest floor. Here was a future.

At the day's end I joined a group at head office for an executive summary of the operation. Its future? They planned to raze the plant and erect one more modern.

2015

Fifty years have passed since Viljo Revell's vision for a new Toronto City Hall opened for business. There is to be a celebratory event in the saucer-shaped council chamber. As I've known members of Revell's family for many years I get invited. The evening unfolds smoothly. The architects' tributes to

Revell are polished — successful architects are salesmen. Two former mayors, Crombie and Miller, introduce each other as David the First and David the Second. They are heartfelt and funny. The evening is a successful tribute to an architect and building that gave Toronto a new vision of itself.

I make a late departure from the event, exiting the building into the evening coolness of the huge square fronting City Hall. Walking south toward Queen Street I see a lone figure on a concrete bench by the pool. He's taking in the plaza, the new and former city halls, the glittering office towers and the whole urban grandness of it all. For the second time in recent months City Hall makes me regret not carrying a camera at all times. The first was seeing the life-sized bronze of Winston Churchill being hoisted by his stomach off his plinth on the western edge of the square. The second was this night's encounter with that lone little man hunched by the City Hall pond, at that moment, the world's most famous living architect — Frank Gehry.

TEN

FIRE

"Flagror non consumor."
I am burned but not consumed.

MOTTO OF THE HUGUENOTS,
16TH CENTURY

"Wretched excess is just barely enough."

MARIO BATALI

1963

My first summer logging on northern Vancouver Island is not proving easy. Some weeks into June the super feels pity and pulls me off an interior-bound crummy at dawn. A stumping fire beside the settlement is on the move. The camp is threatened.

I join an old skidder operator in gray woolen long johns and we toss canvas fire hoses into the bumper box of a former fuel tanker truck. It's been painted red with a brush and equipped with a diesel fire pump. We drive to the edge of town where a field of stumps smoulders. I drag heavy hose toward the tall stump I've been ordered to heroically climb. Balancing 10 feet above the ground, legs akimbo, big bronze valve handles in my hands I confidently nod to the driver a hundred yards away. He cranks the diesel. The canvas hose convulses toward me and I pull the handles. A writhing serpent lifts me off the stump and snaps me around like a flag in a gale. It beats me to the ground and writhes off across the field of shattered brush and splintered stumps. Smoke rises.

Where the river meets the inlet there's a cabin called Henry's. For reasons long forgotten this modest little camp had been built with the footprint of a house trailer — long and narrow. As his retirement loomed Henry decided to fix it up. He worked hard. He even gave up fishing. For an entire summer he went at his place giving it new siding, windows and a coat of paint. As I'd boat by I'd shout, "How's it going, Henry?"

"Super, just super, Mike!"

One fine September day that year while I ran upstream I saw a happy man. Henry lounged in a kitchen chair tilted back against his newly finished siding. The little building glowed in the late afternoon sunlight. And Henry glowed too. He had finished. We shared a wordless greeting.

After I'd passed him by I glanced backwards to the west. The declining sun balanced on an advancing black squall. Several miles upstream I chanced to look behind again and saw lightning. When I returned a week later Henry's perfect cabin wasn't there. Two scorched propane tanks stood above its grave.

For a few days two middle-aged couples in rental canoes have been moving about the inlet. I hear their voices but can't tell what language they speak beyond the sounds and cadences of central Europe. Each night they camp in a different spot, find it lacking in conveniences and move on. Finally they move out to the mouth of the inlet, the big water coast with its long rocky foreshore. They retreat slightly inland to be inside the

treeline that offers fuel and shelter from the relentless wester-
lies. They set up camp.

After they leave the following day I head out in my little motor-sailer to visit friends far to the south. I see smoke,
then flames, then a conflagration. One of my favourite ancient
white pines has become a crackling torch. The fire races
through the mid-summer dryness, moving east on the west
wind, devouring trees. I put in an emergency call but one
of my few neighbours, an army recruiter from Sudbury, has
beaten me to it. She, knowingly, has gotten straight through
to the firefighters.

We all own gas-powered fire pumps. Soon at least a half-
dozen of us are out at the site being amateur forest-fire fighters.
It helps contain the damage. Within 20 minutes a spotter plane
arrives from Sudbury. Minutes later a water bomber arrives,
flying just a few feet above the treetops like a glider. It banks
and descends, running out through the shoals skimming the
surface, taking up water. It climbs, banks and makes a run for
the fire but can't drop because we're all still there, shutting
down our pumps, retrieving hoses and trying to get out of the
way. The water bomber makes three futile passes while we're
scrambling. More trees go.

Finally we're across the inlet and the plane can do its work.
The pickup runs and the low banking and dumps over the
fire are impressive. These guys are very good at what they do.
When they finally depart we are left with a long scar and my
special tree is bone. I move back across the inlet and walk the
fire zone. The perpetrator lies at the western and upwind end
of the burn zone. The canoeists' breakfast fire is still cheerfully burning away. The eggs and toast long ago consumed,
the paddlers have moved on, oblivious to the devastation they
have left.

Some years later nothing has grown back. It's a dead zone,
an ash pit, a bone-yard.

1985

I've promised to help the boys at the old No. 7 fire hall at Dundas and Parliament with illustrations for the fireman's cookbook they hope to publish. At the time it was the busiest fire hall in North America. The kids in the projects across the street would watch the firemen cooking their suppers. As soon as it was on the fire hall dining table they'd pull several alarms and the crew would have to get up from the table while food steamed on their plates and go suit up before starting the trucks. If it was a false alarm, and it usually was, they'd be back at the table in half an hour. As soon as they sat down to their congealing diners the alarms would sound again and off they'd go. Supper could take four or five hours and a great deal of patience. Often when they were gone on the call the kids would cross the street and steal personal stuff from the open fire hall.

If there was a real fire it was often the mattress trick. The kids would stuff a mattress in one of the subsidized Regent Park high-rise elevators, set it on fire and press buttons for every floor. Those fires were somewhat harder to fight, being a moving target with quickly closing doors. The firefighters' suppers were then cold and solidified, soggy or stolen.

Those men were almost saintly. They not only cheerfully put up with this kind of shit but they also had to deal with incredible bureaucracy and insane inefficiencies. When the Toronto Fire Department began to hire women one of the first was assigned to No. 7.

This immediately raised a number of issues that the guys accepted with equanimity.

New recruits become backups for the experienced guys. A veteran would head into a burning building dragging a heavy hose along with a lot of other gear. If they fell through the floor or got overcome by smoke, their backup was supposed to haul them to safety. That's why these guys are big and work out. They're generally much fitter than cops.

Once women joined, the men knew their female backups would never be strong enough to carry a 250-pound man to safety. The men assessed the risk and accepted it. In the case of No. 7 they also had to deal with a washroom issue. It was deemed unacceptable in those days for women to share a washroom with men so the sole woman got the hall's only washroom all to herself while the men had to trudge down the street to the gas station a block away.

I spent weeks visiting different halls doing free food photography. As far as I know that cookbook never got published. This was probably a social good: it probably saved many from heart attacks. Take hamburger pie, a hall No. 7 special, for example. Try to imagine a coffee-table-sized piecrust containing a dozen pounds of cheap ground chuck. Imagine the amount of clogging tallow formed when it cooled as the guys fought phantom fires across the street. Vegetables were for rabbits.

Most of the firefighters I knew were hard-working but unambitious guys. However, one of them studiously hit the firemen's study books to move up the ladder. He got to be a fire hall chief, then a district one and finally got the plumb assignment as captain of Toronto's only fireboat, the *William Lyon Mackenzie*. This was a handsome, twin diesel-powered little ship built by Russell Brothers in Owen Sound up on Georgian Bay. Russell Brothers were famous for their alligator tugs built for the early days of the logging industry. Those tough little tugs would drag themselves overland through the woods from lake to lake.

My pal W became chief of the fireboat just as some joker photographed the *William Lyon Mackenzie* and listed it in the Boats For Sale section of *Auto Trader* magazine. The fireboat station phone rang off the hook for days as guys called in thinking what a neat thing it would be to have a fireboat for their kids to play with at their Muskoka cottage.

As a thank you for cookbook and firemen's fashion photography I got invited down for a cruise on the *Mackenzie* one summer Saturday night. I was told to get into the lift bucket as we headed toward Polson Quay on the east end of the harbour. We tied up to the seawall and the crew boomed me out over the courts to watch girls in bikinis play beach volleyball. Next we went into the quay beside the huge Redpath Sugar refinery. As baffled Filipino ship hands shoveled raw sugar into bucket scoops way down in the bilge of a huge bulker salty I suddenly appeared out of the sky hovering over the giant hatch openings with my cameras. The crew looked terrified. After that, as night fell, we steamed around Toronto Islands in the wake of various party boats that played screaming disco music. The entire fire crew, with the exception of the helmsman, were out on the foredeck dancing to *Saturday Night Fever*. The whole cruise got booked in as a training mission.

As firefighters work long shifts they get quite a few days off. Many of them started various businesses on the side. The cookbook and fire fashions were only a couple of them. For a while the guys I knew had a house-painting business. Then they moved up to roofing. As the captain said, "If ya got a hammer and a ladder then you're a roofer." They did my cabin up on the island for a few cases of beer. One screaming summer convection storm blew off the roofing from the third-floor dormer of my house on Dufferin Grove Park and water began running down the interior walls. In desperation I called my fire buddies. Less than hour later a huge hook and ladder truck came down my driveway with lights strobing and a couple of guys ran up the hydraulic ladder in the downpour with a roll of roofing.

The next time I called them about a roofing issue I was informed they didn't do that anymore. "Now we're driveway sealer guys." It was hard to keep up with their careers. We're told now the big thing in business is disruption — disruptive ideas, disruptive organizations, disruptive technologies, disruptive strategies. The last time I spoke with the captain he'd just been made a Toronto fire chief. "Wow," I said to my former roofer.

"Ya, I know," he said. "Really scary, isn't it!"

The forests of the river's upper reaches are burning — fire drives toward the clearing where we hide our cars. I want to save mine so I jump in my skiff and race through the wild rice and enter the river's mouth. By a couple of miles upstream I can smell it. Soon I can no longer see and coast to a stop against the north bank. Smoke seeps like a rancid fog through the trees lining the other side. It's become hard to breathe. I hear big trees fall. Animals are on the move. The birds are gone. A chopper circles behind a screen of trees. It's a combat zone. My little world burns.

ELEVEN

WANDERING

*"The hinterlands were filling with eccentrics, making
their odd journeys in the belief that certain voyages
out might become voyages in."*
ROBERT MACFARLANE

*"How was I to know that composers had to go up
into the mountains, or to the seashore, to commune
with the muses for six months?"*
DUKE ELLINGTON

1998

Paul, an old friend, calls me and says let's go to China. He's
an architect and wants to explore Beijing's hutongs, the traditional courtyard housing alleyways, before all are razed. One
of our Canadian airlines is trying to establish its new Toronto
to Beijing nonstop and is offering a cheap deal to point holders. I have just enough. After phoning around to my stock
agents and generating some interest in photos of China I agree
to go. We leave 10 days later. The route was too new to be
popular. We had the entire upper deck to ourselves and the
bored flight attendants treated us like grandees.

As this was before the Chinese capital was riven by six-
lane expressways we rent bicycles. After breakfast in our hotel
every morning we'd mount our wheels and ride off for eight or
10 hours. For days we explored Beijing, street by street, block
by block. The hutongs were once occupied by the elite. Each
family had many rooms arranged around a central courtyard.
Now entire extended families occupy each room and the mud

brick structures are rapidly dissolving. Conditions are grim. Every block of these houses has a common toilet where users must wade through six inches of piss and shit to get to the row of holes. The surplus spills over the sills into the streets. It stinks. Moreover everybody has bad skin because of the pollution. They all look sad and sick.

And they seem to treat each other very badly. They push, shove and shout at one another. It's not a civil society. I later ask a survivor of the Tiananmen Square massacre who was teaching in Tokyo why this is so. He explains that most city dwellers had recently come from small towns in the countryside. Those places were basically extended families — everybody in town was related and all public interactions were based on kinship. When they are dumped into a big anonymous city like Beijing they had no social tools to deal with each other. Your neighbour may as well have been a Martian.

On our exploratory rides we often come across particularly nice examples of traditional hutongs and agree to return and document them. More often than not, when we return, even a day or two later, the whole block will be a dusty pile of rubble with a bulldozer on top. The pace of destruction and disinterest in history is mind-boggling.

On some days we separate with an agreement to meet at the south end of Tiananmen at dusk. We have a discovered a little café that serves something resembling a cappuccino.

One day I meet a young local guy there named Dragon. He'd served in the merchant marine, sailing all over the world, even to Toronto. As a result he speaks some English. Paul has been pushing to visit the Great Wall but I've been resisting as the standard trip is to a heavily restored section with a garish amusement park. I'm not interested.

However, since Dragon's between jobs, he agrees to accompany us to a section of wall in inner Mongolia where tourists don't go. We'll pay expenses.

We meet early a few mornings later and board a bus. It proves to be the first of many that day. As we travel out the communities get smaller and the air gets cleaner. Finally, many hours later, we step off the last bus into a village. It's market day and the young country women selling vegetables are radiant. They have round Mongolian faces, clear skin and welcoming smiles. It's a complete contrast to Beijing. They're also very curious. Who are these two white guys and why are they here? Dragon explains. There's a lot of talk I can't follow but eventually Dragon announces that since market morning is winding down a half-dozen of these engaging women have decided to come with us. Our goal is a couple of miles away. A sawtooth range of small mountains lies to the north. The wall drapes along it like a ribbon. It's quite amazing.

We set off on foot with the women joking and flirting and Paul and I doing the same. I'm always amazed by the basic goodwill from one's fellow humans one experiences when travelling. These women are really fun.

After a stiff uphill hike we reach the wall and climb it. Following an hour of walking the Great Wall I look back. The sight of the sharp peaks with the wall snaking over it is memorable. It is at that point that I remember my New York agent saying that if I could get a photograph of a soldier in a Red Army uniform using the then new technology of cell phones on the Wall he could sell it many times. I carry several dummy display cell phones in my camera bag. Two of the market women wear the right uniforms. I ask Dragon to negotiate.

It's complicated. There are several new concepts to explain — the cell phone for a start, especially one that doesn't work. Then there's the idea of the stock photo and, finally, the concept of the model release, especially one in a language they don't know. The pictures must be legally released with payment to have any real value.

Dragon tries but negotiations are clearly not going well. This summit seems to be deteriorating into aggressive giggles on the part of the women and increasing discomfort for Dragon. Being a guy from the West I assume that money is the issue. I offer more. Dragon says no, that's not the issue. For many long minutes I try to tease the answer out of him but he won't say. He just looks embarrassed. Finally, just as I decide to drop the whole project Dragon takes Paul and me aside. They don't want money. Instead they want to see what white guys look like naked.

Paul turns to me and says, "Well, I'll never see these women again and besides I'm gay. So what do I care?" So he and this giggling passel of women troop off along the Great Wall of China to the nearest guardhouse. They disappear through its door. Now even though I'm travelling with a gay guy I'm definitely a conventional hetero. Paul has just taken our friendship to a whole new level.

Ten minutes later the gang returns. The women sign the releases and I make the photographs. Later Dragon explains that the women had heard that Asian guys had smaller penises than white or Black guys. They were truth seekers. Paul claimed that by exposing himself he had more than proven the affirmative. He claimed they were impressed.

This was not the end of the incident. Months later I got a call from the legal department of the big stock photo agency in New York. My rep was very pleased with the images but there's a problem with the releases. I'd left the line listing payment amount blank. Would I please explain the omission.

———

On a cool and damp early September day I run down the river with DH, a fellow photographer. We race to beat a rainsquall and reach the island with a few minutes grace. We run for the cabin — I build a fire as rain begins to tap the roof. As my guest begins to sort out his things I discover he has a secret life. He has packed as a mycologist — dissection equipment, collection bags and a stack of field guides. As soon as the rain stops I will take him to the big back island where I've occasionally seen fungi fruiting under the pines.

When the sun finally staggers out we wade across the narrow channel between islands, pick our way along the shore and enter the woods. It's a revelation. The vast, secret underground network of buried fungal filaments has been exposed by perfect conditions. Mushrooms of every shape and colour erupt through the bed of brown needles and leaves. DH sets to work collecting. He is later able to identify fewer than a third of the dampness's cool bounty. The forest keeps her mysteries.

They arrive every evening just before dusk, these old men pulling small carts from all corners into the vastness of Tiananmen Square. As the day declines into dusk they unpack and lay out their kites in anticipation of the day's end wind from the wastes of Mongolia. When the first breath of the steppes sweeps over the Forbidden City and into the great square the vanguard kites float upwards into a cloudless sky. At every day's dusk I bicycle here to watch the sky fill with paper bats and tissue birds. Next come fish and sea monster kites that swim into the blue so that the sky becomes a sea. Finally the huge dragon kites ascend and the vast sea/sky above the great square becomes the realm of myth and legend until the light falls and the wind fails and the square becomes as bleak as a parking lot.

1979

Magazine editor Charles Oberdorf and I are ambling up Collins Avenue in Miami Beach. We have just spent the morning with the Miami Tourism Department's official photographer. It's his job to photograph the bikini-clad girls who used to wave at you from the southern surf in your local newspaper every winter morning. The cut line under their pictures would tell you the air and water temperature at the beach. The theory behind this was that when you opened your paper in Milwaukee or Des Moines during February and saw the Florida weather you'd impulsively jump on a plane.

The guy who daily did these photographs of nearly naked women looked like a small town accountant. Because he had a phobia about his own legs he had a tailor in Miami make his trousers out of special non-staining, non-wrinkling quick-dry material so that he could wade into the surf with his subjects and not have to roll up his pants. By the time he's gotten back to his car after a session he'd look ready to do your tax return.

He took his job seriously, so seriously in fact that he'd written a whole book about how to take bikini pictures in the ocean. Every photo illustration in it had numerous arrows, diagrams and footnotes explaining the secrets of what he called boob and bum photography. He gave me a copy. He was serious. The book is unintentionally very funny.

As Charles and I slowly walk north along hotel row my jeans and cameras begin to dry out after my shoot of the shooter. Somewhere north of the Fontainebleau we approach a hotel entrance jammed with stretch limos and cabs. Dozens of people wait on the front steps. As we pass the entrance someone shouts, "At last he's here!! The photographer has arrived!" A dozen people rush over and sweep us into the hotel. The photographer: the photographer! Charles looks as puzzled as I am.

After we are escorted into the auditorium atrium off the lobby we discover we have just become the sole media presence at the Miss Teen America pageant. Heavily made-up middle-aged women begin aggressively thrusting their daughters before my cameras. These 15-year-old girls are like little porcelain dolls — absolutely flawless skin, silky hair, molten eyes. Their ambitious stage mothers have shoehorned them into incredibly provocative costumes trimmed with lace, feathers and fur. The little girls vamp like centerfolds for my cameras.

After 40 minutes of frantic photography a master of ceremonies announces the beginning of the competition. The mothers and daughters immediately vanish. We're suddenly alone. Charles looks at me and shrugs. "Let's go for a beer."

Somewhere in my basement are rolls and rolls of little Lolitas and Alices.

1992–93

"Dad, when you go to Kiev please bring back a bottle of the very best Russian vodka."

My assignment involved visiting various Kiev museums and monasteries to photograph Ukrainian treasures — mammoth-tusk dwellings, ecclesiastical jewels and Scythian gold in preparation for an exhibition proposed jointly for the Royal Ontario Museum and the Smithsonian in Washington. It would require a lot of lighting gear. Since the prehistoric tusk dwellings were in a cluttered and rundown museum setting I would be obliged to somehow disguise the backgrounds while working onsite — these were the last analogue days before Photoshop. I bought several large bolts of black cotton to hang in the rooms and wrap the very ugly columns surrounding the installations. A big box of Canadian hockey-stick tape was purchased to secure the fabric. I boarded a plane for Frankfurt accompanied by a stack of aluminum equipment cases.

Journalist friends had warned me that expensive cameras disappeared during customs inspections at the Kiev airport so I requested local government assurances that my equipment would have safe passage. No cameras, no pictures, no exhibition. The Russians had only recently departed and the new regime in Ukraine was anxious to reach out to the West. I was assured that my gear and I would have secure passage.

The Lufthansa flight from Frankfurt was uneventful until the landing at Kiev. As the jet taxied its passage was suddenly obstructed a half mile out from the derelict terminal by a small convoy of military vehicles. Several trucks closed off the runway and surrounded the aircraft. When the 737 stuttered to a stop a handful of soldiers pounded on the door and a pair of grim-looking officers boarded and began to read from an official document. "We are looking for Michael Mitchell." All eyes in the plane were on me when I responded. Escorted off the plane I was taken to the hold where all the baggage hatches had been opened by the military. While the irritated German flight crew stood by, soldiers clambered through the cargo hold in search of my equipment cases. When my extensive luggage was safely aboard an army truck our little convoy headed for the terminal leaving the crew fuming on the tarmac. This was going to be an interesting trip.

The military's tactic for dealing with customs was simple: they drove right by the terminal and onto the highway to Kiev. While this strategy effectively dealt with the logistics of entry it caused me no end of problems when I left Ukraine some weeks later. There was no import record of my gear and no entry stamp in my passport. I had a very complicated departure.

Kiev has a stunning setting high on a plateau above the Dnieper River. We crossed the river and drove up an escarpment into one of the strangest landscapes I have ever seen. The old city was entirely surrounded by dozens of unfinished skeletal high-rises that had been abandoned by the Soviets.

The winds of the steppes howled through the open floors and slowly rotated the rusting construction cranes swinging from the tops of each building. This devastation stretched for miles.

After dumping baggage in the small apartment I'd been assigned as my home and headquarters we went downtown to eat. We parked and cut through a huge butcher shop where dozens of cold cases were guarded by large ladies in white. A lineup of monochrome, exhausted customers gripping plastic bags shuffled across the tiled floor and out into the street. At the head of the line an old couple watched as a single slice was cut from a cylinder of gray meat the size of a drainpipe. This dead thing was the only stock in the entire place. All the other cold cases were empty.

These were difficult times in Ukraine. When colonial powers withdraw they invariably take all portable valuables with them. The newly reborn country was still trying to figure out how to govern itself, accommodate so many different factions and keep everything rolling along without money. A new paper currency had been designed and printed by nice people in Canada who had refused to release the bills until somebody paid for them. Consequently much of the county's daily business was being conducted using little paper tickets like those you'd get at a bingo hall. While, on the one hand, there wasn't much to buy and luxury goods were extravagantly expensive, on the other you could bus all over town on a half ticket that was worth about half a cent. There was a town outside Kiev that had made car tires. In the absence of a circulating currency the local women and children would squat by the roadside with piles of these tires arranged in pyramids like apples and oranges in the hopes of exchanging them for food. They were of execrable quality, crumbling under the touch and blackening the hand. Nobody wanted them.

I began working the next day at the Lavra, a fairytale monastic complex of shimmering white buildings and gold domes high above the river. A network of caves beneath it housed the desiccated ecclesiastical dead of centuries. The many display cases in the Lavra museum protected an amazing inventory of Scythian artifacts hammered out from sheets of soft gold. But the keepers of this treasure seemed astonishingly casual about it all. They'd unlock the cases and then disappear leaving me to choose my 2,500-year-old subjects and arrange them as I pleased. Photographing metal objects can be quite tricky — I recall sweating over the Stanley Cup at the old Hockey Hall of Fame for many hours to get a transparency that didn't reveal too much of the contrivance required to control all merciless reflections in so many curved and polished surfaces. Gold is more gracious — it just sits there and glows.

Every day as I arrived at the Lavra I'd notice a long 18th century building across the street. It looked like another monastic building but wasn't as well maintained. Considerable quantities of smoke and steam issued from stacks in its roofs. Whenever I inquired about its purpose I was told *sotto voce* that it was part of "the military-industrial complex." End of conversation. Finally, toward the end of my stay I found someone who could get me in. It proved to be the home of the industry that made the fake Hasselblad known as the Kiev. Rows of gnomes sat at worn wooden benches fitting tiny screws into tiny holes. It was astonishingly archaic.

I reserved the tusk dwelling for the end of the trip. I wrapped much of the small museum rotunda in black cloth before installing strobes inside the dwelling to give it some drama — it was basically an igloo-shaped pile of bones. With assistants I wrapped the bastard Ionic columns surrounding the installation and was finally ready to begin photography. It was a very long hard day. When I returned the next morning to pack my lighting gear and remove the black wrap from the building I was greeted by a crowd. Word had gotten out that I was finished and perhaps a dozen young women in heels, tight sweaters and very short miniskirts had shown up to charm me out of the bolts of cloth and the unused rolls of hockey tape. Things were that bad. They got what they wanted.

And I only wanted one thing more — vodka for my son Jake. As the job was winding down my hosts offered to take me out to dinner. Until that point I had been making simple suppers at home from whatever I was able to buy from one of the foreign exchange stores. Not far from the downtown empty butcher shop was a large complex designed with exotic Moorish detailing by a French architect in the late 19th century. Its various wings connected with arched passageways. We went down one of them and slipped through a small door into another world.

Outside all was cold, gray and destitute. Within, an elaborate crimson and gold dining room glowed under crystal chandeliers. Beautiful gowned women moved between the tables serving drinks and foods I hadn't imagined were available in Ukraine. At supper I was promised that I'd soon be taken to a place where I could buy the country's very best vodka.

We went down one more arched passageway and slipped through another modest and unmarked door where one was greeted by a floor-to-ceiling mosaic of TV monitors showing lifestyle clips and sports highlights. A long gallery to each side was staffed by men and women in evening dress standing behind counters under beveled glass. French wines and single malts slept on satin cushions within the cases. I was the only customer.

My request was translated and an unctuous young man in a tux slipped into a back room. I would be brought something too precious to be on public display. Several minutes later he returned with an elegant embossed box which he ceremoniously opened and withdrew the vodka bottle — Seagram's.

Back in Toronto a few days later I found myself in the premises of a rare book dealer setting up a session with a couple of graphic designer friends. We'd selected a wall of shelving and were carefully rearranging rows of beautiful leather-bound books so as to create a void on the shelving with a familiar shape. The void was echoed by the stack of removed books in the foreground. I carefully spot-lit the whole arrangement and photographed it with a view camera leaving enough space at the bottom of the image for the cut line that would be super-imposed later — "Absolut Knowledge."

A friend subsequently told me that he'd found a site on the internet that sold original magazine tear sheets of all the Absolut Vodka ads ever run around the world. The rarest and most expensive one? Ours. It ran only once in *Saturday Night* magazine.

2012

I've caught it again — boat fever. Every six months or so I fall in love with a vessel that's just a little larger, or faster, or handsomer than mine. I convince myself that if I acquired this latest love, a 16,000-pound motor-sailor, then my life would be transformed and elevated to another plane. I would no lon-ger have tooth decay, flat feet or thinning hair. So I drove to Buffalo, caught a plane to Minneapolis and hitched a ride with a yacht broker to the banks of the St. Croix River where I was going to rescue this sweet virgin called the *Yankee Lady*. Of course when I got there and met the boat she was a smelly old whore badly in need of rehab.

Her owner was more than a dozen years my junior but he was an American shipwreck. He could barely stand because he'd once fallen down a 70-foot mast and altered his spine; he could barely walk as he'd destroyed both knees in a motocross accident. He'd celebrated his mid-20s by having a couple of heart attacks and now he was overweight with hypertension and eczema. After we'd viewed this expiring vessel we drove to my overnight accommodations, the Thunderbird Motel, on the outer parking fringes of the Mall of America, the world's largest shopping centre. I crashed out at eight.

At four a.m. I was out the door to catch an airport shuttle bus. My plane circled Washington's Ronald Reagan Airport for 90 minutes before landing in the rain. My flight to Buffalo was rescheduled four times so I wandered through the food courts and airport shops. Finally I was on my way again and landed in Buffalo in under an hour. I eventually found my car buried in P8 of long-term parking and drove to the Peace Bridge.

At the border Canada Customs asked me what I have to declare.

"I have three Mitt Romney action figures at $6.99 each — U.S."

"And what action does Mitt Romney do?" the officer asked.

"You wind him up and he waddles across the floor shitting red, white and blue candies."

"Really? Out of his asshole?

"Yes, officer."

"Sir, I'm going to have to pull you over and inspect your imports. I gotta see this."

1990

This year on my annual grind across Canada I've made it as far as Prince Albert, a small raw city of prisons and a pulp mill that always feels like the beginning of the north. The huge, viscous North Saskatchewan River slithers through it in a gorge that separates two worlds, aspen parkland on the south bank and the boreal forest of jack pines on the north. After a long morning trudging through my shot list I cut through the city's very utilitarian shopping mall on my way to lunch. When I reach the appliance department of Eaton's a crowd stops me dead. Dozens of people stand mutely with their plastic shopping bags in front of a display wall of televisions. They are watching Clyde Wells speak in the Newfoundland legislature. Will the centre of this country hold? Will Meech Lake dismantle Canada? This crowd of ordinary Canadians is absolutely still and utterly silent.

While searching for toothpaste in the Rankin Inlet co-op store on the west coast of Hudson Bay I overhear a couple of Inuks in the next aisle exchanging local gossip. Although they constantly switch from English to Inuktitut to English I catch a reference to a drum dance scheduled for that evening. As this was the 1970s drum dancing, once banned by the churches, had not yet undergone the revival now current in Nunavut. It had been some years since a real dance had been documented so I was immediately alert for any hints of time and place. None. A couple of hours later when I mentioned this encounter to the southern administrators in the hamlet office I was assured that such dances never happened anymore. They advised sticking to my assignment list.

It was late February and terrifyingly cold. The days' highs were in the low minus 30s and the drops at night precipitous. If there was a dance where could it be? The only building large enough for a crowd was the wooden community hall near the centre of town. At six o'clock I hustled over to the dark building and let myself in.

I found a corner spot in the big empty hall, laid out my gear on a wooden bench and began loading film magazines and wiring my strobe. An hour passed in the cold empty hall. Then the doors opened and several Inuks looked in. They spied me and retreated. A half hour later a couple more peeked in and left. Fifteen minutes later it happened again and then once more. Just before nine a half-dozen faces looked in, stared at me for a very long minute before disappearing. I was clearly an undesirable but I stayed. Another hour passed.

A little after 10 the doors burst open and every Inuk in the settlement crowded in. Not one carried a drum. A couple of minutes later two more Inuks arrived carrying a 16mm movie projector. They set it up on a chair, threaded the film, turned out the lights and began screening an incredibly bad action film. This plot-free feature was basically just a series of California car chases, shootings, catastrophic fires and explosions. Each time something blew up the whole room would convulse with laughter — people would fall out of their chairs and roll around on the floor. Ninety minutes later when all California buildings had burned down, every car crashed, each yacht sunk and all citizens shot, the lights suddenly came on and the room emptied. Once again I was alone in a cold gray hall.

A half hour later the doors opened, several Inuit peered in and retreated. In ten minutes a few more looked in briefly. Fifteen minutes later, the same.

Sometime after midnight the doors flew back and the entire community poured back into the room. With every *kabloona* save me safely in bed the drum and beater appeared. A half-dozen elders arranged themselves in a row against the middle of one wall. The rest of the crowd formed a higgledy-piggledy circle of parents, grandparents, teens and kids. Gradually the room fell silent and a dancer entered the circle carrying the drum. The elders began chanting as the dancer wove and bobbed around the circle playing the drum. Some minutes later chanters and dancer finished and the drum was placed before the next performer. After four or five dancers the drum was set down before an old lady. As she danced slowly around the big circle several times, I finally got up my nerve and took a photograph by bouncing strobe light off the ceiling. When the flash died I realized that the drum was lying at my feet. This proved to be even more hilarious than the biggest explosions.

It was payback time. I picked up the drum and the chanting began. It looked easy but it wasn't. Those drums are basically a one-metre-diameter wooden hoop with a very short handle attached to the rim. They are totally unbalanced and very hard to control. After several painfully inept circuits of the room I began to get competent. As soon as this was apparent to the elders they doubled the speed of the chant. More hilarity. I wrestled the big drum into submission and caught up with the rhythm. They doubled it again. Now the whole room was giggling. I managed a couple more accelerating cycles before quitting, exhausted. The room fell silent. I rapidly scanned the crowd for a clue. Finally I put the drum down in front of the prettiest girl in the room. She jumped to her feet and ran crying out of the building. The travelling assignment photographer is very much in the world but always so alone.

———

The inlet is mirror still. Every rock and tree are perfectly doubled, the ochre-rose sky is both up and down. No clouds, no waves, not a sound. I kayak out into this perfection trailing a small vee punctuated by paddle dip rings. Mid inlet I rest the paddle shaft across the cockpit combing and still. The boat glides to a stop and then slowly begins to drift broadside to the west. There is still a faint river-driven current here. Soon a small riffle flirts in from the big water and weathercocks my boat toward the setting sun. A southwestern puff gently compasses the boat around toward the just visible polestar. It's a small moment of perfection in a broken world.

1970

Mexico was another way of being. My part of Mexico, my time in Mexico — Oaxaca and Chiapas, the late 1960s — was a life lived on another plane in a kind of timeless state where the deep past was always present and the present was an intense, vibrating and shimmering stasis that made any idea of a future impossible and irrelevant. I eventually stopped wearing a watch because there was no advance of time to record. I lived in an eternal present of a crashing sun, coruscating landscapes and tree-feathered mountaintops framing seemingly mystical horizons.

Our work and residence permits required renewal every six months. We'd drive our little convoy of Jeeps northward up the high central plateau until we reached the Texas border where we'd cross at Nuevo Laredo or Brownsville into the U.S. to renew our supplies, eat American and then reenter the next day and bribe our way into new permits. Sometimes I'd be forced to get a haircut and a shave by the border guards but usually a little bribe, *la mordida*, would swing any door.

On one of these trips we pulled into a bleak gas station and hotel somewhere south of Monterrey. Its dismal restaurant had a small newsstand where a few books cohabited with lurid magazines and week-old newspapers. A thick novel caught my eye. I picked it up, read the first page and instantly entered the world that I was returning to. *Cien años de soledad* seduced me in a way that no novel ever had before or since. However, reading it in Spanish was hard work.

I'd never studied Spanish. Much of my first year in Mexico was devoted to unlearning French as I kept confusing the two Romance languages. I gradually acquired working Spanish by talking to local farmers — *campesinos* — that we'd hire to work on our archaeological excavations. These men were either Zapotecs or Mixtecs who spoke Spanish as a second language. We shared a basic vocabulary and functioned in a world of four tenses — simple past, future, conditional and, of course, present. I could certainly do my business fluently in the backcountry but whenever we went to Instituto meetings in Mexico City I could sense the non-Indigenous, educated *Ladino* Mexicans holding their noses when I spoke. I'm sure I sounded like Don Harron's guy from Parry Sound, Charlie Farquharson.

So when I returned to Canada in 1970 and learned that Harper & Row had just published an English translation of *Cien años* by Gregory Rabassa I immediately sought out a copy. As I was then a broke film and photography student I went to the main branch of the Toronto Public Library. They didn't have García Márquez's book and had never heard of it. I somehow persuaded a procurement librarian to order a copy for the system. I heard nothing for many, many weeks. Finally a call came: the book had arrived and was waiting for me at the New City Hall branch. I rode down on my bicycle and handed in the paper I'd been given months previously. The woman on the desk disappeared. I waited. Five minutes, 10 minutes, 15. Finally four desiccated women came out and stood staring at me. I began to shift awkwardly from foot to foot. Eventually one of them spoke. "So you're the person who's going to try and read this book."

2000

We've been wandering through Seattle's Pike Street Market for a couple of hours, picking up a few groceries and listening to the fishmongers out-shouting one another. I'm with two good-looking British-Jamaicans, the Murray sisters, Sheila and Claire, and they're hungry. We head for a workingman's diner on one side of the market. It has basic booths down one side and a long counter on the other. The only free seats are midway down the counter. I sit between the sisters and grab the menu. It's huge. There are almost 300 numbered lunches listed on its greasy pages. After reading a half-dozen sheets of uninspiring choices somewhere way down in the high 200s I spy something called "The Boss's Lunch." When the counterman passes by I collar him and ask what it is. He stops, peers down at the menu and studies the item.

"I've worked here for 20 years and no one has ever asked me that. I have no idea."

He hails a fellow server, a 30-year veteran. He doesn't know either.

Our neighbours at the counter begin to take an interest.

"I'll speak to the cook."

The line cook doesn't know but the head cook has ducked out for a smoke and he'll be back shortly.

The head cook returns. He doesn't know.

Now there are four staff members staring at the offending item on the menu. All conversation in the restaurant has slowed down. A local matter is becoming of regional interest.

I'm told that the owner of the diner has driven up to Oregon for a couple of days. A decision is made to try to track him down. In the meantime I'm offered a glass of water.

The hubbub gradually returns. After some minutes I ask if I can exchange my glass of water for a beer.

It arrives with the message that they think they've found out what town the owner is visiting out of state. They hope to find a phone number.

Meanwhile Claire and Sheila are enjoying a nice lunch. I have nothing to eat but I can't back down now. The staff and I are committed. I order a second beer.

Forty minutes later the waiter informs me that they've reached the boss and my dish is being prepared and will arrive shortly. The room once again goes quiet.

Then the counter man, the line cook and the head cook emerge through the swinging doors of the kitchen. The cook passes my plate to the waiter who marches down the aisle behind the counter and puts it in front of me. The plate is white, the two slices of naked Wonder Bread are white. Between them lie two pickles. No butter or mayonnaise, just two acrid green, intact gherkins sleeping between two sheets of sterile soda bread. This is The Boss's Lunch.

2014

Sheila and I are on a flight from London to Istanbul. Behind us sits a family, Turkish father, English mom, with their bright-eyed four-year-old boy. It must be his first flight — he can't stop talking. Looking at Sheila's head of tightly curly Jamaican hair he asks her why it's white.

"'Cause I'm old," she says.

We're on this trip as part of her three-continent, three-month long, 60th birthday party.

"But you can still walk!" the boy declares. "Where are your sticks? You're not old."

His parents laugh with obvious pleasure. They're enjoying parenthood.

Sheila beams.

The plane begins its descent. It lands with a bump and lurch at Istanbul's Atatürk airport. The boy looks out the window. "Look mummy, we're finally back to the airport again."

He's right: it's our one universal architecture.

2014

I was lugging my camera bag past Istanbul's Topkapi Palace when I announced my newest career change. I had just decided to become a Grand Vizier.

"What?" Sheila scoffed.

It seemed a reasonable move to me. I didn't have some loud American ambition to be a Sultan with a harem, eunuchs, a three-courtyard palace and pleasure garden. I just wanted to be the éminence grise in second place — sort of Canadian, I thought.

278

Her face was hostile. "Remember your last ambition at which you failed utterly?"

I'd forgotten.

"You wanted to be a bra-fitter but you never got farther than occasionally groping me and you certainly never got the clientele with real power and influence. Were you ever on Hillary Clinton's speed-dial, or Oprah's, or Sarah Palin's? Eh? Eh?"

Sheila and I are struggling through crowds in the Blue Mosque. We keep losing each other. Turning to find her I accidentally bump into a woman in the full black niqab. This dress is always very freighted for Westerners. Bad guys cover their faces — robbers, executioners, evil-doers. Outlaw bikers and riot cops wear black. And Nazis — storm troopers.

I'm suddenly looking into two dark, liquid eyes. She speaks softly.

"Look at my husband over there!"

An arm emerges from her dark presence and points to a guy in bleached jeans and a glitter T-shirt.

"He tells me I'm beautiful but all he does every day is make selfies, only himself in these famous places!"

She giggles and I'm suddenly confronted with an individual, a funny woman, rather than the ultimate other. As we laugh together her husband comes over. When I tell him I'm a photographer he shows me the pictures on his phone — Istanbul's famous cisterns, the Grand Bazaar, the Galata Tower, Hagia Sophia and more mosques. She's right. He's in them all — alone.

———

After a late spring and a cool summer it's suddenly September. Flower stalks turn brittle, the grasses have browned and died: the winter march to monochrome

279

has begun. While sitting on the steps cupping a morning coffee mug I suddenly sense a flash of fire. It
flutters through the stiff brush of summer's death —
the last monarch butterfly.

1998

Some Toronto Februarys give one a break. This year the last
week of the month has been exceptionally warm. Eavestroughs
drip, bare branches glisten and mud patches have appeared in
the garden. I suddenly get sea restless and phone my friend Epp
to convince him to come kayaking with me in Lake Ontario.
He shocks me by agreeing.

We set off early on the last Sunday of the month with two
small boats on the roof of my van. The sky is blue, the sun
shines, the thermometer flirts with the plus zone. The plan is
to paddle along beneath the Scarborough bluffs toward the
Pickering nuclear power plant.

The Scarborough bluffs are a shoreline remnant of the
ancient glacial Lake Iroquois that formed after the last ice age.
Where they now form part of the shoreline of present Lake
Ontario they tower as much as 300 feet above the waters and
run from the eastern end of downtown Toronto for almost
10 miles. They may look like the White Cliffs of Dover but
instead of being chalky rock they are composed of extremely
unstable alluvial deposits of silt, sand and clay. It's a dynamic
landform that is totally dependent on lake water erosion of
its base to remain vertical. Without wave action gnawing the
bottom, it would gradually become just a long muddy slope.

I have an intimate familiarity with the dramatics of the
Bluffs. In the mid-1970s I moved into a small, winterized
cottage on Meadowcliffe Drive in Scarborough. This street
of perhaps a dozen houses located on a benchland halfway
down the Bluffs was the pioneering creation of painter Doris

McCarthy who built her house and studio, Fool's Paradise, there after buying land in 1939.

I knew Doris well because my aunt, painter Barbara Greene, taught with Doris at Central Technical's art school for many years. Barbara and Doris went on several Canadian Arctic painting trips together. My aunt and Doris were probably in one of those relationships that women of their generation did not talk about. Rather than openly sharing a house with Doris my aunt rented a cottage down the street for a number of years. There were plenty of bushes in between. This was the place I took over in the mid-'70s when Barbara, after some sort of falling out with Doris, decided to build a house of her own outside of Perth.

When I moved onto Meadowcliffe the cottage was about 60 feet from the precipitous 200-foot-drop down to the lake. During early spring thaws I'd lie in bed listening to large chunks of the property disappear over the cliff. One evening when I was standing by the living room picture window a whole row of trees at the edge of the lawn suddenly vanished into Lake Ontario's great black hole. On summer nights my next door neighbour would rev up junker cars on his back lawn and let them drive themselves over the brink. These victims of his breakwater building attempts would disappear under the sand and silt in a few days. A few years after actor Billy Van took back the property the little house ended up cantilevered over the cliff edge. This was truly a dynamic landscape.

So my friend Epp and I launched our boats at Bluffer's Park and began to paddle eastward. This may seem like a dumb thing to do in February but I was prepared. Some of my paddling friends call me Belt-and-Suspenders Mitchell because, while I'll do almost anything, like a true photographer, I always have backup. In this instance I had one of the first small cell phones in a waterproof bag along with one of the very earliest portable track-plotting GPS units. I was a high tech Inuk.

The paddle eastward was uneventful but beautiful. The lake slowly undulated beneath the boats, the cliffs towered authoritatively above us and the sun warmed us despite the freezing waters. Somewhere around Port Union we turned around and headed back in order to reach our put-in while the light was still good. We were about 500 feet offshore when Epp spotted a trio of guys horsing around on trail bikes a couple of hundred feet above us. Suddenly one of them disappeared over the cliff edge into a gully. His buddies took off.

When we got no response to our shouts we paddled to the narrow beach at the gully exit and beached our boats. It was a hard climb up the muddy slope to the hanging gully bottom about 75 feet above the beach — we were still wearing our heavy cockpit skirts and lifejackets. We waded upstream in the gully creek until we found the biker lying on his back on a pile of rocks midstream. He was conscious but in obvious pain.

At this point two voices began arguing in my brain. One said this guy is getting hypothermic lying in this icy melt water. Move him! The other voice said never move someone with a spinal injury. He had fallen at least 50 feet.

So Mr. Belt-and-Suspenders booted up his GPS and got out his cell phone for a 911 call. When I reached dispatch and explained the situation the operator asked me at what intersection we were. Now, if you've paddling for miles along a cliff hundreds of feet high you have no idea what's above you. You can't see anything but rim of the bluff and the sky. I gave them our location, latitude and longitude, in degrees, minutes and seconds. The GPS was probably accurate to within 50 feet.

"What's that? What are those stupid numbers?" The emergency operators and dispatchers didn't have a clue what they meant. So here we were, basically in the midst of a city of several millions, but we may as well have been on Baffin Island. As usual, the government was behind the curve. So a lot of precious time was wasted while I instructed them to find someone with a topo map so our "intersection" could be located. Unsurprisingly, it was my buddies at the fire department who figured it out first. They went to Doris McCarthy's property and attempted to climb down the steep gully slope beside it. The combination of the thaw and the clay meant that the slope may as well have been greased. They had to go back and fetch some ropes. Eventually they were able to lower a guy with a backboard down the slope. By the time he got to us our biker in the creek was turning blue.

With time a police boat appeared offshore but couldn't get in because of the beach shallows. Then a chopper arrived and managed to land in the gully bottom. By now enough firemen had descended on the ropes to get our guy onto the backboard and into the helicopter. It took off for the trauma centre at Sunnybrook Hospital.

All this activity had generated a lot of radio chatter. The press and television news people picked up on a good story and soon figured out that we were in the Bellamy Ravine, accessible from Kingston Road. Soon there were cops and cameras everywhere.

One of the officers told the score of media people that I had photographed the whole drama with my underwater Nikon. They closed in on me. Everyone wanted the pictures. Now here's where Mr. Belt-and-Suspenders turned out to be just another dumb guy.

When I looked at the circle of pleading media people all I saw was the blonde from the *Toronto Sun* newspaper. She was bursting out of her strategically unzipped parka. I fell for it. After explaining that I was a professional photographer and had other personal pictures on the same roll of film, I said I wanted some money, a photo credit and the film returned after processing and printing. She charmingly agreed. I surrendered the film.

The subsequent extensive media coverage of the rescue was quite interesting. All the papers did stories about it. They emphasized how strange and lucky it had been that a couple of crazy guys had been kayaking by in February. The television coverage was quite different. They all focused on the technology, the fact that I'd had a GPS unit and a cell phone. What's more the cell phone had continued to work down in the gully while the VHF and fancy 900 megahertz radios carried by the firemen, EMS and the law did not. The steep ravine walls blocked their signals. The whole rescue was coordinated from my phone. I ended up with a huge bill.

For me this rescue was not over for many months. First there was the issue of the *Toronto Sun*. They made hay with my pictures, splashing one across the whole front page and then more on a double-page spread inside. I then asked for my film back. I asked to be paid. Nobody returned my calls for days. When they finally did they couldn't find the film. Finally, weeks later, they announced they'd found the film and would compensate me handsomely. A package duly arrived with my roll and the compensation — five more rolls of film — short ones.

So the camera business was a bust but the cell phone proved more generous. Bell called me and said they had a special program called the Cellular Samaritan. I had been chosen as one of the finalists for a prize. To receive it all I had to do was turn up with Epp at a lunch for the finalists at Toronto's Metro Hall. Premier Mike Harris would present something to all the finalists. I said I would go as long as I didn't have to shake his hand. That would have been like hugging Stephen Harper or Donald Trump. No deal. They phoned me back and said all was clear, his buddy Ernie Eves would come instead. Clearly I was not a great negotiator.

We did go to the lunch. I met the other Samaritans: they'd done amazing things like save people from burning buildings, car crashes, robberies. However, I won the grand prize. It included a year of free cell phone service, a handsome leather travel bag which my wife promptly confiscated and later, when I got it back, Sheila subsequently did too. I was left with a diamond-shaped Plexiglas trophy that for years I used to scrape ice off my van windscreen, as well as framed and signed certificate from Premier Mike Harris saying that Ontario was a better place to live because of heroes like me. For years I kept it beside the toilet in my studio. People would come out of the bathroom asking if that funny framed document was actually real.

A year later a TV network calls me. They want to do a retrospective piece on the rescue. I reluctantly agreed to meet them at the end of Meadowcliffe Drive where Doris McCarthy's house and studio, Fool's Paradise, is situated. Gate's Gully, scene of the event a year earlier, is behind her place. I knock on Doris's door to ask permission to trespass. She opens it, cries out and give me a big hug. Tears ran down her cheeks. It was the last time I saw her. She died in November 2010, several months into her 101st year.

TWELVE

JUST DESSERTS

*"You might as well fall flat on your face as lean over
too far backwards."*

JAMES THURBER

*"Outside of a dog, a book is a man's best friend.
Inside of a dog it's too dark to read."*

GROUCHO MARX

2005

I had decided to read two sections about my father. A month earlier I had published *The Molly Fire*, a memoir occasioned by the death of my parents. Until the last months of their lives I had seen little of them for years. I lived in the east while they had retreated to Vancouver Island and the city of my father's birth. After my father's stroke I began to visit often, flying across the country every couple of weeks and spending days with my mother sitting by my father's hospital bed, talking. He couldn't participate. He was practically a vegetable.

Then suddenly he was gone and my mother only few short months after. The inherited scrapbooks, paintings and boxes of documents that traced their families' lives back to the early 18th century and beyond had suddenly made making sense of it all quite urgent. I'd written the book in a white heat over many months. It got published: it wasn't ignored. Many good books are but I had been fortunate. The *Globe and Mail*'s full-page review led off the weekend book section. It was a finalist for various prizes including the Governor General's. I started to get wonderful letters. I still get some.

So now I was on a plane to the west for my first book tour. The publisher had managed to kite up a ticket from his many stressed credit cards — people don't understand how marginal much of the book business is. I left on a discount ticket following days of rushing about trying to put all my jobs to bed so that I could go. I boarded the flight semi exhausted and endured the takeoffs and landings that slowly moved me farther west. After a stopover in Kelowna I had just one more before reaching Victoria where I stumbled off the plane at suppertime. My loopy friend Michelle picked me up in her latest jalopy to rush me across town to the first reading.

Bolen's is one of the county's largest independent bookstores. It's in a shopping mall. Because this is Victoria and it was a few minutes after six when I arrived the whole mall was shut down for the night. Bolen's, however, was still open. I went in, found the manager and introduced myself. He in turn took me to the back of the store to meet the B.C. novelist Audrey Thomas who would also read. Thomas, much more experienced at this than me, seemed nervous. She asked me to go first and I agreed.

Four or five-dozen chairs have been set up in one of the mall's empty hallways. There's a small stage and a mic. I read a section in which my parents sell everything they have in the east, buy a pickup and trailer and take off on a long looping trip across North America on their way to Victoria where they've bought a small apartment building.

The section culminates with my father being harassed and humiliated by a band of punks in a campground. He's forced to confront his aging, his loss of control and authority. He never recovered from it.

The little full house for this reading in a hallway is elderly but totally attentive and awake. I can really feel that they are with me so I segue into another section in which the *Empress of Canada* grounds while creeping through fog into Victoria

Harbour during the fall of 1929. My 11-year-old father goes with his, an engineer, to see the huge ship driven high up on the shore. It may well have been the moment when he decided he would go to sea.

The audience is even more attentive on this one. I've slipped some quite subtle asides into the text and there's somebody in the back row who's getting them all. I can't see her but I can hear her laugh and see a flash of pink pantsuit. I decide to quit while I'm ahead and turn the stage over to Audrey. I sit on the sidelines while she reads and then get up to go. Michelle and her older friend really want to get home.

However Bolen's asks me to stay. Two small tables are set up at the back, each with a pile of books. Audrey is well known and local. Immediately a score of people lines up to buy her book and get it signed. To my surprise a handful of people line up for me. They are all retired ladies. Each one has family papers and pictures. Each one wants to talk about writing memoir.

As I work through this lineup I'm conscious of the woman at the very end of my line. She bobs from side to side with a grin on her face. It's the pink pantsuit from the back row. Her face is familiar, probably an old friend of my mother's, but I can't place her as I'm really too tired to think. Finally she's in front of me. She too is writing a memoir and wants to talk about the process. Yet another one, I think. Everyone wants to tell their story. And they all indeed have one but at this late hour I can barely respond. I say a few things about how I'd written the book and then excuse myself as I can see that my friends are weary and restless. As we follow the lady in pink and Audrey out the door Pinky turns to me and says I should read *her* book. Her tone when she gave me its title betrays some irritation. I say I will and then promptly forget about it. We go home to bed and I fall into a deep sleep.

At three in the morning I'm shocked awake with a vision of a pink pantsuit and the book she'd told me to read. I had done just that only a week before. "Oh shit!" I gasped. I had ended my very first reading by telling Alice Munro how to write a book.

Over the next couple of days I manage to rationalize it all away. It hadn't been Alice, just some other vaguely familiar face. I screw up my courage and do a half-dozen more readings around B.C. It's a terribly grim business. The last one in a Vancouver Indigo is attended by five people. They were buying greeting cards and cookbooks. They are tired people taking advantage of a free seat. I fly home.

Back in Toronto I wryly tell my publisher and editor about my Alice Munro fantasy and confusion. They laugh and we all go on with life. Some days later I go to a literary launch in the wonderful Victorian mansion kitty-corner from the Art Gallery of Ontario where the Italians have their consulate. The first person I stumble into past the door is the manager of Bolen Books who's in town for the week. He greets me enthusiastically. "Michael, wasn't that totally great at your reading? That's the only time Alice Munro has ever attended one of ours. It was so exciting — she'd read your book and bought another copy."

Patrick Watson, former co-host of *This Hour Has Seven Days* and future chair of the CBC, and I are sharing a stage at the Ontario Science Centre. However, we're not sharing much else. I've just shown several hundred high school media literacy teachers a series of paired photographs recording famous historical events. I'd ended with Joe Rosenthal's iconic Second World War image of the victorious flag-raising on Iwo Jima. Then I'd shown what the actual event looked like — scrubby, messy, confusing. I'd explained that since Rosenthal's original image of the actual moment was so devoid of heroic drama he'd some hours later recruited some all-American soldiers, sourced a crisp new stars and stripes and restaged the event on a dramatic small rise — the perfect plinth for a war memorial, as indeed it later became. Many audience members seemed stunned to see the contrast between fact and fable, reality and myth. While I too could enjoy the theatricality of Rosenthal's famous image I strongly disliked its message — the glorification of war and American military might. What it sanitized and mythologized was ugly. But to Watson it made better TV. We argued.

In 1962 the John Ford movie *The Man Who Shot Liberty Valance* was released. In it the Jimmy Stewart character makes a late-in-life confession to a reporter that, although it made him famous and a senator, he was not actually the man who shot Valance. It was the John Wayne character hiding in the shadows. The reporter had taken careful notes but when the confession was complete he theatrically tore them up.

"You're not going to use the story?" Stewart asks the reporter incredulously.

"No, sir. This is the West, sir. And when the legend becomes fact, print the legend."

1979

An assignment for *Art* magazine has sent me down to 299 Queen West to make a portrait of Michael Snow. Once the Ryerson Press building and now the studios of CityTV, it had become a somewhat dilapidated mixed-use building in the '70s. Snow's studio was on one of the upper floors, the fifth comes to mind but I'm not so sure. I hollow-walk down a dusty corridor of the largely vacant floor looking for his room number. The door is open a crack: I knock and Michael invites me in. At the time Snow was probably the best-known contemporary artist in the country and certainly one of the few with a presence beyond, especially in New York. I was looking forward to seeing this inventive artist's big, well set-up studio. Instead I walk into a little office.

The beige room has a cot against one wall. Snow's trumpet glows on the bedspread. I remember a chair and small table by the single sash window. Beyond these meagre objects I recall only a traditional easel supporting a canvas four or five feet square. Snow had painted a large, bent grid in imitation of the barrel distortion generated by a simple lens. A conventional painter would have laid down the ground of the painting prior to executing the image — in this case the grid — on top. Michael was working backwards. Now that his warped grid was in place he was laboriously painting the ground in the interstices between the grid rules. Wonky. This is what always made his thought process interesting.

We make a portrait in the hallway, Snow leaning against a door jamb as the hallway of empty doors and rooms receded behind him. It makes an acceptable cover for the magazine but I can't say it was my most brilliant performance. However, it is the beginning of something for me as I was to get to know him much better in subsequent years. He was always generous in his comments about my later work. And I remain grateful for the lesson I learned that day, one that has since been reinforced for me many times as numerous self-declared artists I have known have fussed for years over the creation of the perfect working space. That is: the bigger the studio, the smaller the artist.

1982

Sitting in a corner, under the stairs, in the former David Mirvish Gallery on Toronto's Markham Street I'm with a very old man. The gallery is having a brief career as The Canadian Centre for Photography. Over the course of a couple of hours the photographer André Kertész and I talk and watch people who have come into the building to view a survey exhibition of his life's work. Kertész, who began photographing in his native Hungary in 1912 and publishing five years later, had his first gallery exhibition in 1927. A year later he was one of the earliest adopters of the 35mm Leica. At 88 he is still photographing but with a battered Canon AE-1. Periodically viewers of the exhibition, unaware of his presence, will unwittingly arrange themselves into a perfect Kertész photograph. André will stop talking and lift his camera — very slowly. His hands shake, his eyes rheumy. You can see him fighting his old body and it hurts me to watch. He misses every single photograph but he still keeps trying. Between attempts he tells me of his life regrets. There are many including having been "seduced" into handing over his estate to his Canadian dealer. "I shouldn't have trusted her. The book she did was awful. I was a foolish old man."

2011

We are four, driving from Courbières, a tiny hamlet near Najac at the top of the Tarn, toward Toulouse and beyond. I'm at the wheel, Sheila beside me, photographer Arnaud Maggs and artist Spring Hurlbut are spooning in the back. Arnaud has been in my life for over 40 years. Now neither of us is young but Arnaud walks nearly two decades ahead of me. Despite the disciplined clarity and austerity of his art, his life has never been simple. After various relationships he has found final happiness with Spring. They are usually quietly comfortable together but on this French trip Spring fusses and flutters about Arnaud like a small pale bird. He doesn't protest so I'm puzzled. Something is amiss.

We take several breaks on the drive. At each Arnaud leaves the car and does tai chi under a tree. He still cuts a classy figure — skinny black jeans, black-and-white striped sailor's jersey, wide-brimmed black hat — despite being well into his 80s. He has to be the most elegant Canadian man alive. My older artist friends — Arnaud, John Gutmann, David Heath– and

Arnaud and Spring do tai chi on the road to Toulouse

Michael Snow — are my models of how to live a creative life
right to the end. They're heroes.

Although for decades Arnaud's chief medium has been
photography, he remains, at heart, a designer. He loves the
formal properties of objects — letterforms, signs, even funnels and water jugs. He loves the theme and variation. And he
loves assembling and ordering the variants in a grid. Control.
The average designer is not so much a creative person as
one who loves order, craves it and needs it to get by in a
messy world. Although Arnaud had been a very good graphic
designer he became much more than that. He saw the beauty
in mundane things. He could make the quotidian visible,
even authoritative and majestic. He made us pay attention:
he helped us to see.

Only later back in Toronto do I discover that Arnaud has
a secret — cancer. His thin frame has turned against itself, day

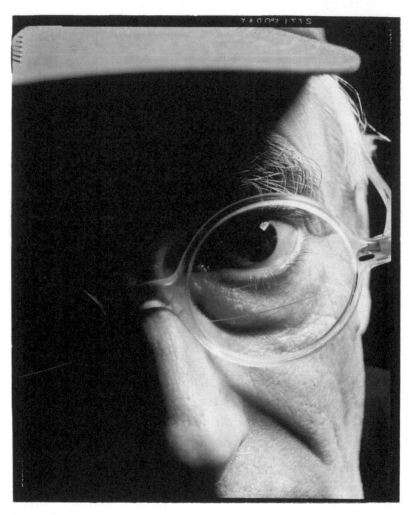

Arnaud Maggs

upon day, beckoning that other guy in black, the one with the scythe, ever closer.

We both once sat in a small boardroom session with a former provincial cabinet minister who was chairing one of those commissions on the state of the arts that periodically erupt like an outbreak of shingles. After Arnaud had described what it was like to work alone, hour upon hour, day upon day for weeks and months producing work that no one exhibited or bought the ex-minister exploded in a rage. Why would one persist? Why make work no one wanted? It was incomprehensible! Who needs photographs that clinically describe the shape of people's heads or reproduce catalogue numbers of jazz albums? It was crazy. You make things that people need like car tires, can openers or toilet seats. And why were so many claiming to be artists?

For me it spoke volumes about the government's commitment to the arts when it would appoint someone with a mickey of hard stuff on the floor beside his chair and a belief that producing artists could be as efficient as training dentists. Arnaud suffered through this outburst with quiet restraint. There was little point in talking to a drunk.

I've now been around long enough to see who succeeds and who falls under the bus. In the early days of organizing exhibitions at Harbourfront, working on a photography magazine, hosting the Toronto Photographers Workshop in my studio and sitting on many arts juries I encountered some wonderfully original talents. They explored unexpected subjects, processed film in unconventional ways and scribbled, drew and vandalized their prints. There was a vigorous urgency to their work.

As the years went by I watched them get ground down by the institutions. Their so-called peers on the granting juries usually argued badly and turned them down. There was a gradual triumph of the academy as more art schools taught photography and promoted various safe, imported orthodoxies. The big Canadian museums were totally deaf to new and local voices, having been mentally colonized by modes promoted by American institutions like New York's Museum of Modern Art or the Visual Studies Workshop in Rochester. The National Gallery in Ottawa bought enormous numbers of prints by second- and third-string Americans all the while ignoring and rejecting a wave of vigorous and original work by young Canadians. The director of one important Ottawa institution eventually used her position to exclusively buy and promote work by her boyfriend. As a result the most interesting young photographers got hungry and backslid into commercial work or gave up all together. It was just too difficult.

And who achieved what is commonly called success in this timid and derivative culture? It seems to me that all too often the ambitious plodders of convention got the rewards. It is true that succeeding requires a complex mix of talents — for self-promotion, a head for business, a desperate hunger for material success, a tin ear to criticism and a vigorous, if uninformed, belief in one's self. It also requires making work that is always recognizably yours, that is accessible and, on some level, decorative. To succeed you built a brand.

The curious, and the truly curious, try many things as part of their journey. This makes it difficult to self-brand. In our crowded and noisy world it is much easier for the public to understand and recognize work that beats the same rhythm on the same drum year after year. Thus in many ways we are served up the second best. Time and history can be a corrective but both can only select from what has been promoted and preserved by the past. The jury faces much pre-selection. I don't begrudge the commercial success of some: they've worked hard for it. But I do regret the losses and the public's confusion of success with excellence.

This, of course, was not limited to photography or the visual arts. I first-hand witnessed the progress of my ex-father-in-law's music students. All his most brilliant students fell off the bus while the driven mediocrities went on to public careers. Their technique was imitative and their interpretations borrowed but they got the concerts and recording contracts. The crudities of the marketplace triumphed in the end.

―――――

Late October morning light slashes through the pines, highlighting some, ignoring others. The woods become deeply dimensional.

I once saw her naked. It was like watching bubbles in a bath — sphere upon sphere upon sphere. Dressed she looked like a rolling tent. What little flesh her screaming prints didn't cover was buried in aggressive jewelry — silver pendants, chains, bangles, bracelets, rings and baubles. Anita Aarons was big and brassy. Chaos followed her everywhere as she swept grandly through life. But she got things done.

Her father back in Australia had been an itinerant theatre organist, a showman playing a flashy Wurlitzer on the road all over the Far East, Southeast Asia and the Pacific Islands. Anita grew up and married a prominent Australian economist. They had a couple of troubled daughters. One eventually retreated into a quiet marriage to a French engineer and the other, Tina, followed her grandfather into show business. For a few years in the '60s Tina was a fey princess on the British folk circuit, *tra-la-la-ing* her way into the fantasies of numerous English boys.

After her marriage failed Anita went to New York to participate in a World Crafts Council conference. It was there that she met Merton, a baby-faced London, Ontario, potter working in Toronto. Being a nice Canadian WASP he politely invited her to come and visit if she ever found herself in Canada. A few weeks later she was banging on his door. He kindly put her up for the night. She never left.

After a few years in Toronto she landed a job with the Extension Department of the Art Gallery of Ontario. Extension circulated art exhibitions to small cities and towns all over the province. Anita's job was to develop some of these exhibitions and get them on the road. She was no intellectual but she was crafty and intuitive. Persistent and inventive, she created numerous interesting shows and gave many young artists their first chance. However, she was a poor politician and when time came for cuts she was out the door.

In the early '70s when the Trudeau government bought up much of the central Toronto waterfront and gave it to the city as a park Anita realized it was a great opportunity. She managed to get appointed to create an art gallery at what soon came to be known as Harbourfront. The Liberals' gift was in some ways an empty one. It was a spectacular piece of real estate but it came with no money to create or operate a big urban park. The various grain elevators along the waterfront were handsome industrial structures but almost impossible to repurpose. Most of the warehouse buildings were at the end of their structural lives and would eventually have to be razed. None of this seemed promising.

However just west of where Bay Street meets Queen's Quay there was a long, low trucking transshipment warehouse. With a lot of scrubbing and some white paint a couple of its bays could be used as an exhibition space. Anita set to work and collared as many people she knew as possible to help. At the same time Greg Gatenby began working there in parallel to develop what became a famous reading series. I soon found myself on the first gallery board and helped Anita swish, bully and beg the gallery into existence. It was soon a vibrant success. It's still there as is its grander offshoot, the Power Plant Contemporary Art Gallery.

Anita's energy and ego kept her right on the edge. She often ricocheted out of control and made enemies. She also made mistakes. When the Gardiner family began poking around Harbourfront to site their proposed ceramic museum Anita fought hard against what she witheringly referred to as "that teacup museum." She succeeded in driving it away to the corner of Bloor and University where it flourished. Quite a few of her artists simply faded away. None of this slowed her down.

It was if she generated her own energy field. Watching her lose it could be fascinating. When this round woman decided to marry the mild Merton we were all sharing a studio building on Queen East. Pat Fulford, a sculptor friend of Anita's, helped create a wedding dress for the blushing bride who then had to be in her 60s. Pat put the finishing touches on the black-and-white gown the morning of the wedding. By noon Anita had become so hysterically excited that she somehow outgrew the dress. Pat hastily added a couple of panels. An hour later it was again too small. Pat added more. I'd check in from the floor above every hour or so to watch Anita blow up minute by minute as the day wore on and the wedding hour approached. It didn't seem humanly possible but she kept getting larger in defiance of all physical laws.

I had a number of encounters with her that were like this. Her new husband taught at a college back in London so she spent most weekdays and nights alone in the studio. On occasion I'd come in around two or three in the morning to process some film. I'd attempt to sneak quietly up the stairs but sometimes woke her up. She'd sweep out onto the second floor landing, see my shadowy ascending figure and start to scream. Even after she realized it was only me she couldn't stop. She'd call out my name between gasping breaths, hyperventilating faster and faster until she'd collapse against the wall. I'd have to watch over her for an hour or two until she restored herself. This high-strung hysteria could be terrifying. It also had power.

Before she and Merton moved into the studio building they'd had a large, comfortable house in the Beaches. At least once a month they'd invite me to a small dinner party. At one of these Merton mentioned Anita's sleeping problems. They'd be in their bedroom under the eaves when Anita would cry out, "It's here again." Whatever "it" was would move around the room, hovering above the floor menacingly, until finally moving over the bed to settle upon Anita's chest so she couldn't breathe. While it was totally real and present to her, Merton never saw it. As he related this story I began to feel cold. My hair felt electric and slowly I became aware of a shadow hovering up by their dining room ceiling. In the beginning it was just a small amorphous mist, but it soon condensed into something darker and began slowly roiling. Anita cried out. She saw it too. Everyone else at the table looked baffled as Anita and I watched it progress around the circumference of the room. The air was electric as the presence grew and solidified. But only the two of us saw and felt it.

After a half hour or so it began to recede. The room seemed to get brighter and become pacific. Finally it was gone and a new conversation began. After a while I got up to go and pee in the basement washroom. While I was down there I felt it again. As the feeling intensified I heard Anita scream in the dining room above. It was back for her too. This dybbuk, this duppy, this spook returned several times that night. It would arrive for both of us simultaneously even when we were in different rooms or on different floors. But it remained ours and ours alone until the first thin light of dawn.

Anita often seemed to be operating on the brink of hysteria. At various times she got illnesses of unspecified diagnosis. I remember a month when she'd whoop to anyone who'd listen, "I'm leaking from every orifice." I never found out exactly what that meant. Eventually the leaks were forgotten, replaced by another pathology.

Life with Anita was never predictable. One year her daughter Tina flew in from England with her Australian friend Jim to stay a few weeks. She sashayed around the building in see-through dresses that somehow made her look angelic. Her friend Jim seemed very studious, spending his days reading music scores. One day he knocked on my studio door with a boxed set of vinyl LPs under his arm. Like many photographers I had a powerful stereo with huge speakers in my studio. He wanted to use it to audit his recordings. They were of one of the warhorse operas — I've since forgotten which one. For the next few days he come up and play the recordings and follow the score while I worked. Finally he revealed that he'd been asked to direct performances of it at the Sydney Opera House. Up to that moment I'd had no idea what he did.

The Rocky Horror Picture Show was playing at the Roxy, a run-down little rep movie house on the Danforth. Tina convinced Jim to go for a laugh. The place was jammed with teens all dressed in costumes from the film. During the musical numbers hundreds of kids would get up to dance, mime and sing the parts. They had the whole film memorized. Jim, who'd been holed up almost as a hermit for several years, was out of touch. He had no idea that this low budget film that he'd directed as a young man had become the object of a teen cult. Jim Sharman was stunned.

In time Anita and Merton retired to Queensland in Australia where she started a local gallery. Back in Toronto planning and building for the Power Plant accelerated. When I'd first walked into the raw building as a gallery board member I was overwhelmed. It had a huge engine hall filled with giant antique compressors — they'd been built to chill the enormous five-storey Terminal Warehouse Building immediately to the east. There were still lunch buckets on the staff canteen table and socks and long johns dangled from lines in the locker room. I regret to this day that I didn't get around to photographing how the light fell on those machines and abandoned coveralls.

Finally the plant conversion was complete and a great opening bash was announced. Anita, who'd often destroyed as fast as she built, was not invited. She was almost forgotten and many of those who did remember treasured the little hurts and slights that she'd dispensed. It was a classic instance of dissing and dumping the entrepreneur who, in many ways, had made the whole thing possible. She decided to come anyway. She flew in from Australia and walked around the party, a short, dumpy, forgotten woman. The managers, the mediocrities, the civil servants had taken over. The crazed creator was left just a shadow drifting in the corners, invisible to all but a tiny handful who knew.

2009

My city neighbour Carmel knocks on the door of our house in downtown Toronto and settles in tell us about her recent trip to meet her new beau's extended family back in the mountains outside Rome. First day there she was emboldened to go for a walk through his ancestral village. She's a lapsed Irish Catholic party girl with bright red hair. Astonished villagers would ask where she's from. Canada. "Ah," they say, "Wood-a-bridge-a. Wood-a-bridge-a."

———

The water sparkles, the clouds scud, wind sings in the pines. There's nobody in the township but me. I spot something moving down the middle of the inlet maybe 1,500 feet from where I master the world from my big screen porch. I run inside and dig around in a drawer for my 10x50 binoculars and train them on the disturbance in the waters. It's huge, it's got a big rack, it's a deer — a buck, no it's an elk, no it's a moose casually swinging its head from side to side as it paddles right down the dotted line in the centre of our boating channel. Wait a minute, those aren't moose antlers. I stare intently through my Nikons. That's the rack of a woodland caribou. It has to be; I've got a set hanging from the collar ties of the room not a dozen feet behind me. They're from in back of Rankin Inlet and have tiny little hunting scenes scratched into the tines. At this distance I can't see hunting scenes but the form is unmistakable. Wow! They're back! Nature can be so forgiving, so resilient, so brimming with opportunity and opportunists.

Now Carmel is getting married to the Italian guy. The wedding is taking place in the backyard of his minor monster house in deepest Wood-a-bridge-a. She's all tricked out in a white 50-year-old-virgin-bride outfit and looks terrified. He's done this marriage thing before and seems pretty relaxed. His kids are there as is his whole enormous, glorious, riotous Italian Canadian extended family. Carmel's section of the guest crowd is centred on her gay buddies from the design world of her work. They swish through the crowd of cabinet-makers, guys in tile, landscapers and house-builders. Carmel's gays are totally relaxed and funny as hell. It's a good party.

The wedding tent covers the whole backyard. I drift toward the back of it and discover tomatoes growing just outside the tent's rear wall. It's only the beginning of July but the plants are already five feet high. Hundreds of huge shiny green tomatoes dangle enticingly from monster stalks. I've got a dozen plants growing in soil pockets on my hard rock island but they're only a foot high. How do the I-ties do it?

"You-a-like-a?" It's the groom's 80-year-old father. Turns out he's the gardener. And he's perfect to type — a short, barrel-chested Italian mountain peasant who's worked hard and made it in the New World. We struggle to talk but it's tough. After more than 50 years here he still speaks little English and I always get by in Italy with my stale Spanish. They're very forgiving.

The groom's sister appears and offers to translate for her father. We begin a talk about growing tomatoes. I've got lots of questions. I'm going to infiltrate these ethnic gardening mysteries. Just because I'm a lapsed white-bread Anglican choirboy doesn't mean I should be damned to bad tomatoes for life. The groom's son now joins us as well. He tells me about the first time he met Carmel at his dad's house. She was determined to master the tomato pasta sauce thing and please her new boyfriend. She wasn't competing with his mum, just learning the basic Italian husband-pleasing skills for the future. He walked into his dad's kitchen at the precise moment Carmel hit the switch on his dad's commercial kitchen blender. She'd forgotten to put the lid on. He offers to take me into the house to see the special tomato speckles effect still on the ceiling. Even new paint doesn't hide it.

The old dad generously agrees to reveal his deepest tomato growing secrets. It seems that you begin in early spring by cutting the lawn on the first full moon. This part is going to be tricky on a Georgian Bay island. Then you get a big tub of a certain type. I can't figure out whether this is some exotic ceramic number or just a garbage can. Then there's stuff about filling it with special water. You toss in the magic grass clippings and drag the whole thing into your four-car garage. It sits there protected through several Ontario freeze and thaw cycles. Finally when the whole thing is bubbling and smells bad you sprinkle it on the seedlings that you've had going in another mysterious part of the house. Next you move outside for the May full moon. Repeat at regular lunar intervals. I think you may have to sleep with the plants to have the best outcome.

Both the son and daughter are simultaneously translating and I'm getting confused. Are these just repeats or are there more steps? How high are the plants by June first? Are there tomatoes yet? Finally the translating slows down to a crawl and I ask if this is the whole secret to growing tomatoes. They translate my last question. No, wait, there's more, the ultimate secret. "Buy Miracle-Gro. Be sure it's the box with tomatoes pictured on the label. Do what it says."

A group of neighbours on the south end of Euclid Avenue have been orphaned this Christmas. All agree to convene for a seasonal meal at our house as we have just acquired a table that can accommodate a dozen diners.

The food is cooked, the table set and candles lit. Everyone is in a party mood. As we move through the courses the conversation sparkles with news, gossip, jokes and lies. During dessert neighbour Rob Gray, who lived across and down the street, suddenly gasps and points to the glowing accumulation of candle wax in the middle of the table. "It's the baby Jesus and his mummy!" he declares. When I examine the gobs of melted wax I could see how he arrived at this interpretation. All the hot air expelled by the diners had guttered the centrepiece trio of candles into a molten mass that is easily as credible a depiction of the blessed mother and child as any of the painted plaster doorstoppers sold in the shops of Little Italy a few blocks away. The whole blobby arrangement is sacralized by an interior glow from the still burning wicks.

"It's a miracle!" proclaims Rob. As he excitedly begins chiseling the sacred wax lump off the tabletop with his dinner knife he announces that, as the original witness to this miraculous event, he has all the concession rights — admission tickets, souvenir photos and keychain reproductions of the Euclid Avenue Madonna. Being almost the co-discoverer of this apparition and owner of the table as well as the original purchaser of the candles I feel that I should get some cut of the action. But Robert is already getting so Holy and Roman about the whole thing that he has begun to affect an Italian accent. Soon he is excitedly referring to himself in the third person as Roberto Grigio, the chosen one to whom this miracle had been first revealed. When I press my case further he finally allows that as all the old ladies in black have to somehow get to the site of the revelation he would allow me to divvy up the primary schoolyard next door and run a parking concession to accommodate the faithful. I try to picture myself shivering in a little lonely booth in the bleak schoolyard accented with dog shit — a tough way to get rich.

On the other hand, if you've ever been to the Museo La Specola in Florence you know that wax figures can last hundreds of years. The booth would be a long-term investment, something even my sons could do after me if their careers as architects ever fall apart. Of course I'd never let them design the booth: their version would require zoning exemptions, consultant engineers and cost millions. While I huddled over a tiny heater collecting quarters at ground level they'd both be luxuriating in their corner offices in a penthouse far above. Not a chance.

I still regret not photographing that dinner. Decades earlier during an assignment in Milan I had taken a break and walked to Santa Maria delle Grazie to view da Vinci's *Last Supper*. It was as faded as a 1950s class photo but was clearly a precursor to the dinner of a dozen some two millennia later on Euclid Avenue. Twelve is a powerful number — think eggs, buns, months and holy suppers. Clearly it makes things happen. And as the big Church knows, there is money to be made.

2015

Carmel has had a handful of good years with Wood-a-bridge-a guy Zio. They have fun together, she enjoys his family. Then one day that old elephant, cancer, lumbers into their new lives.

Zio struggles and tries — new diet, a bit of *ooga booga*, positive thinking and the harsh regime of conventional medical treatments. Don't work. None of them.

I see him one last time at home in Wood-a. He has begun to waste away but is cheerful. He shows us an old album with snapshots that document the days when he was "a real Gino." His hotrod had been a souped-up Gremlin, a solecism foisted on the world by AMC, the same people that inflicted the Pacer and the Matador upon us. We have some laughs. Carmel is admirably brave. Her life ride continued to be a roller coaster. But I've always admired her inner resources, her ability to pick herself off the floor and resume her journey.

THIRTEEN

JAMAICA: SOON COME

"Baby, baby why oh why?
Why did you ever leave me and now
you come back crying?
Why oh why, why oh why,
why oh why, oh why?"
"BABY WHY," THE CABLES

"Heaven for climate; hell for company."
J.M. BARRIE

2012

Friendship and romance can carry us to unexpected places. For over a decade now I've been partnered with Sheila, a British Jamaican. Come every year-end we both repair to her father's house in the hills of St. Ann Parish near Jamaica's north coast. There we read, write, edit and participate in a semi-rural Jamaican life that can be incredibly intense. There is always someone calling from the gate, "Mr. Murray, Mr. Murray."

The Murrays are Quakers, a sect with deep historical roots in Jamaica. Quakers are interested in social justice — they share what they have and help whenever possible.

My father-in-law shuffles down the drive to the gate, steeling himself for the latest tragedy — a stolen goat, a sick cow, a relative in desperate need of medicine, rent unpaid, even bail money. At their most desperate the hailer just needs a slice of bread and cheese, some bananas or an egg. All beseeches eventually get around to some "smalls" — a little change. Or not so little. It seems that Ossie Murray gives away more of his tiny Jamaican

Foreign Service pension than he keeps for himself. Long gone are the days when he was the dashing Jamaican high counsul, dean of the corps in Toronto or the Bahamas, hosting garden parties where white women swirled around him, laughing, flirting, an embarrassment to his two daughters. Now he's barely on the daylit side of 90, a mentally vigorous man whose eyesight is failing him, a former star athlete who must now shuffle carefully in order to detect steps and potholes he cannot see.

The Quaker community that beckoned the Murrays here is now reduced to a pair of very old Black ladies who come to the house every Sunday for Quaker meeting. At 88 Ossie is the baby of the congregation. My place in all this is to take the car and fetch the second youngest. I crawl the car slowly down the washed-out road to Enid's house. The 21-year-old gray Toyota I drive is rather absurdly fitted out with alloy wheels and a trunk-mounted spoiler. "Yanayselly?" shout the touts and higglers in the fields. No, we don't want to sell it although keeping it all running is getting tougher by the month. Paul, a small farmer and sometime mechanic, and I have just spent the previous afternoon taking the steering column apart and making new insulating washers for the horn and turn signals by cutting up an old Joy detergent bottle. We have wrapped the broken door handle housing on the driver's side in wire and slathered glue on the plastic casting. We've bought another few weeks.

I pull into Enid's drive 10 minutes before the meeting. Her housekeeper brings her out slowly as Enid is blind and so impossibly bow-legged that it's a miracle she can still support her own weight.

"Who's that?" she cries.

"Sheila's Michael."

"Ah, bless you, my son. I'm an old, old lady."

"Enid, I've backed the car in so you won't have to feel your way around the car door."

"Who's this?"

"It's Michael, Enid — Ossie's son-in-law."

"I'm an old lady; me mother and father are dead. Me don't have much time."

"Enid, let me take your stick so that you can feel for the seat of the car."

Slowly, slowly, she lowers herself down. Hermin, her housekeeper, lifts her legs into the car and we're good to go.

"I'm a very old lady. Me the only child alive. Both my brothers have passed."

"How old are you, Enid?"

"I don't know. I'd have to work it out but I can't find me papers."

"I guess it hardly matters now."

"I'm an old lady now, my son. How are the dogs? I love that Mitzy so much."

Mitzy is a weimaraner named Misty but nevermind. The dog doesn't care. For most of the silent Quaker meeting Enid will caress the dog she cannot see. While Ossie and the ladies make their silent peace with spirit and the universe I retreat to my room and write.

I know meeting is over an hour later when Glenn Gould begins the Goldberg Variations on the stereo. This signals that all will now have tea. It is Gould's last recording that we hear — meditative, slow, reflective, tinged with nostalgia and regret but still life-affirming and always so beautiful. The music is loud because the ladies are going deaf. Bach sends his solace out into the garden, over the frangipanis, the orchids, through the banana trees, the oranges and ortaniques, our coffee bushes, the coco palm, the valley behind and the green hills of St. Ann. Glenn plays to the hills of Trelawney and Cockpit Country and over the graves of a million slaves, of the rich planters and the more recent patient poor and long suffering. You may not be able to eat it but this is still Toronto's no mean gift to a very tough world. I drive Enid home. It rains hard.

It's an occasion of great moment. We have all assembled in the damp and dim basement of Huntley Crescent, St. Ann Parish, Jamaica, to witness The Great Uncrating. My father-in-law, Ossie, had been a diplomat, not a handyman. His kitchen tool drawer was largely home to the careworn corpses of broken hardware items — cracked knobs, half hinges, retired water shutoff valves, lonely screws and nails — junk. The few tools that lived in the tool drawer were all challenged — by wear, neglect and lack of love. The opened drawer presented a sombre iron oxide palette.

However, we have managed to excavate a claw hammer (missing one), a large slot screwdriver (rounded bit) and what I would call a "safety" chisel, i.e., terminally unsharp. For nine decades Ossie kept his faith — not only in God but in the threat posed by any tool with a keen edge. If a knife couldn't cut butter he believed it would never harm a human.

The deliverymen attack the crate with these Neolithic tools and slowly *it* emerges from the box — a shimmering white cube — the new clothes washer. Many weeks ago this machine left an assembly plant in Kentucky, rode an 18-wheeler all the way to New Orleans, boarded a ship, crossed the Gulf and the Caribbean Sea to land at Jamaica's container port at Kingston. A snarling, smoke-belching, vintage highway tractor had hauled it across the interior mountains to the smaller ones in St. Ann where its crew muscled it down our path lined with ortaniques and oranges to this house.

I volunteer to step forward, hook up the hoses and insert the power plug. The white cube is shoved into place and shimmed to an approximate level. The week's dirty sheets are loaded in the top and the lid closed. I respectfully withdraw and let one of Ossie's daughters push the button. A row of twinkling coloured LEDs instantly brighten the back panel and the white cube begins to make sanitary noises. We are hypnotized. We all stand respectfully in a solemn semicircle to witness the full procession of small coloured lights marking the full virgin cycle of the white cube. This great moment has been made possible by transatlantic, transcontinental finance — monies raised in England, Ontario, British Columbia and from a tiny Jamaican Foreign Service pension issuing from Kingston. It is one that none of us will forget. It's a truly great day.

———

There's a small stone hollow at the edge of Sulkers' Rock. It's perhaps a foot from the shoreline and barely an inch or two above the water level of my inlet. I wash my socks, a T-shirt and gotchies in this spoon-like depression. The several pails of water it contains have been warmed by the rocks of the basin and the late morning sun. As I knead my clothes in the tepid water I suddenly sense the presence of all the women I have photographed over the years doing exactly what I am doing. And we are now doing it together, I by the Sweet Sea, they by the far off streams and rock pools of Mexico, of Nicaragua, of Peru and my other island home, Jamaica.

We Canadians like to think of ourselves as goody-two-shoes innocents keeping the world's peace while minding our own business. It's false. Here in Jamaica where I'm writing this both the north and south coasts are intermittently disfigured by bauxite loading piers. At the paradisal harbour known as Discovery Bay, Columbus's reputed landing there on his second voyage of 1494 is commemorated by a mountain of ore, an enormous conveyor belt and a grimy pier. A long line of rusty freighters chugs in through a channel blasted in the coral reef and are bullied, bow out, up to the shore. They have poetic names like *Bulk Patriot* and are invariably registered in Panama or Limassol. Each is only around for a day or so while ore is dumped into its hold for transport, often to Russia. Others ship to the U.S. and Canada. While this loading goes on another ship waits offshore.

It has been estimated that Jamaica has reserves of 2.5 billion tons of bauxite "red gold" — a hundred-year supply. The Second World War's demand for aircraft aluminum stimulated this industry and by 1957 Jamaica was the premier source of alumina ore in the world. Many of these mining operations have Canadian names — Alcan and Noranda. Alcan is the biggest in the country but American companies such as Kaiser have been involved as well. All of them used a predatory technique known as transfer pricing to cheat Jamaicans of their fair share of the country's richest resource. Their Jamaican subsidiary would internally sell its processed ore to the parent company in Canada or the U.S. at a bargain rate and pay royalties based on that price. You can get an idea of the significance of this and its impact on a very small country with considerable poverty when you understand that during some years in the 1970s bauxite royalties were nearly 30% of Jamaican GDP and over 45% of the country's net earnings. Yet it employed only 1% of the native workforce. Whites from North America had all the significant jobs. And every day this little island, never more than 50 miles across and less than 150 miles long, gets measurably smaller.

In the '70s PNP leader Michael Manley negotiated a fairer deal for Jamaica, tying the ore price to the global price for aluminum ingots as well as gaining 51% ownership for the government. But North America got him back. By leveraging a temporary $500-million IMF loan into deals for other sectors, especially agriculture, it utterly destroyed the local dairy industry and put countless small farmers out of business so that American ones from Ohio and Iowa could sell their subsidized surplus potatoes, carrots and powdered milk to Jamaican distributors. Even the humblest Jamaican farmer understood exactly who was undercutting their very production costs and bringing them to their knees.

When I buy frozen fish in my local market in St. Ann Parish it has been packaged in Toronto. I'd like to have local and fresh but it's not there. And every year the signage of Canadian banks marches farther across the country. Scotiabank has been here for a long time — it had branches in Jamaica long before it ever had one in Toronto. But now the Royal Bank has absorbed local banks as has the Bank of Commerce. I suspect that many locals don't understand that these banks operating under cryptic initials — RBC, CIBC — are Canadian.

———

My little harbour has hosted many of what we once called god's creatures — buffleheads, loons, beavers and beetles, muskrats, minks, garpikes and enormous black water snakes. I once saw two snapping turtles screwing in it. At least that's what I think they were doing as they roiled around and around stirring up mud like a pair of bulldozers.

But today when I stare into the shallows all I see are catfish. They float tail down, languidly gumming the surface and swishing their barbels. There are dozens and dozens of them. None of them looks much like lunch.

2014

I pull up to the front door of the big agricultural feed store on Brown's Town's main street and enter. When I'm languidly accosted I explain that I need a 15-kilo bag of dog food. I'm sent to a young man who drags it off a shelf in the middle of the store. He directs me to a centrally located desk while he lugs the heavy bag toward the front of the shop. While I stand at this desk various entries are made in a vintage desktop computer. After some minutes an old printer at the back of the store begins to slowly regurgitate an invoice. Eventually it is fetched and handed to me. I'm then directed to another desk at the far side of the store. I wait while the cashier finishes a patois conversation with another woman who's carrying a bundle of scandal bags, the local name for the opaque black plastic bags that disguise their contents — groceries, toiletries, medicines, occasionally even secrets.

I may pay by credit card only if I show two pieces of photo ID. I'm prepared for this. Ten minutes later I'm carrying an expanded sheaf of papers back to another centrally located desk where after waiting my turn — more conversations — my papers are examined, a new sheaf added along with a prominent stamp in purple ink. I'm next directed to a desk near the door where a uniformed security guard examines my paperwork and passes it on to door-side clerk behind a desk. After careful inspection he adds the imprint of an even more impressive stamp to several papers in the pile. They're returned to me. I'm told to locate the original retriever of the bag. I do. Seven people beside myself, the lone customer, have now found employment through this transaction. Forty minutes have passed. I finally own a bag of dog food.

I know this system.

When I worked in Oaxaca in the late 1960s we'd set aside one whole day a month to do banking. Our money was sent down by the National Science Foundation in Washington and the University in Chapel Hill, North Carolina. The morning of banking day was spent slowly shuffling from desk to desk with a thick wad of papers. At each station a clerk would prepare a fat sandwich of forms and oily carbon paper and wind it through the rollers of a big black manual typewriter. This ever-expanding paper stratigraphy would migrate slowly from desk to desk as morning drew to a close. Finally, by siesta time, our monthly deposit was finished. We'd leave for lunch, returning a couple of hours later to repeat the process in another room of desks. By evening we'd have a withdrawal. The blinking ATMs that I used last fall in Oaxaca represent many vanished jobs.

Driving into the centre of Brown's Town I park across from the market under a No Pissing sign and slip through an iron gate into St. George's Anglican. Norma, the local justice of the peace, will witness 32 signatures on my sheaf of estate documents. We sit in the front pew as various old parishioners come in to practice hymns on a battered upright. Norma witnesses and embosses the first pair of signatures. "B flat on your other hand," she cries and sings the note. She turns and whispers to me, "She's got arthritis." I watch an old Black lady wearing a ball cap and flowered blouse hunching over the keyboard. She picks out "You in your small corner, and I in mine" so slowly that no one but Norma would ever recognize the melody. "Sharp! Sharp dear." Norma coaches and corrects. Another signature and seal are embossed. Thirty more to go. This will be another Jamaican soon come.

This Jamaican Great House I'm visiting crowns a hill above the Black River plains. Where its owner's slaves once laboured at its base their descendants now drive goats and grow poor root crops and bananas. As dusk descends tiny white lights limn the distant Santa Cruz mountains far to the east. And to the west and north where the Lacovia and Nassau ranges border this great plain, huge cane fires are burning. Devilish columns of black smoke vanish with the fall of night but orange flames remain visible, surrounding the dark plain like an invading army rolling across this often uncivil and troubled island. Local newspaper headlines tell the stories:

Man Chopped In Front Of Son
Jacket Man Kills Father
Man Held Prisoner Under Woman's Bed
Madman Beaten For Taking Off Child's Panty
Woman Vows To Spread Aids
J'can Drugs, Rapes Girls For Porn
Molester Prays For Victims
Woman Beats Man With Broomstick
Man Loses Lip In Fight Over Battery
Mom Burns Son For Dirty Uniform
Man Vows Never To Steal Mangoes Again
Male Teachers Flee Classrooms To Escape Female
Student Predators

2016

We're travelling north up the A3 from Kingston through Red Gal Ring, Stoney Hill and Golden Spring toward Toms River. This highway stretch is like loose string in a drawer — a tangle of multiple hairpin turns and cliff-hangers hacked through the steep hills and valley cuts immediately west of Blue Mountain.

I'm also driving Jamaican — too fast and furious — dodging each pothole surprise at every blind corner. It's a video game until an apparition suddenly menaces up behind — a big-shouldered, black SUV limned with strobing strings of purple LEDs. Its driver pounds the horn — he wants by despite the big bus barreling toward us on the niggardly narrow blacktop. I dip around a washout just before the bus rockets by a mere hand-width from my mirror. As I enter its black exhaust nimbus the flashing dark brute at rear pounds past, thundering music from two pairs of 18-inch woofers flush-mounted just forward of the chromed landau hardware on its rear quarter panels. This high-risk move is now explicable — the speeding, big, black speaker-box is a hearse. The formaldehyde marinated corpse inside is being dubbed and dance-halled into ground chuck. The dear departed has nothing to lose as this sound-system death-chariot leans hard into a blind turn ahead and disappears toward Devon Pen. By the time that midnight chariot reaches the north coastal delta the departed will be pureed. There's an old local joke: "Why did the Jamaican pass on a blind corner? Because he couldn't see anyone coming."

There is nothing subtle about Brown's Town's settlement patterns. The elite public buildings and institutions along with houses of the rich are built on the heights. Thus Hillcrest, an Anglican retreat centre, St. Hilda's Girls School, the library and the courthouse have the high long views while the market and the banks occupy the lower middle ground. As Main Street descends into a valley running into the interior the shops and bars get grittier. Down there is where I hang out when passing time in town.

Today I'm having lunch in Jerkies, an unassuming lunch place across from the Live for Now Bar, a loud dark hole papered with glossy posters of women with big brown bums and thunder thighs. I grab a takeout beer from the bar and cross the street back to Jerkies to order a late breakfast of ackees and salt fish. As I sit down farmer Paul's son Marco pulls up in his latest hot car and joins me at the table. He's a big affable guy with dreads who builds and tunes racing cars for the Jamaican circuit. He learned all his mechanical skills from the internet. He's a modern Jamaican guy.

He's also all too typical. Although he's not much past 30 he already has five kids with four different mothers. "Ya gotta have fun," he tells me. This fun has created an island of overworked single mothers with not much time for parenting. And the guys do little more than drive-by fathering. The result is an uncivil every-man-for-himself culture. The country spins its wheels, moving neither forward nor back. So the smart and ambitious leave "for foreign." There are more Jamaicans living in Toronto, Miami and London than on the mother island. The culture stubbornly refuses to change.

Driving Jamaica's north coast highway I hear a siren. So I look in the mirror of my now 24-year-old Toyota Corolla Sprinter and spy an ambulance behind with flashing lights coming up fast. Now even though I've been driving on the sinister side in Jamaica for a decade and a half, at heart I'm still a sucky Canadian. I pull over to let the emergency vehicle pass.

But nobody else does. All those vengefully insecure Jamaican-behind-the-wheel male maniacs driving the long row of additional two-decade-old Toyota Corollas, mini buses and dump trucks laying down smokescreens hold their ground. They're not going to take any shit from some agony patient. We're all running one of the two lane sections of the highway that's equipped with those sharp hills and blind corners that are perfect for passing. The ambulance tries but just doesn't have the power when all the Corollas put pedal to metal. And the only way to pass a big-shouldered Jamaican dump truck is to take another road. The ambulance with its pathetic emergency is just gonna have to grind along burning oil like the rest of us.

When I get home sweet Hermin, the housekeeper, is there and, as always, brilliantly avoiding cleaning anything above waist-height or behind furniture. Dead roaches add interest to the floor. As I start my standard rant about the lack of basic civility on Jamaican roads she rocks back and forth on her bare feet using the string mop as a stabilizer. "Number One" is what she always smirkingly calls me. "Did you read last week's paper about the guy who a few days ago wouldn't let an ambulance go by?" No surprise I had not. "His mother was in it. She died."

I can complain about Jamaican guys but if you have a flat tire on a potholed highway — something that only happens every couple of hours — it's always going to be some dreadlocked guy piloting a totally crapped-out vintage Corolla who's gonna stop and help you with the change. It's never going to be the I-shop-in-Miami, have-family-in-the-U.K.-and-Toronto middle-class Jamaican who stops. "Fuck you, Sunburn. I gotta get on with my blingy 4x4 and my success."

2016

As the plane climbs it swings over the gridiron of warehouses and light industry immediately west of Toronto's Pearson Airport. Soon Lakes Ontario and Erie will slip below as course is set for Jamaica. Like a kid I still book window seats so I can watch the world roll out when the sky is blue. Jamaica bound — port side southbound, starboard on the return — I anticipate the swirls and drifts, some two hours ahead, of the reefs and bars that escort the Bahamas through a robin's egg sea. A lifetime of flying has still not dulled my interest in the land and seascapes that pass beneath the plane.

I have long abandoned queries to flight attendants — what's that river, that bay, those lakes, those mountains? They seem an incurious lot. A flight is a takeoff and landing, home and a hotel with some troublesome service in between. Their flight could be a subway ride for any interest in geography.

Past Cuba the sea roughens as the descent begins. Suddenly one can see through it to reefs and rocks, then coast clips by, and returning Jamaicans begin to crane at the windows. Velvet hills rise as we arc toward the Sangster airstrip just east of Mobay. We skim past my favourite bar and the wheels hit. We're down.

While in the long line snaking slowly toward immigration three uniformed Amazons single me out from the crowd. The largest of the trio is what Jamaican men call fluffy — dangerously overweight. She dangles my entry form like a dead rat and shouts for the benefit of the hundreds of badly dressed tourists in the holding area.

"Mr. Mitchell, you have been to Jamaica many times and should know by now that red ink is reserved only for government officials! Go back outside and fill in the form in blue or black before you come back!"

At least 500 people turn to regard the geriatric slow learner with the red pen.

I'm forced to beg and borrow from a large, hairy tourist in flip-flops. His pen is from a lumberyard in Sudbury.

A couple of hours later I'm at the house. At 94 Ossie is old and ending. The water pump has died, the phone is broken, the car tires bald, the water heater leaks, the propane cylinder is empty, the toilet is broken and his computer has quit. There is no food in the cupboard, and the fridge is empty. I find only a few ounces of powdered milk mix and crusty leftovers from my last visit three months prior. Only the dogs have been fed.

The next morning I'm up early and open the door to the cage — the elevated barred-in patio-deck overlooking the back garden. At that moment I'm suddenly home. The early morning light burrows through the heavy vegetation, highlighting a branch here, a frond there, then twists off to bring another plant to stardom. In defiance of weeks of drought, the vegetation is exuberant — the leaves glisten and everywhere there are flowers. Huge poinsettias drape like velvet, thousands of magenta blooms cover the 25-foot-high bauhinia and one vine's yellow blossoms garland across the many crotons and banana palms. The mahoganies shoot skyward while the 80-foot guango towers protectively over all.

And above it all five cirrus clouds hang like hooks in the new blue sky.

There is so much presence in this yard — so much *is*-ness and *there*-ness, just sheer *being* everywhere. And the light continues to flutter through the trees and brush, creating highlights before shading them so as to show off something in behind making the scale change endlessly so the depth pistons in and out. There is so much going on. This is why we take photographs, to arrest ephemera, the temporary and the evanescent so that we can capture it like a caged bird and examine it, understand it and own it in an album or on a hard drive. I have utterly failed hundreds of times to capture all this garden's *is*-ness. I have set up cameras before first light programmed to expose every five seconds all day long until the light fails and the data card fills, but the garden is still not really there the way it is when you quiet yourself and just sit.

But life moves. White and yellow butterflies dog-fight through the bush. A flock of glossy black cling-clings peck through the grass and bathe in our little water bowl while jabbering crows boss from the bushes and streamertail hummers buzz the blossoms. A flock of parakeets briefly rattles through the treetops and moves on. All is well. And with our arrival it has begun to rain. More riches.

———

A mid-September morning of hard, brassy light in which every limb and needle is edge-enhanced on the acrobatic white pines. A crystalline cold grinds down from the barrens. One of my transplanted red pines has already died.

I have come down the river alone. The river and its inlet have been abandoned. I'm the only one for miles. The trees still show no sign of autumn but when night comes on sharply I know it's waiting in the wings. The sun slips away at half past seven and following a suddenly cold night it doesn't return until the following seven. Night and day, dark and light, are now near equals.

2015

After running the north coast highway for a couple of hours the consensus in the car is that it's time for lunch. A further vote is for a sit-down place by the sea that'll be more comfortable than rebar stools in a jerk joint. A few miles on near St. Ann's Bay the perfect place appears a few hundred feet off the road and right on the beach. It's new, freshly painted, with bright, gauzy swagged drapes hanging between white-washed pillars. The entire place is enclosed by a decorative railing. There are no walls. The place has a certain country elegance.

We chose a table on the waterside. The dazzling blue Caribbean descends toward us from the far horizon — a faint line separating the sea from an uninflected sky. Two-thirds of the way down from that level the waves curl and flash on the offshore reefs. Then the waves recompose themselves and run the rest of the way to the lip of the sand beach mere yards away. The white sand slopes up to a windrow of chip bags, pop bottles, plastic toys, takeout containers and condoms just a few feet from our wicker table and chairs. It's the standard 21st-century beach shoreline of any place on Earth.

The place is big. It takes a waitress 10 minutes to get to us. We are the only customers. She seems surprised that that we've entered the restaurant because we wish to eat and drink but she does go off to see if she can locate some menus. Another 10 minutes. She returns with two menus for five people. Then she vanishes. We'll manage. We study the eight-page menu carefully, eventually choosing drinks and dishes. Ten minutes

323

later she is again surprised to discover that we want to order. She vanishes to locate an invoice book. Soon come.

Ten minutes later she returns with an order book, sheets of carbon paper and a ballpoint. We begin to tell what we want. Her ballpoint doesn't work. She vanishes. A few minutes later she's back with reliable technology — a pencil. We order — beer, wine and a couple of the cocktails luridly illustrated in the menu. She laboriously writes it all down and disappears.

Twenty minutes. She returns to announce, "White wine finish." The wine drinkers then order Red Stripe beers. "Gin finish." The cocktail drinkers switch to beer. She retreats.

She returns in half an hour with a tray of tall drinks that look like vanilla milkshakes surmounted by a red cherry and a leaf. This shipment would be clearly intended for another table if another were occupied. We accept the mystery drinks and enquire about the food. She leaves. Ten minutes.

She returns with a menu. "Conch finish." I reorder something else. "Red snapper finish." They reorder something else. Twenty minutes later she returns with the intelligence that "shrimp finish." I order the most basic and ubiquitous Jamaican staple, rice and peas — white rice and red beans cooked in coconut milk. Ten minutes later she returns. "Rice and peas no ready for an hour."

We've only been here an hour; it's now coming up to two p.m. We finish our drinks, pay 50,000 Jamaican dollars for the big white drinks and drive to the Juici Patties takeout in St. Ann's Bay. "Soy patty finish. Fish patty finish." I'll make toast when we get home.

2016

If I'd been on this clifftop 622 years ago I'd have seen Christopher Columbus's little fleet searching for a channel through the reef that guards Discovery Bay. However it's 2016 so the only ship I see is an exceedingly ugly Chinese bulk carrier loading bauxite at the Noranda pier on the west side of the bay. The ship lists hard to starboard as ore spills through a mid-ship hatch and a cloud of red dust rises. Its young Chinese crew wash down bowls of rice and peas with Bigga pop at the clifftop jerk centre during this loading. When their ship clears the reef early next morning Jamaica will be thousands of tons smaller. A replacement ship riding high offshore waits to haul more of the island off to Houston.

Few Jamaicans seem know just how much of their beautiful island Prime Minister Portia Simpson-Miller is giving away. She has surrendered a pair of ecologically protected islands on the south coast. Reefs will be destroyed and endangered creatures vanquished so the Chinese can flatten the pair of Goat Islands for a new Panamax deep-water container port. And over a thousand acres of land have been passed to the Chinese in return for a four-lane, 42-mile-long toll road across the island. There is little transparency or public discourse when these quiet deals are cut halfway around the world in Beijing. A supine Jamaica has agreed to be the stepping stone for future Chinese investments throughout the Caribbean. The red flag with the yellow star flies over an indebted little nation.

2016

On this bright Sunday morning I'm driving through the mountains of St. Ann, ricocheting from cliff to chasm on tiny ill-paved roads in a hummocky landscape dashed with dazzling greens. Every handful of miles a hamlet emerges with its ladies making their way to church wearing bright spangled dresses and extravagant hats — wide brims, ribbons and sequins, satin and bows. Still this rural world's biggest buildings, these holy houses gush music and song — tambourines and drums, pianos and small organs — flowing from a reassuring faith that moves lives forward day by day despite sickness, poverty and disappointment.

2016

After weeks alone at the Brown's Town house I get a call from a friend asking if I'm free for Christmas dinner. I affirm that I am. Where's the dinner? It turns out it's at rocker Keith Richard's house overlooking Ocho Rios. I offer to pick up my friend on Christmas morning and drive us both to the house.

Richards has figured out how to maintain his privacy. As I turn up the road inland from Ochi's cruise ship terminal I find myself on a series of branching dirt tracks climbing up into the bush. With each unassuming turnoff the road gets worse. Several times my vintage Corolla gets hung up in washouts. The wheels spin as the little car pivots like a compass needle on humps on the roadbed. The track gets steeper and rougher as we crawl into the hills. Finally, just as the track begins to give in helplessly to the bush we encounter a pair of enormous steel gates flanked by razor wire. They majestically swing open by remote control and I scoot through only to get hung up on another hump in a very steep washed-out drive. There is still no sign of a house, just jungle.

We grind slowly uphill, the body pan, transmission and muffler yowling every foot of the way. Finally a bright blue wall appears around a corner and my little-car-that-could finds a resting place next to Keith's big 4x4.

While the wrinkled rocker isn't home his old buddy S. is. He's been in the kitchen all morning but there's still time for a drink on the long balcony cantilevered over the swimming pool and all of Ocho Rios a thousand feet below. Then it's dinner for three with the best view in the world. Why would one ever wish to leave Jamaica?

FOURTEEN

BAD DADDY

"Life is bullshit and it's your fault!"
BEN MITCHELL

*"Only a thin line divides the articulate man
of wisdom from the windbag."*
JOHN KENNETH GALBRAITH

1977

An unexpected pregnancy, at least for me; a horrendous high forceps delivery after a 36-hour labour and I'm suddenly a married father. It's very intense. Despite sleepless nights and exhausting days, the first few years of parenthood go quickly. In no time at all I have a four-year-old son in daycare. But this is the late 20th century so it's called an early childhood learning centre and it's part of a community college in a northern part of the city near his mother's work. She takes Jake in. I pick him up. The young women who run it are intelligent, committed and sweet. My son is happy.

Then one afternoon I arrive to retrieve him and walk into a freezer. Jake seems normal enough but the women avoid eye contact and are brusque. This continues for several days. By the end of the week I've graduated to a few glaring glances. The following week his mother discovers why.

There'd been a kind of show and tell. "And what does your mum do?" Jake had given a somewhat credible account of his mother's work as a designer. "And your daddy — what does he do, Jakey?"

"He goes away."

"But he must come home sometimes. What does he do then?"
Long pause . . . "He drinks a beer."
"But after that what does he do?"
"He drinks another one."
"Then what?"
"He gets sick."

This told them the whole shabby secret — an absent alcoholic father who'd occasionally stagger home to hurl abuse and barf on the broadloom. They'd been warned about these fathers. They could imagine the whole thing — the unpaid bills, the smashed brown station wagon and the table dancers. Poor little Jakey. A storyteller like his father.

1994

The premier's limo is idling in my driveway. The economy has tanked and Bob Rae is daily beaten up by the press. I've been doing his official photography for a while now, watching him look older and heavier week by week. I would never, ever want his job.

A few times on his way home in the west end he stops by my studio to do a photo session and have a beer. He's an odd mix of smarts and naivety. Jacques Parizeau has recently visited Toronto and upon returning to Quebec complained loudly and publicly about his treatment by Ontarians. He saw himself as a foreign head of state: Ontario treated him like just another visiting fireman. He's deeply offended and particularly annoyed with the Ontario Provincial Police. Bob gets busy on my studio phone discussing security arrangements with the head of the OPP and a member of his cabinet. I finally manage to catch him between calls and point out that every layabout in my neighbourhood can listen in to my cordless phone. It's not remotely secure.

Finally his business is finished and the beer has started to erase the day. We get to work. We're in the middle of a portrait session when my younger son, Ben, sashays into the building, cuts right across the seamless setup and demands his allowance. I fish for some change and he turns around and spots Bob. "What are you doing here?" he says. "Why aren't you on TV?"

1982

My friend Charles and I slip down to the Toronto's lakefront railway yards at dawn on a chilly Sunday morning. We are met at a back gate by a co-conspirator, a CN locomotive electrician. With my young son Jake in tow we sneak quietly into the yard. Soon our little gang of four is hustling between the long lines of boxcars in a silent freight yard. The famous but troubled high-speed train, the Via Turbo, is to be quietly scrapped the following week. Built at the Montreal Locomotive Works, this sleek, gas-turbine-powered aluminum passenger train had set a Canadian rail speed record by racing toward Gananoque at 140 kilometres an hour. That record still stands.

We dodge under a coupler between some old wooden boxcars and there it is — a crimson-nosed dolphin with a long pale and pearly tail shimmering under the early morning overcast. Our inside man pulls a ring of keys from his jacket and unlocks the last car. We slip down through the cars, single file, two seats on the left, two on the right until we reach the engine fronting the train. In a few minutes the Pratt and Whitney Canada ST6 gas turbines are winding up. We all crowd into the control cab and Canada's fastest train ever slinks forward on its last run — some 200 feet — driven by a six-year-old.

2001

I think I remember how I met the pair of Italian Canadian guys in the shoe business. It was when my older son Jake called and persuaded me to drive him to a peeler bar out on the Queensway for the Miss Exotic World Universe competition. Jake has always had a refined sense of the ridiculous and I suspected that this event qualified. In spite of knowing deep down that this would be another of my "Bad Daddy" moments I agreed. We got in my minivan.

The room was packed but Jake found us a table right at the end of the long runway projecting out from the stage and the announcer's booth. The competition began.

The first dancer came out with a handful of radio-control remotes and distributed them to members of the audience. When her music began she started to remove her clothes while grinding around suggestively on the runway. Once she was down to a G string and heels she introduced a new element — a motorized dildo on four wheels. The idea was that while she languished on the stage guys in the audience would use the radio controls to pilot the rubber erection to the appropriate destination. She was always faster than the rolling radio-controlled stiffy. It was hard not to laugh.

The next act had a Mayan theme. Two life-sized pre-Columbian sculptures were wheeled out on dollies and set on each side of the runway. One never knows when one's background as a Mesoamerican archaeologist is going to come in handy. This was one of them, as I immediately recognized these figures as chacmools, the recumbent figures that are feature of the late classic Maya site Chichen Itza in the Yucatán. The original chacmools were carved in stone. They are male figures lying on their backs, knees drawn up with the upper torso supported on their elbows. The idol's heads are always turned at right angles to the body. They usually support a sacrificial bowl on their stomachs.

The chacmools at this event were cast in ice and cradled enormous erections instead of ceremonial bowls. As soon as the dancer emerged in her feathers and jade it was clear there were problems. The runway's hot lights made the erections drip and then droop. In a couple of minutes both hard-ons had crashed to the boards. The music stopped, the dance ceased and four burly guys came from backstage and reinstalled the boners. The dance and music resumed. As soon as the dancer shed her upper feathers the stiffys sagged and fell once again. The music stopped, the four guys reemerged, did the bodywork and vanished. When one of the erections finally rolled off the stage and disappeared into the crowd the dancer was disqualified.

Following this foolishness I left Jake and went to the men's room. At the end of the corridor I encountered a shoe display. It was amazing. Several dancers were picking through the racks of spike-heeled sandals, pumps and thigh-high lace-ups. The girls told me that a salesman came every month with samples of the latest exotic dancer styles. The shoes were lurid but very well made — beautiful leathers, double stitching with studs, chains and heels of solid brass. They were built to be comfortable for an eight-hour shift. And they were designed and crafted right here in Toronto.

I phoned the shoe company owners the next morning, explaining that I was a writer/photographer interested in doing a story about their business. They agreed.

A few days later I parked outside an industrial unit in the north end of the city. Inside I met Marino. He and his partner were each born in the Marche region on the Italian Adriatic coast. However they didn't meet until both attended a wedding in Wood-a-bridge-a just north of Toronto. Many towns and villages in the Marche are focused on shoemaking. Both partners had apprenticed there, one as a shoe production mechanic, the other as a designer. When business got slow there they had immigrated to Canada and found jobs with different local shoe companies. But when the recession hit at the end of the '80s both men lost their Toronto jobs.

They got talking at the wedding and agreed to explore a partnership. The economy was still weak so they had to find an unexploited niche. They eventually settled on the stripper and hooker sex worker market, leased a factory, bought equipment and hired staff. They soon found the market was bigger than they thought. Orders began to come in from New York for many of their styles but in men's sizes up to 14. Manhattan apparently had a lot of cross-dressers and queens. While in the plant I watched rows of old Italian ladies in black busily sewing chains onto enormous slutty shoes.

Marino invited me to join him for a few late nights at the plant. Once the ladies in black went home he would sit alone at a drafting board under florescent strip lights in the bleak front office and design whips and chains shoes while Verdi operas blasted out of the office stereo. It had proved to be a high stress, very competitive business. As soon as he released a new design to the local peeler bar circuit, spies from China would sweep up pairs and courier them overnight across the Pacific. Within 10 days precise copies would be back on the North American market. However they would be vinyl instead of leather, have breakable plastic heels and hurt your feet. But they were cheap so they sold. Thus Marino was under constant pressure to innovate.

Eventually they gave me a dozen sample pairs for the photo essay. While I had fun pairing the shoes with sliced fruit and certain vegetables in tabletop setups, I also wanted to make some photographs with live models. This proved to be a problem since most women don't like to admit they have big feet. Shoemakers cater to this by making all samples in size six. Buyers think they look better. I began furtively glancing at the feet of women friends and colleagues in the hope of finding someone with small feet. I was beginning to get a reputation as a foot fetishist. Eventually I got a well-known literary publisher and poet as well as a doctor friend to model. While they clearly had fun staggering around in the tarty crotch-high crimson-and-black numbers both swore me to secrecy. I mustn't show their faces.

Sworn to Secrecy

I started shopping the story and photographs around to magazine editors that I knew. It sold immediately. A few months later I sold it again. And then again. And again. Each time the publisher, fearing a feminist backlash, would get cold feet. To date I have been paid four times for that story and it still hasn't met a printing press. Its soles have yet to bump and grind across a page.

———

Morning coffee on the cabin stoop. A swirling in the pollen-streaked waters of my harbour lures me down to the shore to investigate short streams of large bubbles that erupt randomly around the bounded waters. Looking down I spot sex and a quarrel. Three male longnose gars are roiling with an enormous female as she scatters her eggs. This very public sex has riled a largemouth bass that is attempting to protect its nest and eggs in the shallows by the shore. The bass repeatedly attacks the tailfins of the gars who are too busy bonking to notice.

2015

Months later I step from my cabin into the incomprehensibly black October night. The brisk wind is warm, the sky shot through with a spray of white-hot stars. My younger son, Ben, has recently phoned and asked if I would go halves with him on a 10-inch Schmidt-Cassegrain telescope. "We'll keep it at the island, Dad. Everyone thinks it's nerdy but I think it's cool."

I have no memory of seriously discussing astronomy with him, of telling him about my long winter nights as a teenager walking a tight circle around a stool with a big glass disk glued to it, slowly over many months making my way through graded pots of jeweler's rouge as I ground it into a parabola to be silvered and mounted into a tube. I had built several astronomical telescopes with a friend. Now, through some sleight of genetics, Ben also wants to be awed by dark immensities.

1994

Ben has been bugging me for weeks to take him to an astronomy lecture at U of T's Hart House Theatre. One of those popular village explainers of science will be onstage revealing the dark infinite secrets of the universe. Ben really, really wants to go. In my needy quest for parenting points I finally buy the tickets by phone and we're all set.

Now Ben is a guy who worries about things. There was a period when he'd spent hours each day watching the Weather Channel so that he'd be the first to know if there was going to be an earthquake. Back when I was doing graduate work in anthropology, against the counsel of my advisors I insisted on taking a graduate course in geology. However, despite the fact that I had none of the science prerequisites and schedule conflicts prevented me from taking half the classes or any of the labs, I'd managed to squeak through a pass. This made me an expert. I repeatedly tried to reassure my son that southern Ontario was geologically quite stable — there was little danger of a Lake Ontario tsunami sweeping over Toronto Island to topple *La Tour CN Tower*. And any attempts by me to suggest that since seismic events traditionally were not part of weather systems, he might better get advance quake warnings from another source didn't make any difference: the Weather Channel was always on with Ben hunched anxiously before the flickering screen.

On lecture day Ben was dressed and ready to go hours ahead. I was too old, adult and dim to understand the urgency of getting to U of T several hours in advance. When I finally capitulated we arrived sufficiently early that a janitor had to admit us. The holy grail was a seat in the front row. We had no competition. The room was dark. As it gradually filled Ben repeatedly squirmed around in his seat to watch. When the auditorium reached capacity and Ben turned to me and announced in a gale-force stage-whisper,

"Dad! They've all got pocket protectors! Why didn't you warn me? The place is full of nerds!"

———

Rain has fallen now for three days. The new roof on my cabin has surrendered. Gray skies and the east wind have won, allowing a million tiny drops to make

their way through the cedar shakes, the asphalt sin-
gles, the weather membrane and the pine cladding to
drip on the counters, the big oak table and varnished
floor. In some places the water is spackled into bright
droplets, in others it forms glycerin tongues teasing
across the tabletop. I have learned a life lesson: never
build cupolas, they always leak, every single one in
all of history has leaked. Keep it simple.

2017

My architect son Ben has recently called me a couple of times.
He knows I'll soon be moving out of Toronto and he'd like to go
through the stock of my photographic prints in the basement.
This is a strategic advantage-taking of my need to downsize
for life in a condominium after the big house. He gives me his
criteria — no unmatted or unframed items, all pieces of my art
must be hang-ready. And while he's willing to bang nails into
the walls of his new condo himself, I'm also expected to provide
delivery. This is a requisite part of parenting. I accept his terms.

Ben arrives for his shopping trip accompanied by his partner, Sharon. They let me know how busy they are and quickly
descend to the basement storage. They're gone for a couple of
hours. When they finally emerge I ask them how it went. As
Ben puts on his coat he replies, "I'm sorry, Dad, we've decided
to go with another artist."

This morning when I boot up my laptop and check email I realize that Ben has sent a message the night before. Understanding
that I'm on duty for my two sons on a 24-hour, seven-day-a-
week shift — they're only 35 and 40 — I immediately write
Ben back. His reply takes a mere minute to reach me. "Too
late. Unreliable parenting."

FIFTEEN

THE DEAD AND THE NOT YET

"Don't get old. There's no future in it."
JERRY EVOY

*"Life's a tough proposition, and the first
hundred years are the hardest."*
WILSON MIZNER

"I have tried existing, and I do not like it."
AGNES MARTIN

New Year's, 2015

"Don't die on me, Dad." My elder son Jake is at the door,
departing for Pearson and Louisiana where he has been living
and teaching for the past year. We've spent the week together, his
first visit since he left for the States. Our shared times have been
the brief pauses between his visits to old friends, mostly ones
prefixed with "girl-." On his first morning here he'd descended,
tousle-haired and deeply dark around the eyes, inquiring as to
whether he had "missed the continental breakfast?" And at
what time would his laundry be picked up? Once each day we
wedged in time to have a drink together. He'd always been an
enthusiastic sampler of exotics from various microbreweries. A
year on the Gulf Coast has made him a drinker of Bud Light.
The crime and decline of continentalizing has set in. However
he does leave me with a half-pound of Slap Ya Mama Cajun
seasoning from Ville Platte, Louisiana, as an opinion reviser.
Then he's off for his plane. Despite my aversion to crossing the
U.S. border I promise a spring visit. He's gone.

This airport is under construction — there are temporary walls, barriers and closed corridors. I search for the Toronto check-in, very tired, as I've been trudging for several hours — going up and down curved ramps, taking stairs, escalators, elevators, running into dead-ends or doors too small to enter. People, intent, busy, rush by toward the end of their lives.

I remain lost. There are no arrows, no signs. I've long ago stopped lugging my bags having abandoned them on a ramp up to the roof. Even travelling light I still move in circles, occasionally passing a place I may recognize but I'm not always sure. So I continue to move with the current, letting the river of people carry me to where the planes will never arrive and never depart. This dream is a nightmare.

———

I'm drawn out of the cabin by a glass-rattling thunder. An enormous Hercules aircraft stampedes toward me a couple of hundred feet over the pines across the inlet. It lumbers ox-like out of the noon sun, advanced by a cruciform shadow that plows the waters before it. The sun is briefly eclipsed, my pines toss, then the huge aircraft vanishes into the northern woods trailing a long tail of black smoke. It is searching for a capsized vessel that is never found.

2014

Pat the Beggar

"Hello Michael, it's Pat the Beggar. How are your cats, Ziggy and Billy?" Patricia, the caller, is a big bag-and-cat lady that Sheila and I have known for more than a decade. Superficially she's what you'd expect — she wears several hats at once, various layered coats, sweaters and shirts and lugs an assortment of plastic bags containing, as far as I can tell, more plastic bags. She's a sight but one that's all too often invisible in a big city downtown. And she doesn't smell like a flower arrangement.

We give her money when she's desperate, I drive her and her stuff from one transient hotel to another when she's forced to yet again move and we chat with her on the phone when she's lonely or in crisis. Most years we take her out for lunch on her birthday. This can get tricky as numerous restaurants along Queen West where she begs and we live won't seat her. The hipster places are the least tolerant, donut shops the most. The best birthday lunches have been at the Free Times Café up on College where the staff always treat her with dignity and voluntarily produce a birthday cupcake with icing and a candle. She's big and can really pack food away. In recent years she's developed a taste for sushi.

Who is Patricia? She gives highly articulate accounts of her past. She's entertained royalty, has had lovers like Raymond Massey and John Lennon. There have been husbands. She knew Einstein and Freud. As a result of a past career as a painter she has pieces in the Louvre. When she had to initiate a lawsuit against her wrongdoers she was represented by her old pal Paul McCartney who was a lawyer before becoming a Beatle. When she was finally moved into a home following an extended hospital convalescence the matron of her floor told me that Pat was their very first resident theoretical physicist. This all sounds like a rich interior fantasy life but when you question her about her travels she's able to give very vivid and accurate descriptions. The small details couldn't come from movies or books. There would seem to be some real travel experience behind them.

Pat's dream has always been to move out of the home, get away from the shouting crazies, the disabled, the sad and lonely lives. She would announce that her inheritance had finally come through and she was moving into an apartment

339

of her own. Each move would go pear-shaped. There was no wheelchair access, her keys hadn't arrived, the public trustee wouldn't release her money. Pat was marooned again with a ranting roommate.

This past summer when Sheila called Pat's refuge to say she would drop in for a visit in a few hours the receptionist announced that Pat was dead. An online search revealed a three-sentence confirmation. Pat was gone.

Who was she?

One of the most consistent elements in her tale-telling was that she came from the Bear Island Reserve in Temagami. So far our enquiries, including one to a JP from the reserve, have revealed no friends and no family. It's as if she's never existed. But she did and for nearly 70 years. Three tall garment boxes from movers Tippet-Richardson still stand in our basement as testament. They contain all her worldly possessions. We've only peeked in one. It's stuffed with teddy bears.

2002

Joking Joe

I'm back at my table in the cabin picking away at what will become my memoir *The Molly Fire*. Both my parents have died within a few months of each other and I can't believe that they're gone. Every word I write is a stepping stone to my own understanding and acceptance. Little do I know that in a few short months my own heart will stop for 81 minutes while my chest is sawn open and new plumbing installed. I have four bypasses that are said to be good for 20 years. That warranty lapses five and half years later and in I go again. Ten days after that I'm back again in the cath labs at Toronto General for stents in my stents in my bypasses. As my gurney squeaks back into the operating theatre several nurses wave cheerily. "Nice to see you again. Have a nice day."

Now 10 years have passed since those 81 minutes. I hike and kayak but always listen when my body tells me to forget it and take a nap. Life is pretty good but the ever more frequent exits of old friends and colleagues are numbing. Many have left so fast there were no goodbyes. Today's breakfast news brightener is that an old work colleague, Joe Bodolai, has killed himself in L.A. He was 63. Last time I saw him he was still working in a Toronto art gallery but writing his first "funny," a country-and-western song "dedicated to all the good folks in Montevideo, Uruguay." He called the song "TV Mountain." After some successes in Canada, Joe tried to advance his career by attempting to scale the television comedy heights of California. It hadn't worked out so he'd taken comfort in the bottle and then finally death. Long after I'd lost touch with him I remember driving to Montreal listening to him on the radio describe how to fit legs to a coffee table book so that it would support your cup and saucer. It was stupid but it made me giggle in the car. When I hear that Joe had two sons, as do I, his death suddenly rears up in dark relief.

A Pair of Laurences

Margaret Laurence and I are jammed into a very tiny room down by the lake. She's smoking. I'm trying to do her portrait. She won't be photographed with a cigarette.

Each time I pick up the camera she lights up and asks me not to shoot. I wait until she finishes then reach for my camera. She reaches for her lighter. I'm totally frustrated.

Almost two decades later while working on a project for the Perimeter Institute with her daughter, Jocelyn, I describe my attempts to make a portrait of her mother. Jocelyn sighs and lights a Gauloise. I tell her how much I'd admired *The Stone Angel* when I first read it and how stunned I'd been some years later when, in response to a request from a well-known American writer friend curious about CanLit, I'd sent him a package of a half-dozen favourite Canadian novels. He'd loved Findlay's *The Wars* but found Laurence old fashioned and unreadable. Jocelyn lit another cigarette and told me that she and her brother used to anticipate Margaret's posthumous royalty cheques every year. However recently they'd gotten smaller and smaller and finally trickled to zero. Nobody bought her books anymore. She'd even fallen off university courses into the abyss of the forgotten that follows death. And now sadly, halfway through the 21st century's second decade, Jocelyn has followed her.

———

After a dusk arrival at the island I unpack, fill the fridge and drag my duffle into a bedroom. Those rituals complete, I pour a drink and open the door to the big screen porch by the water. It's become dark and cold.

Far across the inlet a single light flickers from the low fringe of bent pines separating invisible waters from the faint luminance of the sky. Beyond that I'm alone with the unseen sound of unquiet waters. It's fall — mid-October — so the world is unstable, unreliable, not to be trusted. It's transitioning from benign heat and sunshine to turbulence and the gray gods of winter. This small place on the great curve of the planet has only two witnesses — me and a single small light far across the inlet.

Macbeth

My old friend Macbeth has come down with me this time to Jamaica. It's his first time on the island even though we've known each other for over 40 years. We don't talk much now that we're old men whose friends are dead. On this trip I've twice thought he was too when I caught him on his back during the day, body stiff, mouth open, pale, scrawny and very still. But he wasn't. We pass in the hallway with few words and go off into separate corners to read. At midnight his room light is on, as is mine, while the rest of the house is dark. The night creatures shout outside the windows and something big huffs and roars; I'll never know what it is.

He's become an all-inclusive resort guy rather than the adventurer of his youth. He likes everything to be taken care of so he can concentrate on his creature comforts — booze, tobacco and lunch. Like a dog, he needs to be fed regularly and like a dog he'll hang around the periphery of the kitchen totally focused on the preparation of his next meal. Sometimes I expect him to dart into the room to wolf down dropped scraps. It seems to me that his world has become very small.

Jamaica and Brown's Town can be very intense. The market in the centre of town is like an ant colony until you engage a higgler and an individual quickly emerges. I don't think that Macbeth has seen that yet. He seems defensively withdrawn, almost stunned by this mountain town's frantic, African alienness. I can't seem to get him interested in the small local sights — the produce higglers' homemade carts with their wooden drag brakes and rebar steering wheels, the Westwood High School girls in their crisp jumpers and jaunty little straw hats or the wizened old Black ladies in huge hats and cat's-eye glasses. He just seems disengaged and stunned. When I take him out in my ancient right-hand-drive Toyota, rally-driving down the narrow, potholed mountain roads he says nothing until I pause and he declares that he'd like to go home. He needs a quiet drink, either coffee or neat gin on ice.

It's 7:30 in the morning and we're both sitting in the cage, the barred-off, roofed and tile-floored deck over the cistern at the back of the house. The new-day sun is dramatically spotlighting the dense plantings in the garden. A golden yellow croton suddenly glows in a beam of light against the dark greens behind. The magenta blossoms covering the tall bauhinia tree shine like Christmas lights and the poinsettias are intensifying as the milky dew burns off. The background of all of this is an 80-foot-tall guango tree. The still rising sun paints a shifting theatrical light rapidly across its many spreading limbs, making the big tree seem to advance and retreat with every passing minute. While all this showy chiaroscuro is unfolding hundreds of bright birds — streamertail hummers, todies, bananaquits, orioles, warblers, parrots, parulas and parakeets — flit, soar and flutter through the glossy trees and bushes. But Macbeth remains hunched in his plastic chair, head down in a magazine, coffee at his fingertips and a roll-your-own in his mouth. Everything beyond the bars is just background noise.

More than a quarter century ago Macbeth talked me into quitting tobacco. We were on the phone — he was out on his toy farm an hour north of the city and I in downtown Toronto. "Yup, that's over," he said. "Finished." This was a few days after another friend, sitting cross-legged in the middle of his sitting room carpet while grinding coffee by hand, looked up at me critically and said, "You still sucking on those things?" So I decided it was time to quit.

This wasn't so easy. I had been a small child in my grandparents' country house, a big Maxfield Parrish kind of place with fan windows, elaborate gardens and a handful of staff to keep it all going. Where did my grandfather get the money to run that huge place as well as a big Victorian just off the Avenue Road hill in downtown Toronto? Tobacco. He was president of a major Canadian cigarette company. He'd built the big country house in 1928 when everyone was smoking their way through the Depression. He did well. And I grew up in a cloud of smoke.

I was probably addicted to tobacco by the time I was five; however I managed to get on for years by occasionally bumming smokes, until I was 27 when I went to a store and finally bought my own pack. A loud voice in my head said, "Bad idea, jerk!" But I did it anyway and smoked for the next decade and a half until my buddies shamed me out of it.

I did it cold turkey and was miserably sick — dizziness, hot flashes, headaches and the runs — for almost a year. I was always desperate for a smoke and relief but simultaneously so horrified to witness how smoking had altered my body chemistry that there was no way I was going back. I eventually safely made it out. It was like reaching land after a long desperate swim.

A year after I quit Macbeth was back on the weed and has been ever since. He smokes his own rollies made with French papers and cheap pipe tobacco from a reserve. He uses the cap from a ballpoint stick pen as a cigarette holder. He and his wife have money so that's really just an affectation. The whole operation takes up tons of time and makes him stink. Someday soon it's going to kill him.

Puffing Peter

Three artists are crammed into a little basement studio in the old CBC building on Jarvis Street. We are trying to explain the seductiveness of photography to Peter Gzowski on his *Morningside* show. I had agreed to join the others because when he was really cooking the listener had the sense that for a couple of magical hours our enormous, empty country was held together by a shared curiosity, generosity and common goals. Canada was an endearing and worthy experiment. Through Peter we could all talk to each other across thousands of miles of bush, prairie and stone.

But today I'm having a hard time. My fellow photographers are being relentlessly conceptual and academic while

I'm trying to hold ground zero as a classic documentarian and purist. The table we sit around supports the largest and ugliest ashtray I've ever seen. And it's full. In case it's not quite at full capacity Gzowski has a couple more smokes on the go and a little stack of fresh packs at the ready. The air in this studio is so blue that my throat burns, my head pounds and I'm beginning to get chest pains. I desperately want to be out on Jarvis Street breathing fresh auto exhaust. As we stumble along I can see the producers sweating behind glass. None of us are on the same page and none listen. Gzowski finally allows that he's amazed that there are people who think so hard about photography. It's clear that he has not. It's like puzzling about blue sky.

———

It is now well past mid-August: I've never been alone on the island for so long. I sleep not in the cabin but in my favorite room — the big screened porch fronting the Bay. Waves break barely 10 feet away, air whispers through tall screens that admit all the songs and smells of the northern woods.

I dream vivid, visual, dreams peopled by all those who have floated my life — friends, colleagues, lovers, family. These dreams are so detailed and intense that they pull me back to consciousness, leaving me wide awake and watching a waxing moon throw confetti on the waters. Another two nights and it will be full and fabulous. So many people from my life have filled these dazzling nights of dreams that it's all beginning to feel like a long goodbye. Then the dream pops like a bubble and I'm suddenly back in the world, awake.

Eli

I've been to this Mount Pleasant Cemetery chapel too often in recent years. Today's funeral is for my ex-father-in-law's second wife. She has died just a year older than me. Her husband, a well-known professor of classical guitar, has been wheeled out of Baycrest, the big Jewish home for the aged, to attend this ceremony. He's in his 90s. He sleeps in his wheelchair.

The chapel event is run by a funeral host. Essentially an MC, it feels as if she graduated with a C from theatre school so she went into funerals. Her execution is trite and glib but professional. Once the chapel part of the event has concluded the family trudges across the street to surround a deep hole. Its depth is designed to accommodate her husband above her when his time comes. His younger daughter trundles him to the edge of the pit. He wakes up.

"Who are all of these people?" he asks.

"Family and friends attending the funeral," his daughter replies.

"This is a funeral?"

"Yes, Dad."

"Who died?"

"Your wife."

He falls back asleep.

Frenchie

By the beginning of the 1970s Rochdale College was a tower of lost souls. Conceived as a free university during the previous decade, the 22-storey residence on Toronto's Bloor West had quickly devolved into a crash-pad and HQ for the hippie homeless. If you were young and lost, it was where you went to get found.

In the fall of 1970 I had returned to Canada after a couple of years walking the deserts and thorn forests of southern Mexico.

Rochdale seemed the perfect place to regroup and recharge. I took what I thought was a simple job as a floor sweeper and toilet scrubber but within a few months I was co-managing the crew of some dozen or so misfits who mopped the elevator lobbies, vacuumed corridors, disinfected washrooms and shovelled garbage out the back door.

The biggest expenditure in my budget was not for garbage bags or urinal pucks but for fire doors. On Saturday nights the drug squad would kick in the entrance to the sixth-floor east wing on a search and first thing many Mondays I'd order and install a new one. Sometimes we'd also have to clean up after a weekend jumper.

Midweek we'd take City of Toronto health inspectors and their friends on an official tour of the communal washrooms. They came not so much to investigate infractions as to ogle the girls in the showers and observe men and women mingle in the same toilets. Other intruders from officialdom were much harder to please — the building department, the mortgage-holding CMHC and, as always, those bottom feeders of social order, the police. It all proved to be the most stressful job of my life. After doing my shift I'd often walk all the way home to Queen and Broadview just to unwind.

The men of this so-called maintenance department included a Tennessee draft dodger, a Regina runaway, a New Brunswick petty thief, various middle-class dropouts and an agitated and intense floor swabber named David French.

Most of the crew had mastered the dress code of the '60s — long hair, low-rise bell-bottoms, tie dye and clogs — perfectly. Not Frenchie. He had a short mustache rather than a beard. His jeans were too high-waisted, wide, straight and short. He was older and thicker than the rest of us who were all Jagger-thin. And he wasn't cool and relaxed.

While most of us drank, swore, fornicated and smoked anything that would burn, David demurred. Weekly we had an extended lunch hour so that most of the crew could cross Bloor to the Medical Arts Building and get their doses doctored.

David kept more to himself. He mopped his designated half-dozen floors of elevator lobbies, only occasionally joining the crew for morning coffee in Rochdale's street level café. Like several members of the department he wanted to be a writer but as the building was full of hapless hopefuls I don't think any of us took that too seriously. We were all in some smoky anteroom to the rest of our lives.

My relationship to David came to be based on several things. Since the two of us were the only crew-members who regularly talked books and had actually been published, we began to collaborate on certain linguistic experiments. Hippie brother and sisterhood was largely based on a vocabulary and phraseology that was so limited and generic that it always seemed that all were in agreement not only in their opposition to parents, conventional careers and the cops but also about pretty much everything else. If some stoner rode his chopper through the front doors, into the elevator and disappeared into the upper floors the loafers in the lobby would nod sagely when someone declared the biker was "out of sight." The crucial noun/verb/adjective/adverb in these pronouncements was always "fuck" as in "out of fucking sight."

In the Rochdale sub-dialect "fuck" was ubiquitous. Frenchie and I worked together to make it even more so. We would invent a new usage or insertion and then casually toss it out while swabbing the crowded ground floor lobby so that we could watch to see how long it would take to infect the patois of the entire building. "Far fucking out," "too fucking much" and "out of fucking sight" were soon superseded by stealthy infixes such as "fanfuckingtastic." Our linguistic innovations didn't always catch on but many spread like a virus and we both had a good giggle when they took. We even worked for some days on an attempt to infix fuck into fuck as in "fuckucking." But we never quite got one that worked.

The other thing that distinguished Frenchie was his passion for one woman. While everyone else was vigorously "free-loving" it, Frenchie only had eyes for a reedy blonde girl with a most beautiful face. He was completely obsessed and smitten with L. She, in turn, seemed to find his intensity a bit terrifying. If she left the building and walked off toward Yonge on the north side of Bloor, Frenchie would scoot along a little behind her on the south side, dodging from mailbox to newspaper box half-wanting to be discovered, half-craving invisibility. He was just crazy about her. While such obsessiveness is scary — it's like stalking — it can also be hard to resist. In the end he was successful and got the girl — for a while.

After months of Rochdale craziness during the winter of 1970–71, it began to warm up and spring finally arrived. Frenchie announced that he was going to quit and head out to PEI for the summer to try to write. As I recall he disappeared sometime in May and I hired a replacement.

Another member of the crew, RH, used to run a movie program on the second floor of Rochdale every Friday night. After one of his screenings RH, myself and Ralph Osborne, who'd moved on from maintenance to become general manager of the whole place, got to drinking and talking about the departed Frenchie. Around midnight it got decided that we should go visit him. Ralph phoned Wilf Pelletier of the Nishnawbi institute around the corner on Spadina and asked if we could borrow that aboriginal organization's Travelall van. In the spirit of the times, Wilf gave us the keys at one in the morning and we were off. We drove through the summer night, taking turns, and by lunch time Saturday were on the ferry dock on the Northumberland Strait. We crossed and a couple of hours later located the little farmhouse David was renting to write. L. was there as was her best girlfriend, a beautiful young Black woman from L.'s hometown, Regina. Those two women together, L. willowy, pale, blonde and blue eyed and her best friend deeply dark, angel-faced and voluptuous, were an unforgettable sight.

After we all went skinny-dipping on a north shore beach, RH, Ralphie and I were as obsessed with L.'s girlfriend as David was with L. We spent the night on the second floor of his rental house trying to seduce that Caribbean princess by whispering sweet nothings through the hot air heating ducts. Unlike Frenchie's success with L., we failed.

The following day we took off for the long drive back to Toronto and Bloor West. When David returned to the city some weeks down the road he failed to rejoin the crew. Instead we all joined him a few months later in the lobby of the Tarragon Theatre to see the first run of the play he'd written that summer in his little PEI farmhouse. *Leaving Home* was a hit. I had never seen Frenchie so happy.

Almost four decades and numerous Mercer family dramas have passed since that night. During those decades I'd see him perhaps once or twice a year. Some of those meetings were simply encounters on Bloor Street. It seemed he never really got that far away from Rochdale, he just hung out down toward where Bloor met Bathurst instead of where it crossed Spadina. Those encounters were usually just quick catch-ups but a few were something more.

One night in the early '80s we found ourselves at the same dull party in a new loft conversion of a tall industrial building on King Street East. Frenchie and I were catching up in a corner when suddenly one of the guests — a transplanted Jewish New Yorker with a therapy practice in Toronto — started to howl. The party went dead silent while this guy gave us a play by play as he watched Jesus Christ himself float in through the fifth floor window. I began to giggle but David stopped me. He was suddenly on high alert, concentrating on every detail of the moment, filing away the dialogue for future use. Becoming a photographer after leaving Rochdale had taught me how to see. That night Frenchie gave me an important lesson in how to listen.

Some of the subsequent encounters had a kind of sweet justice to them. David and I raised a glass together when Ralph Osborne, the former Rochdale manager, had a book launch at the Red Room on Spadina. One of the legions of would-be writers in Rochdale, Ralph had finally put bum to chair and began to publish books. The Red Room launch was for his second and it was all about Rochdale. Not long after that I published a memoir. Predictably I ran into David at Bloor and Brunswick. "That book of yours," said Frenchie, "is not bad. Actually it's really *fucking* good."

My last encounter with Frenchie was just a few months later on his well-walked section of Bloor West. I congratulated him on the revival by the Soulpepper company of *Leaving Home* and his other Mercer family dramas. "Yes," said Frenchie, grinning as he had on the opening night of *Leaving Home* so long ago, "my old plays are being performed again and this time they're all over the world." David died on December 4, 2010.

EL

"Hold my hand. I want to die right now."

I reach across the hospital bed and take hers. She begins to cough violently. For a few seconds I think that she might actually go but after several violent minutes she haltingly recovers.

"I just want my mum to come and hold me — tell me that it will be alright."

At the moment this wouldn't be easily arranged. She still hasn't even told her 96-year-old mother that she, her daughter, has been terminally ill for over a year.

EL was a tiny person with a big presence and an even larger life that almost beggars description. Physician, photographer, musician, restless searcher and, above all, traveller, she cut a jagged path through the lives of people in many parts of the planet. She did things that no other woman I've ever met would consider — travel the deserts of Mongolia a handful of times, most of them alone; hike by herself into the Atlas Mountains in winter to photograph rocks; sleep out in the great deserts of the American southwest; slurp soup in Kowloon; climb and shoot in the Himalayas and travel, travel, travel.

Like many of us she had trouble peeking out beyond her immediate life to comprehend the big picture. She loved nature, the Canadian North, remote mountains and deserts and the very rocks that anchor the continents. She travelled to them all many times seemingly without a thought to the enormous and destructive footprint generated by all her restless air travel. She was a small person who left a long shadow.

As I got to know her very well over the course of several decades I became intimate with her essential traumas — her childhood displacement from a room of her own when her brother was born and her subsequent night terrors sleeping alone by the courtyard woodpile in her family's Hong Kong compound. Later on when her engineer father left for Canada to prepare a family base in the New World she felt abandoned again. Even when established at last, he sent for the family a handful of years later she could never forgive his absence. Not surprisingly this coloured all her subsequent relations with men and probably contributed to the erosion of two marriages and relationships with various boyfriends. Her simmering pot often boiled over.

Numerous times after agreeing to meet her for lunch, the encounter, having begun affably enough, would degenerate into a shouting match as she began to broadcast, for all in the restaurant, my many crimes. I hadn't told her about a party to which I'd been invited. I'd recently had everyone but her up to my little island. I'd ignored her at some event. She'd missed a dinner. And so on. It mattered little to her that she'd usually missed these occasions because she'd once again been on the road in a distant country. It was still exclusion and abandonment, the great wound at the centre of her being.

These hurts became a loop that was always running and often made external dialogue difficult. You'd be attempting a short answer to her query when she'd suddenly interject, mid-sentence, with a remark that was totally off topic or inappropriate. She hadn't heard a word you'd uttered. Her running abandonment loop had blocked it.

I know that many friends wondered if she ever truly listened to her patients. Many complain that their doctors are poor listeners but with EL it must surely at times have been the case. When she withdrew from her working-class and immigrant practice in the outer reaches of the city she took on a downtown practice that was legendary for its difficulties. At its core were over a thousand lonely and angry, divorced Jewish women. They spent their time imagining pathologies, researching them on the internet and demanding their physician schedule endless tests for them. It was a plea for attention and caring but EL would have none of it. From her first month that practice began shrinking. Eventually hundreds of her patients stroked off for more sympathetic shores. Finally EL herself was encouraged to leave. She happily went back to the relative simplicities of suburban pregnancies and babies.

Why chose to be friends with such a person? Well, in many ways she chose you and kept in contact to nurture the relationship. She worked at it and could be incredibly generous while maintaining it. Unlike many women on a "date," she always insisted on paying her share if not footing the bill. If you could get her telling work tales she could be very funny about her practice and patients while always carefully protecting their anonymity. There was the huge and hairy trucker who liked rectal exams. Suspecting that a teen patient was pregnant she asked if she was sexually active. "Oh no! I just lie there." Many of them drove her crazy but she loved all the babies despite maintaining that she wasn't the mothering kind herself.

Her photography practice was conceptually and formally quite simple. She chose a theme — for years it was rocks — placed the subject in the centre of the frame and pressed the button. These photographs often seemed blocked to me. They had no foreground activity and backgrounds that were merely an unfocused fringe around the central subject, frequently a huge stone. These objects, whether natural or anthropogenically altered, filled the middle ground of her photographs, standing almost like policemen halting traffic. They were barriers to entry into the larger world. It became difficult not to see them as expressions of an emotional state. The continent and literal content may have changed but in an essential way she was always taking the same photograph. She was trying to get through a door that remained closed to the end. She was stuck in her loop.

It was only toward the end of her life that she began to include people in her pictures. In her African baobab photographs the figures beside those enormously inflated trees seemed to function as little more than measures of scale. In her late African pictures people posed rigidly in a short row, like the old slow-emulsion photographs in early geographic magazines. Real humanity only showed in the photographs of Mongolian nomads that she took late in her life. They were still centre-balanced and formally posed but they betrayed a certain reaching out and emotional identification with her subjects. They were nomads like her — always on the move.

While I do have one of her Mongolian pictures on my photo wall a family photograph that she sent me some years ago still fills me with wonder. It records her extended family in Hong Kong. She and her brother are in the front row, tiny figures dressed in traditional clothing. The old ladies, including her great grandmother, have bound feet. When she told me about it she described how her great-grandfather's concubine was allowed to join the family only after undergoing the public humiliation of approaching his house on her knees and asking permission of his wife. All these things gave EL a more intimate connection with an ancient past than many of us. We live in a land of forgetting.

A couple of years ago a persistent summer cough took the doctor to a doctor. There were tumours in her lungs. She was told she had a month. Further investigations identified the tumor type — a congenital one largely confined to Chinese women. The good news: there was a drug known to quickly shrink the tumors. You could even buy it at Shoppers Drug Mart. The bad news: it had never worked longer than 18 months. But she had bought time and hope. The drug did rapidly shrink the tumors and EL resumed her normal life. She began travelling again. She tried to practice medicine one day a week. She was going to beat it.

The 18-month mark came and went. The tumors began once again to grow. This time the drug cupboard was bare. She began to plan her last trips. She asked me to go with her to the Serengeti. Was she really serious about dragging her oxygen tank through the heat and dust of an African plain? It was crazy. I declined. The plan she finally settled on was a cross-Canada odyssey by train. Her niece signed on and arrangements were made for fresh oxygen to be delivered at stations along the way. She had worked in many parts of the country as a young doc and stayed in touch with colleagues scattered along the route. They came out to see her as she passed through. It happened: she was happy.

But when she returned the sky began to darken. Soon she was in Princess Margaret Hospital. She phoned me one day and ordered lunch. I took care to arrive at the Baldwin Street sushi joint she'd chosen well before noon to order her takeout.

The callow staff there were not very organized and had trouble interpreting her order. By the time they got it together half an hour later people were starting to arrive for lunch. The officious young woman running the place exited the kitchen and gave me back the order form. Now that they were busy they would do no takeout. They had no time for dying people. I was shown the door.

I finally got something close to what she wanted from a place nearby and made my way to her large hospital room that faced west over the city. The sun was pouring in and she had her main staples in her lap — white rice and noodles. She was happy. People began to come and visit.

One of them was a medical friend of mine that I'd introduced her to a few years earlier. He was now director of a cancer research facility. This made a bond. However, during his visit he casually mentioned that she was on the terminal floor. She hadn't known this and she wasn't going to take any of that shit. She certainly wasn't going to die or do chemo, the last resort. Many such patients were on her floor and she didn't want to ever look like them. Hell, she was a doctor. She checked herself out and went home. Serengeti crazy.

But she couldn't breathe on standard portable oxygen. She needed supersaturated. Back to the hospital and last-ditch chemo. It was brutal. Some day — it can't be too soon — poisoning tumours and the body by chemotherapy will be as crudely obsolete as trepanning and bloodletting. When I next went to see her at Toronto General Hospital she had shrunk like a mummy and was wearing a wig. The future was clear. There wasn't one.

As a physician she was no stranger to death and she faced her own without fear or complaint. In her nearly three score and ten she had lived several lives and always flat out. She'd extended each day by only sleeping four hours a night so that she could practice her cello or piano or edit her photographs before commuting to her patients. This pushing hard exacted its toll. She could fall asleep in her noodle bowl at one of her favourite Chinatown joints or in the middle of a noisy party. She had often shared her beloved brother's unused symphony tickets with me. I always kept an elbow at the ready to arrest her snoring two bars into the overture. She once lost her OR privileges because she fell asleep during an operation. She was perpetually exhausted.

By the time one has reached the three score and ten there have been many losses. At least half of my colleagues in photography are gone. I think of them all periodically. They'll suddenly come to mind at the most unexpected times. They are each missed but some weeks on I'm surprised at the space that her death has left in my life. Several times in the early days she asked me to marry her but I couldn't imagine being in such a relationship. More than once I swore I never wanted to see such a difficult woman again. Now I really wish I could. I can't believe that such a vital person is gone. She was a force.

———

The great clock and calendar that once sent these birds north and later south chimes no more. The cranes reach this inlet and fly no more. The geese have forgotten their Vs. The seasons turn to a different tune.

Jeremy

A photographer friend has just called with news of another death. Our years of lying to ourselves that 60 is the new 50, 70 the new 60, is catching up with us. None of us has seen Jeremy, a fellow photographer and spiritual searcher, for some years. And those years, like many before them, of his patient, craftsman-like master printing of black-and-white negatives, bare hands in the chemicals, breathing heavy metal vapours while compulsively chewing his blackened nails have rendered their due. Now we are gathered in an unctuous funeral home far out on Bloor West staring down at Jeremy in a padded box. No amount of makeup can disguise the leaden cancer look on his face.

I have always found the practice of open caskets barbaric — the body is not the person. This one is particularly discomforting. I turn to take in the précised survey of his work clumsily strung out around the viewing room — large format urban views, a series of Lake Ontario reduced to horizon and sky. One of his last shows had been an old series done in 1960s Montreal of a young woman named Suzanne, she of the "tea and oranges that came all the way from China." After an hour we slip out just before the service to try to resume the rhythm of our lives. It's our knowledge, subconscious and unspoken, that we're going to die that allows us to create what we do — in defiance of death. Otherwise we'd be like any other animal.

————

It's a spectacular morning with an uninflected blue sky. As the land's big granitic shoulders begin to heat, columns of rising air spiral up from the heat-sink rocks of the Shield. I can't see these vortices but a dozen circling turkey vultures are drawing them for me. Their gliding paths on the thermals reveal the invisible.

"Dave Heath, Photographer of Isolation, Dies at 85." *The New York Times*, July 1, 2016

"A haunted genius behind the camera Dave Heath: Photographer/teacher, 85." *The Globe and Mail*, July 23, 2016

"He's a creep!"

"No, he's a jerk."

"Well, David, I find him extremely creepy."

"The problem with you, Mitchell, is that you never use language precisely. The man is a jerk!"

"Creep!"

"Jerk!"

"Creep!"

"JERK!!"

Heath's face is turning red. He's shouting. I'm in trouble. For the next couple of minutes we yell at each other until I suddenly have a vision, a kind of mirrored infinite regress of three decades of arguments with David Heath about photography, photographers, movies, books and now an extremely creepy American lawyer, photo collector and aspiring photographer. It's all finally come down to whether this guy is a creep or a jerk. I can't help myself. I start to giggle. Heath flies into a rage. Heath is the most intense human being I'll ever know.

We first met in 1970. David had just arrived in Toronto to teach at Ryerson and I'd just made a big life decision to abandon a career in field anthropology to see if I could become a photographer and filmmaker. Dave Heath was to be one of my teachers. It clearly wasn't going to be easy.

No more tweedy, pipe-smoking academics supervising my Mexican doctoral thesis. No more predictable, anonymous hurdle jumping. Suddenly who I was as a person had become everything. Did I have any talent, any vision, any original ideas? This guy could read my photographs and tell me who I was — and what I wasn't. I had entered the program with a couple of degrees and the slimmest of portfolios. I'd swallowed my pride and enrolled at a mere polytechnical school after years at University of Toronto and UNC at Chapel Hill in North Carolina. I'd worked in Mexico alongside colleagues from University of Michigan, from Stanford and for an elite Mexican university. Now I was at "Ry High" and it was harder.

David taught me how much more a photograph could be than a mere formal statement. A great image could resonate down through the years, its meaning shifting to suit the times. Without question some of his did that. But this seeming facile medium was not generous. The lifetime work of the medium's greatest practitioners came down to perhaps a dozen memorable photographs each — at most. It was tough.

David wasn't always right. One of the earliest photographs that I brought to his class was one I'd made in a five and dime. In 1970 some of them still had a burger and soda bar down one side of the store. In those days the east end of Toronto was a working-class cultural backwater. The women behind the counter in my picture wore clothes and hair from the late 1940s. Heath launched into a technical attack, singling out areas of my print where I'd clumsily burned and dodged the image. I didn't have the courage to tell him that I'd only been photographing for six months prior to entering his class and I didn't have a clue what burning and dodging were. It was just a straight enlargement.

We got through it — two years. And then I left to try to survive taking pictures. I had the sinking feeling that nothing I ever did would meet Heath's standards. They were unobtainable.

Our paths continued to cross. I'd meet him at openings. We ended up on the same magazine editorial board. I organized an exhibition of his SX70 Polaroid work at a gallery I'd helped start at Harbourfront.

One evening in the late '80s David invited me over to his little house in Riverdale. We spent all night drinking liqueurs and going through boxes of his vintage prints. They were black-and-white masterpieces, virtuosic examples of burning and dodging, bleaching and toning and, above all, seeing. When I got up to go home he pulled a beautiful 1962 print of Allen Ginsberg and Barbara Morath in the old village's Seven Arts Café. He took a Rapidograph and carefully wrote a dedication on the border of the print. It's a stunning image. Many years later when he'd finally surrendered to digital photography he did the same with a colour image of the legendary photographer Robert Frank and artist June Leaf and gave it to me. The interesting thing about these images is that although made many decades apart, both have exactly the same formal structure. The later print substitutes Frank for Ginsberg and Leaf for Morath. I have a salon wall of photographs in my dining room that slowly changes as I acquire new images or tire of the old. The Heaths are always up there.

And despite the many tongue-lashings I got from him he could be very generous with praise when he felt you'd exceeded yourself. In the mid-'80s he unexpectedly phoned me to tell me he'd gone to see my Nicaragua exhibition and that it was a "beautiful show." He was also very generous in his praise of my *Molly Fire* book. I can't deny what those calls meant to me.

But the bumpy times weren't over. As the years slipped by David's belly got bigger and his scowl deepened. Gossip had him harassing his female students. He was said to have abused one and thrown another off his porch. There was a restraining order against him. Whereas he'd once turned up for any event related to photography he was now seen walking the streets less and less. Always a troubled man — he'd been an orphan — he became angrier and depressed.

In the early 2000s there was a period when various people would ask me if I'd seen Heath. What was he doing now that he'd been retired? I was curious myself so I decided to organize a dinner. It would be in David's honour. As the guest list expanded — there were fellow photographers, curators, professors — I realized that I couldn't cook for so many. I hired a chef with an assistant. I spent serious money. It would be my thank you to David who was feeling somewhat neglected and abandoned. Everybody came, a couple even flew in from Paris. The long table was beautiful, the food excellent, my Heaths were on the wall. At the end of the dinner I returned a book that I'd borrowed and failed to return some 35 years earlier. It was my little joke. He couldn't handle any of it.

Many months later he sent me a long email. He said that none of the people at the dinner cared a fig for him. That the evening had been the most embarrassing one of his life. That I'd done it all out of ego. This was all in the first couple of sentences. As I read it I thought, "Here we go again." Now I'm the one who can't deal with it — with him. Without reading the balance of the letter I pressed delete. I had crossed the transom at the end of a long corridor in the middle of my life.

Arnaud

He lies motionless, wrapped in a white sheet on a hospital bed. His eyes are closed.

I look down at Arnaud Maggs's body. It is frighteningly frail, incredibly pale.

Then he opens his eyes.

Recognizing me he whispers, "I love you, buddy." And asks me to turn him over.

I don't really know how to do this. I don't fully understand the nature of the cancer that's killing him. I mess it up. He screams in agony.

Arnaud and I had known each other for a very long time — decades. I don't even remember how or when we first met but we had definitely long ago become photo colleagues and good friends. As he came from a graphic design background he often had technical photo questions to which, in his mind, I would always have answers. I sometimes did. Also, he would occasionally call to borrow a wide-angle camera I owned in order to document his impeccable gallery installations of his work. The installations shared equal intention with his art.

That camera, a 1966 Hasselblad Superwide, had a very sharp lens plus fit and finish like a great Swiss watch. I'd bought it from Kryn Taconis, at the time the only Canadian member of the legendary photo agency Magnum. Kryn had several times lent it to Magnum's great master, Cartier-Bresson. I liked the idea of sharing a tool fingerprinted by so many giants of the medium. Arnaud was definitely one.

He mined a very narrow theme in his photography — comparative typologies. Initially he'd gotten interested in the shapes of people's heads. After trying to draw them he realized that photography would be a superior medium with which to document their form and a gridiron layout the best for comparatives. He remained true to this interest until the last year

Arnaud Maggs in his Toronto studio

of his life when he broke ranks with himself to masquerade as the great 19th century Parisian portrait photographer Félix Nadar's Pierrot. Arnaud's self-portraits as that master's clown were supremely beautiful pictures.

Another longtime friend, photographer Geoffrey James, used to speak of "keeping the faith." This meant believing in oneself and carrying on despite no support, no money, no response, no glory. Arnaud managed to do that. He'd had early financial success as a celebrity designer. He'd done famous jazz album covers and hobnobbed with the greats. He was profiled on society pages. Then he decided to become an artist.

That's when it got wobbly. "I'm living on air," he'd say on the phone as he called from his latest austere studio in yet another half-abandoned industrial building with no heat on weekends. "Nobody calls anymore." But he kept working. Kept the faith. I loved him for it.

"Michael, do you miss fucking?" Arnaud was 80 when he asked me this. I was just a pup in my 60s. There were so many assumptions peeking out behind the inquiry that I was still flipping through sticky index cards in my brain when Arnaud saved me a reply. "I just discovered Viagra." He smirked.

My family doc, who was almost my age, told me the year after Viagra became available that almost his entire downtown practice became writing scripts for guys who could no longer get it up. He'd had no idea what a huge and ubiquitous gender issue this was. I thought of all the years I'd listened to young women making disparaging cracks about men and their erections and then the same women decades later saying, in the wake of failed marriages and bored singledom, that they just wanted to get laid. Suddenly there were no guys to do it. Some women I know began seducing teenagers.

Arnaud's late life relationship with Spring Hurlbut, despite the decades that separated them, seemed to have been a happy and enduring one. They were both collectors of objects destined

365

for later elevation in their art-making. Having gone prospecting in a flea market in the south of France with them both I can report that it was conducted with near military precision. Arnaud especially worked the tables like a strategic campaign. Years of doing this had yielded many "Maggsian" treasures — collections of enameled steel water jugs, of three-dimensional letters, of funnels, diagrams, death notices. He had very high standards, all of his own creation.

A few years before he died he gave me the last oil lamp he'd saved from years of accumulating a vast range of examples. It was beautiful but lacked a glass chimney. Assuming that he hoped I'd use it at my cabin, a place he visited yearly, I set out to replace the missing part. As it required a non-standard diameter, this was no simple search. Many months later I finally found a fit at the big Mennonite hardware store in Kidron, Ohio. It was a straight glass cylinder with a global bulge a third of the way up that echoed the lamp's round oil reservoir. The following September when Arnaud encountered it at my island he made the stentorian announcement that he didn't like it. So the lamp now stands uselessly without a chimney. I wouldn't dare.

When I sold my last house I had a little money and bought a small motor-sailer. This funky little vessel had a beautiful sheer line, a vertical stem and an hourglass transom. Designed by one of the 20th century's greatest yacht designers, Canadian William Garden, it had been very well built in Collingwood. However, a previous owner had sullied the stern with a stupid name, *Minnow*, and some cartoonish graphics. As the river I travelled down to reach my island was crossed by a bridge that sheltered many swallow nests I renamed the boat after them. I asked Arnaud if he could do the type for *Swallow*'s transom. What he did was simple, original and very handsome.

In the end Arnaud triumphed. During his last couple of years he produced the strange and wonderful series of Dada

Arnaud Maggs and his lettering for *Swallow*

portraits based on a most unlikely source — antique French construction drawings. He had a radiant retrospective at the National Gallery, won a major prize, was published in his own monograph and starred with Spring in a wonderful documentary. Finally, he was vindicated. He'd kept the faith.

The last time I saw him he was wheelchair-bound in a beautiful hospice, a converted church, just off College Street. Eve Egoyan had come to play for Arnaud and the small group of friends surrounding him. She might have played some Bach and Satie, I don't precisely remember. Arnaud then asked if she could just play and improvise. She did. Later, driving me home — we're neighbours — Eve expressed regrets about her improv. For her it had been a mere pastiche. She was being professional but her music had put Arnaud at peace even though less than a handful of days remained. It was a generous act.

For a number of years Spring and Arnaud would join a

small late September gathering on my little Georgian Bay island. It is from those get-togethers that I have the most enduring image of him. Every year Arnaud and Spring would be up at first light and while others slept they'd launch my canoe and paddle into the morning mists. It was a photograph that I never took and never needed to. Unforgettable.

Mary

I don't really remember exactly how it all began. Mary and I would find each other in a corner during a party and end up talking all night. I'd known Marcus, her photographer husband, for many years. He and I had worked on several book projects with photographer Ed Burtynsky. So we were well acquainted but I was just getting to know Mary.

She was dying. Like all too many of my women friends, she was struggling with breast cancer. However, Mary's was truly running amok, metastasizing everywhere. She was very, very ill.

But she glowed like a ripe peach. She radiated energy, enthusiasm and even hope. She embraced a strong Buddhist faith, using it to help her cope with her increasingly bad hand. Mary was determined to maintain a quality of life and remain a productive artist right to the very end. We were both focused on the same question — how to live. But also on its corollary, how to die. We decided to make a film about the last year of her life.

Initially fate smiled on this voyage. I owned all the gear necessary to record and film her journey and Sheila had a sophisticated editing suite. Best of all, it turned out that we lived only two blocks apart in downtown Toronto. This was the most important element because it meant that whenever Mary had energy and felt like talking, she could phone me and I grab my camera bag and walk over. I could be there in under five minutes, crucial timing when her energy was at a premium and fugitive. I'd roll tape and she'd speak her mind and describe her journey.

At the time I had other friends — longtime ones — who

were also dying. They were angry, irritable, hostile, confused and fearful. They had shitty lives in their last months. Their lack of a good life ending made me sad. But Mary didn't. She worked hard at life, embracing whatever light and pleasure she could get from each moment and her friendships, even while her body was abandoning her. She was amazing.

Documentary films can cost serious money to make — hundreds of thousands. How were we going to finance this one? I'd long ago come to accept that my personal art-making time, my energy, my ideas and my skills were worth diddly-squat. I'd founded organizations, sat on arts boards and written books for free for years. And Sheila and I would work gratis on this one but materials had to be purchased and labs had to be paid. We began to approach various funding agencies.

In film this is a brutal process. The very important, wise and all-knowing, extremely powerful and impressive people in Ottawa want binders full of forms, plans, schedules, budgets and rationales. You even have to do their photocopying for them. Then they make their very predictable decisions and further the ordinary.

We decided to focus on TVO and the Ontario Film Development Corporation. Both have significant offices. At the time we applied to fund Mary about 60 other filmmakers also did. There was really only a slot for one. We made a short teaser, filled out pounds of paperwork and sent it in. *Mary, Mary, My Last Act of Love in the World* made it into the final three. We went into an impressive boardroom for an interview. A half-dozen organization people sat around a boardroom table asking questions. Finally one of them, a woman, asked where Mary's husband was in all of this. Our treatment and sample footage had focused almost entirely on Mary. Sheila and I explained that her personal journey was *the* story and we'd decided not to focus too much on Marcus because their struggle to get through all this — it had been the focus and challenge to their relationship for about a decade — was their private matter. Mary was our main story: she was the one who invited us into her life. Marcus was willing to go along with us and try to make the best of it. The commissioning producer at TVO finally said that if we'd build the film around the drama of their struggle as a couple facing death then they would give us the money. This, he said, would make better TV.

When I looked at Sheila I could tell by her eyes that she felt the same way I did. This man's idea was invasive, insensitive, even cruel. Their struggles after years of dealing with Mary's slow decline were theirs, not Sheila's and mine and certainly not the viewing public's. Mary's triumphant coping, her gathering wisdom and willingness to share what she was learning were what mattered. Her journey would help others. While Marcus certainly was there and important, it was Mary's thoughts and emotions that would be the primary message of the doc.

If that was our position, then our interrogators said they would give the money to somebody else. And they did so. We left with nothing in hand. Some months later I ran into that producer at a photography event and he began asking about Mary. He remembered every detail of our submission and recalled our footage vividly. Finally I inquired as to who had won the competition for funds and what their film was about. He stumbled. He couldn't remember either. That was a depressing moment.

Nevertheless we continued to make the film. When we got desperate a couple of times an old friend of mine, Michael S., stepped in and wrote the cheques that got us to the next step. Other friends in film donated time and their services. The project inched forward as Mary inched downwards. At times it got very intense as the end got closer and closer.

And there was subterfuge. Several times I had to sneak my large shoulder-mounted video camera into her room in palliative care when it was against rules. When the final summer came around Mary and I increasingly had sessions where we didn't film, we just talked and I kept her company. It was all she could deal with. Me too.

In mid-summer I filmed a birthday party in Trinity Bellwoods Park that the entire Pocock family held for both Mary and her sister Kate. Mary's many sisters and brother flew in from Europe, the U.S. and Ottawa. Despite Mary's dim prognosis the event was joyous. It was a very beautiful day despite omens. That party is part of the film.

Not many days later my younger son, Ben, called and asked if Sheila and I could drive my van to Montreal where he was living and help him move. As distance had kept us apart for some years I readily agreed. We drove down and began hauling his stuff from storage in the north end of the city. It was pretty hard work.

After a day or so I began feeling an unease. I think that Sheila and I both did. I talked to Marcus by phone. The situation was getting critical. We quickly wound up the move and set off on the long Toronto drive. We got in very late.

Early the next morning the phone rang. It was Marcus. Mary was in critical care. Her lungs were filled with tumours. She was struggling to breathe. If we wanted to say goodbye we'd better get over there. We dressed, made coffee and set out. We were too late.

Now this was all wrong. Mary and I had still more plans for the film. Its arc was not finished. I didn't know what to do. Our intimate filming sessions were over. Forever.

This was where Sheila really stepped in. She went down into our basement editing suite and sat there alone for days, weeks and months, cutting all the footage I'd shot. Several times she needed to start all over again. She did. And the film I'd been unable to finish began to take shape. She saw it through to the end when I no longer could. She did a wonderful job. The movie is now out there and it moves people but it's been a very hard sell. Nobody likes to witness death unless it's in Hollywood.

A couple of years ago Sheila and I went to a lecture at the City of Toronto Archives during Black History Month. When one of the speakers related the story of Toronto's first Black postman I remembered that somewhere in my vast basement studio archive was a beautiful little crimson box of Kodak Canada Royal Dry plates. They were century-old glass negatives of that Black postman's funeral. He lay in state in an open coffin surrounded by large floral offerings from various organizations. I told the archivist and asked if the city would be interested in a donation.

It is not easy to give something away to most institutions. I'd once offered Ryerson's film and photography department a dozen or so signed vintage Karsh portraits that a colleague had salvaged when *Saturday Night* magazine trashed its archives. They were fascinating because they held all the crop-marks and stamps from all their appearances in print. Ryerson's curator said they weren't in their mandate. They only collected (American) masterpieces. I'd once offered the Art Gallery of Ontario a 45-print set of elaborate little 17-colour silkscreens by the Group of Seven. They were all mounted in mats that had been handmade by A.J. Casson for my grandfather. He'd known all the Group members and had at one point employed Casson. The prints were a make-work project printed by Sampson Mathews to help artists survive the Depression. The AGO's curator of prints and drawings rejected them because the Group had silkscreened their signatures onto the pieces. Therefore they weren't art. In both cases the pictures got sold to private collectors. Stupid.

It took the city months to come around and have a look at

the glass negatives. They took them away and some months later announced that they weren't records of what I said they were. Before I got around to taking them back they informed me that they'd like to have them anyway. I suggested that if someone made enlargements from the plates or examined them with a magnifier, the type on the ribbons securing all the funeral wreaths would identify both the date and the dead. Months later the archives got back to me. I guess that someone had finally done just that. The plates in the box were indeed what I had said they were.

All this is to remind us that photography was once a mortuary art.

2017

Reeves

John Reeves, portrait photographer, drinker and, above all, marathon talker is gone. When his favourite watering hole, the Waterfront Tennis Club, was closed down by the city's development ambitions, John moved his monologue down to the Keating Pub where the Don River awkwardly elbows into Toronto Harbour at Cherry Street. It was the perfect site for his memorial service.

I drove in late that day from Hamilton, found the last parking spot and entered the bar. The moment I slipped into the hushed room I realized that I was in the wrong place or had missed the right day: the place was full of gray, balding men and faded flowers. However, within a few seconds I began to recognize faces. Once again I had forgotten that I too was old. His people were my peers. John was dead as were many of his sitters like Leonard Cohen. We survivors were at yet another rehearsal for our own exits.

2011

Overcoat

He sits at his command post in the kitchen with his oxygen tank beside him on the floor. From this high extension of the kitchen counter Charles Oberdorf can see down the hall to the front door. To his right he can supervise his dining room while behind him glass doors give on to a small deck before his beloved garden that ends in a deep cut hiding the Yonge Street subway. Once a globe-circling travel writer, his whole world has shrunk to this little outpost in a corner of his North Toronto house. He has emphysema. It will kill him.

We used to share a studio and smoked together. He was a pack-a-paragraph writer and I was a pack-a-picture photographer. I managed to quit. He didn't until the damage was already evident. As he'd started much earlier than me and was also older, his tobacco career was considerably longer than mine. Also, he really knew how to inhale — deeply. I was an amateur.

Although we largely worked independently, we did collaborate a handful of times to create magazine stories. He was already a well-known journalist and editor when he sublet a writing room in my studio on Downtown Toronto's Queen Street East. As I was just beginning to establish myself as a freelance photographer, I was barely earning a living and spending much of what I made on equipment. In those days you needed cameras in various formats and various prime lenses for each of them as contemporaneous zoom lenses were still drawn out on paper and weren't very good. Since the cameras were mechanical and prone to break down, one had to have at least a second body in each format for backup. Film stocks were slow so you needed lighting gear, both hot lights and strobes, as well as a darkroom to process film and make prints for publication. All this was a big investment. The few hundred thousand I spent in those first years gave me tools

374

that last year fetched less than $10,000 at auction. It's all now obsolete. Today's freelancer can get going with a single camera body, a couple of zooms and a laptop.

Hence I was quite willing to pose as the hot woman across the table when Oberdorf did restaurant reviews for newspapers and *Toronto Life*. He was still single in those days and I was hungry. My only obligation was to order a different dish than he did and pay close attention to what I ate and give a critique. I remember on our first "date" I had to ask what crudités were. After a couple of years of this cross-eating I got quite sophisticated about classic dishes. We had some laughs and a few disasters.

Sometimes a review produced a regrettable outcome. By accident I'd found a pizza joint way out on the Danforth that made amazing pizzas. The immigrant guy who opened it was fanatical about quality. Prior to opening his dream restaurant he'd spent an entire year driving all over North America eating pizzas and talking to their makers. He had thrown everything he'd learned into his creations and every cent he had into buying the best ovens.

This had left him with no capital to renovate his leased storefront. So he'd opened his pizza palace with the previous tenant's lurid erotic murals still on the walls. It looked like a whorehouse. Our review celebrated not only the food but also the Freudian excesses cavorting on the walls. The publisher loved it and so did the readers. A couple of days after publication the pizza guy phoned us in a panic. His phone was ringing constantly. People wanted to make reservations. He couldn't cope.

His new customers from Playter Estates and Rosedale would order their pizzas and snigger at the artwork while they waited. He felt ashamed so after 10 days of exhausting work he decided he had to renovate. He borrowed money and put a sign in the window. The renovation took weeks. When he reopened, ready at last for his new clientele, they'd moved on to the next review and several after that. Toronto's still the same. He went bust.

We also did some travel pieces. When we did a piece on Mardi Gras the U.S. Travel Service put us up in a grand hotel in the Vieux Carré. We arrived tired and hungry. After leaving our bags with the porter we headed for the dining room. No jackets, no ties — they wouldn't let us in. Defeated we took the elevator up to our room. A well-dressed guy in a pinstriped three-piece rode up with us. Still thinking about my stomach I asked him if I could borrow his suit and tie so I could eat. He stiffly refused my feeble joke then exited on our floor and vanished down the hall.

When we got into our room the phone rang. Three-piece pinstripe was on the phone. "I won't lend you my clothes but I will take you guys out on the town for dinner." After we accepted we discovered that he was a corporate lawyer for a huge aluminum corporation. As we walked together to his restaurant we found out more about him. Although he lived in the Southwest he'd grown up in New Orleans and knew his way around. When he found out why we were visiting from our northern icebox he stopped in the middle of the street and said, "What you guys gotta understand about New Orleans is that she's a grand old lady with really dirty underwear."

At his great Cajun seafood restaurant I asked him about his job. There was an enormous pile of aluminum ingots sitting in a parking lot out in the desert. This valuable heap was the subject of an ownership dispute. Our new friend's entire decades-long career had been focused on this one case. As a matter of fact his was the third generation of lawyers fighting to recover this treasure.

"What do you call that kind of work?" I asked.

"Rolling the turd."

Returning much later to our hotel we stepped out of the elevator to a hallway full of screaming girls. Fonzie, a sitcom actor named Henry Winkler, was in the room next to ours.

One day Charles called me to say he'd been asked to do a travel story on Mexico. Since I'd lived and worked there he wanted me to partner on the piece. A self-described piazza man, he had an aversion to any developing-world location. He'd once flown to Africa for a travel piece. When he stepped out of his plane into a hot weird world of Black people and funny trees he immediately turned around and flew back to Toronto. Although he'd lived in Toronto for years he remained, fundamentally, an American. He never did take out citizenship and every time he returned from some exotic locale he'd rush off to the McDonald's at Yonge and Dundas to eat a hamburger and get grounded.

So naturally I suggested that we do a piece on my old hometown of Oaxaca in southwestern Mexico. I knew it well and could tour guide and provide local dirt. On this trip I made some myself. On Oaxaca's main square I ran into a stripper from Shanghai on holiday. Lily was clomping around this little conservative Catholic city in her stage outfits. Since she was having trouble connecting with locals she asked if she could join us on our tour. Before Charles could open his mouth, which was already open, I said yes.

She proved to be a lot of fun. Totally innocent of any education but that of life, she was full of curiosity and absorbed every boring archeological lecture I gave Charles and asked challenging questions. She travelled with us all the way to the Pacific coast, at that time a 10-hour switchback odyssey over the coastal sierra. Inevitably we ended up bonking on a remote beach near Puerto Escondido. We later discovered we'd had a supportive audience of a half-dozen *campesinos* on horseback.

Our Mexican travel story was published in an august Canadian magazine during the late '70s. Once it was on the stands we got a note from the Mexican consulate. It pointed out that Mexico's Ministry of Tourism sponsored a prize every year for the best piece of international journalism about Mexico. It was a huge competition. They thought we should submit our piece. We ignored it. A few weeks later a second letter arrived. Same thing.

One day when my wife, Annick, was visiting the studio she discovered the second letter on Charles's desk.

"Have you acted on this?

"Nope."

"Stupid!"

She tore out the article, filed out the form and mailed it.

A few weeks later we got a registered letter. An international jury of eminent journalism professors has chosen our piece as one of the three best in a field of 450 entries from all over the U.S., Europe, the Far East and Australia. Our presence was requested at a dinner in Acapulco a month hence.

We ignored it. We had no money that spring and no way to get there.

The Mexican consulate called and told us to show up at Pearson on a certain day. I'd looked up Aero Mexico flight schedules for that day. There weren't any. As I was overly familiar with the fragility of Mexican arrangements I expressed my concerns to Charles when we were in the airport cab. Did he have any money? I had only $25 Canadian cash. It turned out he was almost twice as rich as me. He had $48. Neither of us had a credit card. We were fucked.

After much bluffing and temporizing at the Mexican check-in desk we were led down a back corridor and onto the tarmac. Mexico had sent a DC8 to Toronto to pick us up. We were the only passengers in a 200-seat aircraft. I sat in the cockpit playing cards with the pilots the whole way down. We burned $3,600 worth of fuel — American.

Mexico. Nobody met us at the airport to tell us where to go. After many phone calls we reached someone who told us to take a cab to a beach hotel south of Acapulco. The Princess proved to be a gigantic concrete "Aztec" pyramid that towered over an otherwise undeveloped beach. Nobody expected us at check-in. More phone calls. Finally we were ushered into a vast penthouse suite.

Now I was really getting nervous. We started to charge stuff to the room — meals, sunscreen, a bathing suit each, booze and cigarettes. How were we going to pay for all of this if we remained persons unknown? I knew something about Mexican jails. On our third day we got a message from the Ministry of Tourism. Be sure to show up in a week's time at the Acapulco convention centre for dinner. In the meantime just charge whatever we wanted to the room. Go crazy. We did.

I chartered a boat and went way offshore to scuba dive in a reef. I'd lots of experience snorkelling in Mexico but no diving instruction or certification. My boat guys used the air tank nozzles to open our beers. When you suited up to dive the tanks and regulators leaked like soda fountains. When I got down 50 feet I suddenly ran out of air so I decided to go parachuting instead. I went up in a light plane, struggled into a parachute harness and jumped out. It actually opened but the groin straps nearly severed my thighs. The next day we rented a car and drove inland to Taxco, the silver city way up in the mountains. Driving back in the dark via a lonely mountain road we hit a bonfire roadblock. As soon as I stopped some guys appeared out of the gloom and stuck pistols to our heads.

I babbled away in my back-country Spanish telling them we were special guests of Miquel A., the Minister of Tourism, and if they didn't let us go with our silver and sombreros the entire Mexican army, backed by the Princess Patricia light infantry, would suddenly materialize and kick the shit out of them. After a conference in the ditch they put out the fire and waved us on.

Charles was beginning to regret having teamed up with me. I got grounded. He insisted that from then on he would be in charge of our activities. They proved to be a Mexicanized version of his famous piazza man routine. We sat all day on

Charles Oberdorf

underwater stools at a swim-to bar trying not to swallow the
paper parasols floating in our pink drinks. I wore out the bums
of two bathing suits by sliding repeatedly down concrete water
slides to reach other bars. I started to put on weight.

When the big day came we cabbed to the convention centre
and waddled in. Dinner was set for 3,500 guests — tourism
people from all over the globe. For the very first time we were

actually expected, welcomed and led to one of three tables by the lip of the big stage. One had a flag that said *National Geographic*. Another one said *Sports Illustrated*. Both big round tables were ringed with publishers, editors, circulation managers, publicists. Even the legendary Grosvenors were there.

Then there was the third enormous circular table. It had a hand-lettered sign naming our magazine and a score of seats for Charles and me to sit on. We looked so pathetic at our lonely table that the Grosvenors invited us over to theirs. We brought our own chairs.

Dessert after dinner was the announcement of the winners. Third place: *National Geographic*. There was some irritated shifting at our table. Second place: *Sports Illustrated* — more awkward shifting. Grand prize winner: Charles went up to represent both of us. So we left Mexico having had a deluxe 10-day holiday with a thousand bucks (U.S.) each in our pockets and an incredibly ugly two-foot-high silver trophy.

Halfway back to Toronto Charles turned to me and said, "You know, Mitch, since the story was your idea and you did all the driving and provided all the information I think that the trophy properly belongs to you." He then took the monstrosity which had been restricting his legroom and made it affect mine. However, when the approach to Pearson was finally announced he turned to me with irritation and announced that since he was the real professional travel writer and I was just a photographer, the trophy was really his. He leaned over and extracted the prize from my crotch.

In the immigration and customs lineup an officer spotted the big trophy, examined it and announced that since it was 99.9% pure silver Charles owed a whack of duty. Charles immediately dumped the monster in my lap and declared me to be the true owner — he'd just been helping me out with luggage. His name was on it so I declined ownership and to this very day it sits, heavily oxidized, in his old office. It is accompanied by a second

In 2013 I returned to Oaxaca after an absence of 36 years. While photographing students during preparations for Day of the Dead celebrations I suddenly realized that I was recording the children of couples I had watched courting every evening in Oaxaca's main square during the late 1960s.

iteration of the same prize, as we won it again a few years later for a piece I dictated on the Maya in the Yucatán. Now you know that there's big money in archaeology.

Now I don't want to leave you with the notion that Charles was a piker. He was usually very generous and taught me much. Listening to him do his assignments I learned how to work the phones, how to find people and how to find out about . . . He was a real pro.

After stints editing various magazines Charles retreated to the Valhalla of exhausted freelancers — college teaching. He was very good at it and persisted even after emphysema stuck its ugly head out the closet. He'd wheel his oxygen tank into classrooms and deliver his lecture between gasps for air. It was heroic and taught one the true value of the ordinary, small things in daily life.

Bill & Billy

My cat Billy has a secret. Actually he has a number of secrets. He's never told me where he came from or how he came to live with my friend Bill the Human. And I don't know exactly when feline Bill joined forces with Bill the Human. Moreover I have no clue if Bill the Human named him after himself or if Bill came into Bill's world as Bill fully formed. The feline Billy may have been an avatar and may now be a duppy, a manifestation of Bill the Human's spirit because the bigger of the two Bills is now dead.

They looked alike: both were stocky, thick limbed and friendly faced. Both liked girls and eating. Neither asked too much of the world: they accepted their small part in it and its many disappointments without complaint. The main area in which they diverged was sartorial. Bill the Human was one of those guys who was always rumpled and disheveled — his fashion sense was indeterminate. But Bill the Cat always wore a tux — by day, by night, even on weekends and holidays. Feline Bill was a sharp dresser although I did take exception to his insistence on white socks with formal wear.

They also diverged somewhat on the subject of possessions.

Stuff stuck to human Bill. He had many expensive tools — the full set of Snap-On wrenches and drivers, for example. He had dubious taste in music but loved good sound so he owned racks of exotic McIntosh preamps, amplifiers and receivers. He loved vacuum tubes and reel-to-reel tape decks. He had once loved Ducati motorcycles to the point where he bought a dealership so that he could possess many of them. He quickly bankrupted it and lost his house along with his steady girl. These were things that just happened along life's trail. He didn't dwell on them or complain. They just happened.

On the other hand Bill the Cat merely owns a cardboard scratch box that he has converted into a bed. He also owns a stuffed white Ikea rat and has recently acquired a stuffed panda named Lin Lin from the Toronto Zoo. He tosses both rat and panda into the air and likes to bat the rat across our tasteful designer-gray hardwood floors. The rat skids from living room to dining room and down the hall with Bill in hot pursuit. He calls bouts of this activity "the rat race" and has to sleep afterward. Most importantly, Bill owns a bowl that says "CAT" in caps. It's decorated with multi-coloured fish skeletons. Bill loves it, especially when it's full. Like Bill the Human, he used to have a girlfriend, a big soft angora sweater that he liked to bonk. But he lost her when we moved. I can take credit for all these things because I bought all of them for him. He's very happy with his few possessions but would like me to buy him another soft sweater. Despite this one deficiency he's basically a happy cat.

However, Bill the Human was a bit of a sad case. He came from a family that grew rich in the 19th century logging and lumber business. They had a huge multi-storey head office building with their name carved in stone right on Yonge Street downtown. But the family got tired. Human Bill kind of drifted from job to job and place to place never quite finding himself although I don't think he ever looked very hard.

When I first met him over a quarter century ago he was working as a yacht broker. In fact he was the only yacht broker in southern Ontario who would talk to me. I was in the fortunate position of walking around with a bunch of cash I wanted to spend on a boat at a time when there'd been a big recession and the Great Lakes were lined with large locked yards full of repossessed yachts. You could buy anything for 25 cents on the dollar. Since I didn't wear a captain's hat or blue blazer, didn't look like a commodore or drive a Mercedes, the majority of yacht salesmen pegged me as a keel kicker — a dreamer, another loser. So I bought my yacht from Bill. We became friends.

Bill and I would get together for lunch several times a year and shoot the shit. Bill always ate huge hamburgers with greasy chips and drank several pints of Guinness. When the yacht broking business got very slow he became a boat service guy — work that was seasonal and marginal. He ended up living in a basement out in the Beaches. His little apartment was chaotic. There were tools and toys everywhere along with Carrara marble statuary that his family had bought in Europe for the family mansion during the Gilded Age. Now those white fauns and fops lived with Bill in a basement in the Beaches.

One day Bill woke up in his subterranean lair and discovered that he couldn't move. He'd had a stroke. He managed to call an upstairs neighbour who got him to a hospital where he partially recovered. Not long after this Bill had a stroke of luck — sort of. His mother died in Calgary and left her sons and daughter a bunch of money.

Donny the architect, another friend of Bill's, knowing that Bill was no banker, insisted that he spend some of his inheritance on a condo so he'd always be housed. He helped Bill find a nice top floor unit in a nice building on a nice part of Queen Street in the nice Beaches. Bill moved in with all his stuff and then complicated things by getting a cat. She was some sort of expensive exotic from Southeast Asia — lively, smart and very loud. This tiny cat got into all sorts of trouble. She opened boxes, jars and cupboards, adding her chaos to Bill's. Bill claimed that she even opened the condo fire doors.

Whenever I went to visit Bill I'd buzz him from the ground floor entrance and he'd shuffle down to let me in. We'd take the elevator to the top floor and each time we stepped out the cat would be waiting for us in the elevator lobby. And each time Bill would swear that he'd locked her in his unit. As he was not quite running on all cylinders since his stroke, I always assumed that Bill had been forgetful. That is until one day we ran a test. When the cat was sleeping in the front bedroom Bill and I announced that we were leaving. Bill left the unit but I didn't and concealed myself in the little condo kitchen that was right beside the entrance door. After that door closed behind Bill that little cat came streaking down the hall, scrambled up a tall bookcase and leaped off it catching the lever handle of the fire exit door. Despite her featherweight she had enough momentum to release the lock. She then darted into the hall. Despite being only a V7, Bill was right.

This condo period was a scary time for Donny and me. We seemed to be his only friends so he called us whenever he needed things done or documents signed. We were both uneasy when Bill needed our support to get his driver's licence back. In the end his doctor signed for him and he began to drive his big van again. He regularly sideswiped power poles and columns in his underground garage.

Donny and I got really nervous when Bill became fascinated with guns. He started ordering fancy long rifles, the kind with lots of engraving and exotic wood stocks. He asked both of us to sign as witnesses when he applied for a gun license. This was very uncomfortable for both Donny and me. We didn't trust Bill with a gun; he was forgetful and at times confused. However, his passion was, on some levels, clearly good for him. His obsessive research on guns helped him recover his reading skills. And taking apart and reassembling all those complicated mechanisms was helping his brain recover and tuning his small motor skills. Besides we couldn't get him interested in anything else except his raucous little cat. So we both signed but with a caveat. He had to join a gun club, get proper training and only shoot on their ranges and under supervision. He kept his word.

Then one winter Bill decided he was interested in yachts again and was going to drive from Toronto to Florida for the annual Miami Boat Show. He didn't tell anyone of this plan. He just hobbled into his van, scraped his way out of the underground garage and took off — alone. Before leaving he'd calculated how far he'd get the first day and pre-booked a hotel room just off the interstate in northern Tennessee. He managed to talk his way across the border and arrived in Tennessee late that first night. When he spotted his hotel glowing on a hilltop west of the highway he took an exit ramp up the hill. As he got to the top he realized that the exit he'd taken didn't actually lead to his hotel so he pulled over to call the desk for directions. The cell reception wasn't very good so he opened the car door and got out. He had to lean on the door because his left leg had still not recovered from the stroke and was gimpy. He got through to the desk but as he was talking the van began to roll back down the hill. He'd forgotten to set the brake and put the van into park. As the van picked up speed Bill struggled to get back inside but his gimpy leg wouldn't let him. He got slowly crushed between his car door and a lamppost while gasping to the desk clerk. Bill died.

I hated Bill's funeral back in Toronto. His siblings came out from Calgary and each used their 15 minutes to tell stories about what an idiot Bill had been — the yacht he'd lost, the failed Ducati dealership and relationships, as well as his inept financials. By this time he'd lost his condo and car and was living in a low-rent tower on the Danforth, one where new immigrants went to begin their new lives. Depressing.

A few days after the funeral his brothers showed up at our place with two cat boxes. Two?! Before returning to Calgary they were going to put me in charge of Bill's cats. Cats?!? This was the first time I met Billy. Where the hell had he come from?

As I already had my cat Ziggy, having a second and a third cat proved overwhelming. That little girl began to raise hell at Sheila's and my place just as she had at Bill the Human's. Meanwhile the other Bill hid for six weeks under the claw-foot bathtub on our second floor. I suspect that little smarty-pants cat knew she was driving us crazy because when friends from the country dropped by she snuggled with each one of them and then curled up in a cat carrier and waited to be transported to their farm. That little squawker never even said goodbye.

Up at the farm she bolted out the front door and got eaten by a coyote. So she's gone, Bill the Human is gone, but Tuxedo Bill sits beside me as I write this story. He's proved to be a wonderful cat. He pays close attention to both of us, tries very hard to be good and to make us laugh. He does roll-overs and somersaults upon request. And he reminds me of the other Bill every single day.

Dougie

Photographers tend to be collectors. Most people travel through life experiencing the world in successive moments — moving on to the next and the next — remembering some, barely noticing others, acting, intending, moving on. Photographers, however, stop to concentrate, preserve and collect certain of those moments. This is how they connect to the planet, its inhabitants and the stream of time.

After a working life of image-making, some photographers finally put down their cameras and just *are* in the world. Some forsake images for objects. The great American photographer of Depression-era America, Walker Evans, after years of documenting commercial signs plastered on the barns and fences of the rural South, devoted his last years to prying real signs off walls and spiriting them home for his own private enjoyment. Why have a mere picture when one could have the real thing?

Doug Clark was the quintessential collecting photographer. His successive studios were treasure troves of signage, machine parts, molds, toys, goofy objects and 19th century photographs. He loved all that stuff. His things taught him how to see and, in the last decade or so of his life, much of it became the stuff of his own photographs. The constructed photographs of his *Gio* and *Articles of Faith* series are full of those objects. They are there not to be just what they are but also to become part of a larger private message, a projection of what it was like to be *Doug*, made available to the larger world.

Clark's career was launched by his studies at Ryerson in Toronto. When he was a student there in the film and photography department during the early 1970s, only a couple of approved modes of serious photography were considered. The main one was a kind of arty photojournalism derived from the early 20th century work of European Leica photographers like Henri Cartier-Bresson. Its North American heroes were the rebel Swiss-American photographer Robert Frank and the *Life* photo-essayist Eugene Smith.

The other dominant mode favoured the much larger view cameras, which produced at least a 4x5 inch negative, if not one that was 8x10. These big camera photographers were craft-obsessives who argued for hours about developer formulas, exposure systems and elaborate printing techniques. Every print they made was overflowing with high art ambitions and had significance that transcended the literal content of the image. Edward Weston converted vegetables into existential presences and the California coast into eternity. Ansel Adams deified mountains and the American West while Minor White deified just about everything.

There were regional variants and hybrids of these approaches. A particularly influential one in Toronto during the 1970s emanated from the Visual Studies Workshop in Rochester, New York. Headed by the photographer Nathan Lyons, it used the tools and materials of the Leica people but spiced them up with largely urban-based formal games, the occasional use of colour and heavy doses of irony.

An ambitious fine art photographer of Doug Clark's generation had to absorb and pick through these modes and influences and find something for himself in them. During the late 1970s Clark did some of the obligatory black-and-white "street" photography, using hand-held 35mm cameras, but soon moved on to a more individual use of the medium. Doug's was an extremely oral personality. He spent a lot of time stuffing things in his mouth — fast food, donuts, cigarettes and endless cups of coffee. And lots came out. All those stimulants made him run fast and chatter. He was always bouncing off the walls, talking, joking, enthusing, exclaiming. He photographed the same way, cranking huge quantities of film through his Leicas and Nikons.

This personality soon attracted him to working in colour. It was sensual and delicious, and the world was full of weird mysterious tableaux. Its store windows, urban signage and the strange nooks and corners of people's homes and workspaces were best recorded in its full range of hues and chromas — not in the more abstract black and white. With the aid of the new fast colour negative films, a wide-angle lens and on-camera flash, these odd little corners of the world could be lifted out of the ordinary and made strange — and beautiful. During the early and mid-1980s, Clark made thousands of photographs this way, many crazy, sensual and inventive. It was exciting.

By the late '80s these visual acrobatics had begun to wear thin for Clark. He wanted more control over what the world threw at him. Instead of just documenting the odd little corners of evidence that he found out in the world, he began to construct his own.

The strange juxtapositions that he occasionally found out there in the world could be built by cutting up individual negatives, joining them together and masking them around the edges so that they became the towers and totemic stand-ins for the human body that make up his *Articles of Faith*. To make the component negatives he ransacked his own overstuffed studio and those of others to find "hot" objects to arrange and light under a copy stand.

The techniques and materials employed to make these assemblages were Clark's caveman version of high tech. Many people were beginning to use computers for this work. Clark used razor blades, yards of Scotch tape and kitchen aluminum foil. His results were just as good or better. He took delight in the polished beauty that could emerge from kindergarten technique. Its manual primitiveness suited an oral personality. Doug had always loved things. Now he was trying to understand why and what meaning these objects had for him. He was trying to increase their power by rubbing them up against each other. He was also beginning to think about leaving evidence that he had existed. He used the nearly adult-sized photographs of *Articles of Faith* to ask basic questions:

"How do you remember?"

"Does time change the picture?"

"Do you enjoy being watched or watching?"

"Do you believe in what you see?"

"What kind of objects do you collect?"

"Do you have dreams that you hide?"

"Do you kill time?"

Articles of Faith was a popular show, touring Canada and

making its way out into the world. Clark was no longer just a taker of photographs, he was now also a maker. He had never really been a true documentarian.

He wasn't above a little diddling, a little adjusting of reality as he found it in order to make the picture more successful. In 1983, when he found a spherical glass vase of lilies next to a desk lamp in a Venice, California, living room, he tried making the photograph several times — with the lamp on and with it off. The change had a significant impact on the depth and focus of the photograph. He was rehearsing for *Articles of Faith* and beyond.

Clark, however, didn't totally abandon his documentary impulse. During his many travels in Europe and Asia at the end of the 1980s, he encountered things so foreign and beautiful that he simply recorded them, using a panorama format of his own construction that mimicked the experience of scanning the visual field of the world. These are among his most beautiful pictures. He loved being alone in an exotic place, drinking in all that new strangeness and the evidence of other ways of being.

By the early 1990s Clark had begun working on a kind of sequel to *Articles of Faith*. He returned to his low-tech cut and paste. These new pieces were simpler, more graphic and less exuberant. While a few of them retained the vertical format of the *Articles*, many ranged off horizontally or at angles. Several of them seemed to take on the shape of letters in a primitive alphabet. He arranged three of these in a sequence to come up with the name of the series: *Gio*.

Gio was less obviously figurative than *Articles of Faith*. In some of the pieces we're not really sure what we are seeing, whether looking at the components or the whole. *Gio* is more like a private alphabet. We recognize that we are seeing runes, but we don't know what they represent. Doug has left us with only a partial explanation for just one of them:

Madonna is based on the 1450s Stefan Lochner painting *Die Mutter Gottes in der Rosenlaube* (*The Madonna in the Rose Garden*). This votive painting of the humility type originated in Sienese art and relates to a myriad of spiritual symbols. Here the "Queen of Heaven" wears the crown and the blue robe of paradise. The roses in the image are meant to represent pain; purity and chastity are represented by the lilies; modesty and humility by violets; strawberry leaves represent the trinity of the divine.

Imposed on the surface I have recorded a Hopi winged-man and plastic leaves. The metal devil figure is wonderfully technological and the plastic leaves further extend a comment on this irony of paradise. Paradise came to mean the most perfect, the most secure part of a garden — here a garden of plastic leaves, a garden of reproductions. At the top and bottom of the frame, the negative has been cut and flipped. This is another direct intrusion of myself into both the factual and symbolic memory of the photographic process.

Here, an already heavily freighted image, Lochner's *Madonna*, is further loaded up with iconography from another culture (Hopi) and then skewed by a material analysis (a tinned steel devil and plastic leaves) into an ironical commentary on paradise and photography. It's easy to get lost attempting to understand what Clark was trying to do here. He seems to be questioning the veracity of the photograph and its ability to carry meaning beyond those meanings assigned by, for instance, Christian convention to depictions of the rose or lily. If we do not have established manmade meanings assigned to images, then what do they mean? Is there meaning without the impositions of cultural convention?

Looking at the other pieces that make up *Gio*, it seems difficult to believe that they were all meant to carry forward a dialogue about meaning, but it may be the case. The message seems so hermetic that most viewers will be tempted to simply enjoy the forms, textures, colours and moods that they encourage rather than struggling with speculative interpretations.

Clark's life was soon to change radically. In 1992 he was awarded a residency in the Canada Council's studio in Paris. Exploring the city's contemporary galleries, he began to encounter artmaking practices that were more based in ideas than on raw perception, sensation and the affection for the curious that had previously informed his work. Other artists like fellow Canadian Robin Collyer, also visiting Cité des Arts at the time, encouraged this shift in Clark's thinking. A blossoming romance with the Hamburg-based artist Martina Oehmsen led to collaborative work on a three-dimensional project. When he went to Germany he discovered that conceptual work was everywhere.

Clark had always enjoyed punning titles with double meanings. He titled his 1984 show in an Edmonton elevator cab *Upward Mobility*. The *Articles of Faith* were both objects and clauses or stipulations as in a written document. In 1994 he produced *Stock Market* and *Counter Fit*. Both played on double meanings — *Stock Market* inserted a cowboy into the NYSE newspaper listings and *Counter Fit* carefully collaged (fit) faces lifted from various international paper currencies. The following year while living in Germany, he produced *Shelf Life*, a piece in which expropriated images of hands from *outdated* magazines were converted to photographic reproductions and wrapped around 120 large cans arranged on a dozen shelves, like groceries that presumably had *expiry dates*. Puns on puns on puns: it was classic Doug playfulness.

Shelf Life became an important component of Clark's last major public exhibition. *North of America* was installed at the McMaster Museum of Art in Hamilton during the fall of 1997. Although his journey was soon to be over, this show clearly demonstrated how far he had travelled in a quarter of a century of active practice. Sombre, formal and monochromatic, *North of America* was an exhibition in which things disappeared into the walls and technology was used to ask more questions. The numerous clocks in the exhibition struggled to tell the truth about time. It was as much a show for the ear as for the eye. While new original work in photography now took a backseat, colour was right off the bus. Clark was getting ready for new travels.

Our rational minds pooh-pooh foreshadowings, but in Clark's case they were totally rational. His father had died of a heart attack in his 40s as had his grandfather. Doug's solution was to live and work fast. He packed a lot in — not just art-making but also travelling around much of the world as well as lots of passing on what he had learned to his many students during the last few years of his life. And then it came to the foretold midnight ending in a Muskoka cabin while holidaying with his wife and son. Like his father and father's father he had his fatal heart attack at 47.

One of the qualities that made Doug special was his generosity to others. Not financially, for years he seldom had enough to feed himself regularly and well, let alone to give, but he gave of his time and his energy. He always praised and promoted the work of his peers when he thought they'd done well. Peripatetic and gregarious, Doug knew many people in many places. He always made sure the ones who could profit by each other's company eventually met, and he initiated many collaborations.

From his career beginnings as a 25-year-old curator of photography at the Edmonton Art Gallery, Clark worked enthusiastically to showcase the photographic work of others, often in quite imaginative ways. His 1981 publication, *Keepsake*, combined public submissions of amateur photography with documentation of selected communities by commissioned camera-artists to celebrate the 75th anniversary of the province of Alberta. In 1983–84 he filled buses in Edmonton, Winnipeg and Vancouver with fine art photography. *Gallery-in-Transit* stripped buses of all the hectoring and intrusive advertising and filled the card slots over passengers' heads with images that gave rather than took. He organized other projects. People loved all of them.

For nearly two decades Doug Clark was a prime animator of Canadian fine art photography. He thought that the invention of photography in the first half of the 19th century was a seminal event in human history. No other visual medium was capable of recognizing the phenomenal strangeness and beauty of the world with such fidelity. Photography changed how we saw and how we communicated. It introduced us to places, people and events we would never encounter first hand. *It was amazing!* Through exhibitions, teaching and his personal photography, he communicated this wonder to others. His excitement was a great gift. Doug often joked that he was going to trade in his personality for a new one. Photographers from one coast to the other are glad he couldn't.

Toward the end of his life Doug decided to take himself more seriously. He began to dress in charcoal and black. His clothes were even ironed. Early in this final phase he yelled at me one day, "Don't call me Dougie." He was turning into Douglas. And he was now Mr. or Professor Clark, not Clarkie as many knew him in western Canada. Before I had time to adjust to this change he was gone. Miss you, Dougie. I miss Clarkie too.

I want Dougie back. I want EL too and Mary and David and Volker, Jeremy, Patricia and both Johns, Bill and Charlie and Arnaud — I want them all back.

It's been an unsettling day in the cabin. Each time I look up from my laptop a strange shadow flickers in my peripheral vision. When I turn my head to catch it — the shadow's always gone. When it returns there are movements on the margins. I hear steps and feel ghosts flutter.

SIXTEEN

A SLENDER SUMMA

"Stare, it is the way to educate your eye, and more.
Stare, pry, listen, eavesdrop. Die knowing something.
You are not here long."

WALKER EVANS

Early photographers worked at the forefront of the information age. In a sense, their medium continued and expanded the information dissemination and storage revolution begun by the printed book. A large glass plate or a strip of film is a massive storage medium, so massive that it is frequently difficult to manage the message.

We have always modelled our world and the universe in order to understand it, manipulate it and control it. The handprint on a cave wall is a simple *I am and was here*. The cave image of a prey animal is more complex — *this is what I hunt, how I do it and how I survive*. A Gothic altarpiece is a statement of *how I believe the universe works and what I hope will happen after death*. A Dutch portrait painting of the 17th century models an individual's place in a social order, their values and their economic achievement. It records what people of that time and place thought was important. Everything else was ignored and omitted. It was invisible.

Photography took modelling to a whole new level because it took in everything, not just the immediate subject and one's responses and associations with it. It also took in an enormous quantity of ancillary and adjacent information that, while perhaps not of interest or concern at the time the exposure was made, may speak volumes to future concerns. Those things

397

were not mediated by the artist's consciousness, they simply got recorded as part of photography's omnivorous gaze.

Photographers must accept this complexity and mystery and the currently unrecognized, in a way that no other visual medium demands. This extra evidence can be mined for many different interests and intents. It is open-ended data collecting that serves not just the present but can also serve the future in unanticipated ways. This is why the meaning of individual photographs can change through time.

Most users of cameras try to control the extreme data hunger of the camera by putting the subject squarely in the centre of the frame as an indicator of what's important. When doing portraits the American photographer Richard Avedon set his subjects on white seamless backdrops, even when outside, so as to control the distracting, indiscriminate and unruly data recording inherent in photography. But even with that radical act of environmental elimination he still recorded much that a traditional painter would have customarily ignored or not seen. Avedon still had to live with signs of wear on clothes, its wrinkles, blemishes and postural flaws and so on. There's plenty of extra information in his portraits.

Really, truly *seeing* a photograph can be quite taxing. When teaching I have locked students for hours in a classroom with a single photograph projected on a screen and asked them to make observations. A half-day later they were still finding new things in the image. Sometimes we'd be at it all night. Photographs can be very rich.

Friends who still teach tell me that many current students of photography are more interested in manipulating found and borrowed photographs than in taking their own. It's as if they believe there are already enough pictures and all the best photographs have already been taken — there's nothing left. Whereas the wonderful thing about being a photographer is that it gives you a license to be curious, to be, as Les Murray once said, "interested in only everything."

So what does a life as a photographer add up to? What has it meant?

We went everywhere, did everything and were fortunate enough to have a purpose. That purpose forced us out of ourselves and attached us to the world. And it allowed us privileged access to many otherwise closeted and closed worlds. We were allowed to enter those worlds because we made a practice of staying awake, of being alert and caring about people and the whole huge, messy business of being alive. And each of us leaves behind a paper trail of photographs, our individual footsteps through our tiny gift of time.

And ever since digital technology released us blinking into the light from the darkrooms of the world we have ridden the crest of an image wave that swells by an estimated three billion new pictures each day. It constitutes a vast "language" that we all share. What began with a red ochre handprint on a cave wall is now the most exhaustive and definitive statement of *I am, I saw, I was.* Nothing is now forgotten.

SEVENTEEN

THE WAITING ROOM

"We are the killers. We stink of death.
We carry it with us. It sticks to us like frost.
We cannot tear it away."

"Terror seeks out the odd, the sick and the lost."
J.A. BAKER

"It's not dark yet, but it's getting there."
BOB DYLAN

Getting old was something that happened to other people. It wasn't going to happen to us, we had an infinity of time ahead of us; besides, we were busy idling in an eternal present.

————

The first of September arrives and it's suddenly cold. The morning breeze still drifts out of the east making the waters of the inlet dance and sparkle but it is met in the middle by urgent gusts from the northwest. And they are dark. Over the next few weeks one will triumph over the other. The clinical clarity of winter light will soon rule. Things will start to die.

A shadow lumbers through the forests of the south shore. A black bear that understands latch buttons and door knobs, exits the bush and enters our buildings, bulldozing through rooms like a vengeful nimbus. Once inside it clears shelves, empties cupboards and eviscerates fridges. It has laid waste to four cabins in a week and has begun returns. Suddenly there's fear on the islands and all along the shore. Guns I knew nothing of appear. Death crouches impatiently under the pines.

On a brand-new and perfect day Sheila and I paddle kayaks out to the mouth of the inlet and begin to explore the many new channels created in the low glaciated foreshore. A pair of extreme winters has dramatically raised water levels. We enter a new little inlet and a hundred feet in we beach our boats on the sloping shore to go for a walk. When we return the space between the kayaks is occupied by a large bowfin with spectacular, glowing, lime green–indigo fins and a peacock's eye on his tail. His long dorsal fin undulates like a snake in water. A strange misty purple head sports a pair of barbels. For a while we watch him guard his myriad tiny offspring in less than a foot of water. He's a survivor from the Mesozoic, a messenger from an ancient past like the nearby garpikes and snapping turtles that carry genes from the Cretaceous. And above them sandhill cranes call, a weird gronking from two and a half million years ago. In a time when three-quarters of freshwater species have become dodos their message is adaptation and survival: the former we're failing to do, the latter seems less and less hopeful.

The dark bear returns once more. The police have suggested the cruelty of feeding the intruder corn cobs glazed with molasses and cement powder. As the powder slowly sets in their stomachs it kills but D. has opted for something faster. He loads his gun with heavy buckshot and slips around back of his cabin, cornering the invader in a dark hollow. Death reveals the intruder, a sow bear and her little cub, hungry in a bad year for berries. The bodies are carted in a wheelbarrow back into the bush. Vultures circle.

It's an upstream run. Macbeth and sculptor John McEwen sit on the mid-thwart of the skiff while McEwen's big dog Babe up in the bow scans the river with her nose. A mile past the last cabin we bank into a turn and spy a muskrat crossing the river between two stone cliffs. I cut the engine and we sweep toward the swimmer. The closer we get to it, the stranger it looks. It's no muskrat or beaver.

It turns to us, struggling hard, grunting and crying. I lean over the gunwale and come face to face with a baby bear no bigger than my cat Bill. If the mother watches we can't see her despite the open bush. I'd reach down and pull this exhausted swimmer into the boat but for the big dog barking excitedly from the bow so we elect to be an escort and secure the tiny cub's arrival on the north shore. It struggles out of the water and clumsily scrambles up the cliff face. This tiny bear is far too small and inexperienced to be alone but incomparably competent against a bobble-headed human baby.

A light offshore breeze has purred from the east all morning. At noon it dies and all is still for a score of minutes and then it begins — first a hiss far back in the pine forest that grows and nears. A few leaves tremble, then needles on the white pines and finally one feels the air beginning to move. The day's prevailing wind builds in the west, the land is heating and a hundred miles of water shoves cool air toward the heating land of granitic rocks and tortured pines. This builds hour by hour until the day begins to expire and the light warms and the air once again stills. The dying needles are touched with fire. The horizon moves out to infinity and every god that has ever existed is right here, right now.

This landscape appears primeval and eternal but in reality it was covered in a mile of ice a mere handful of millennia ago. Moreover, the wind-bent pines staggering across it are less than a century old as this inlet was stripped bare of trees to rebuild Chicago after the great fire. The rocks of the Shield may be a half billion years old but the trees upon it are babies. This is a recovering landscape, a message to the present about nature's willfulness and ability to heal. This gives me small hope for the careless present but also makes me fearful that it encourages abuse, a lazy irresponsible attitude toward the land. For what comes back is never the same as what went before.

Today there's a scudding cloud cover that encourages the sun to engage in theatrics. It spotlights selected rock faces and highlights certain trees but only for seconds before moving on to new targets. I'm gob-smacked.

The first day of autumn has arrived and so have the killers. They slice down the inlet before dawn in their camo death-boats — low freeboard, mini landing craft with four-stroke Hondas humming like velvet drones. In this Dunkirk of the Ducks, hunched hunters advance under cover of darkness toward the coastal wetlands, their shotguns and two-fours of Bud Lite at the ready. Come dawn the ducks will rise magnificently; the guns will bark and the bright birds will pinwheel out of the sky into the jaws of dogs. At noon the landing brigades retreat upstream between windrows of duck-down to have hot lunches prepared in their man-camps by mourning grandmothers in black. There's a grim military precision to it all. It's another job.

And it's one we've been hard at for millennia. We were the last of the large mammals to cross the Bering Strait: bison, deer, caribou, moose and elk all beat us to it. But we quickly got even. Even before Europeans arrived, serious slaughter was underway and species elimination had begun.

We reached peak efficiency in the late 19th century. Everything was the enemy — every shimmering fish, all the great beasts, the bright birds, even the land itself. We dammed, blasted, logged and stripped it clean. When the land got ugly we left and moved on. There was always more of it to conquer.

We're the only species to have ever caused the total extinction of another and we were proud of it. 1886 may have been the true *annus horribilis*. Five million birds were slaughtered to decorate American women's hats. A Wyoming cowboy claimed to have walked 20 miles on contiguous cattle corpses from overgrazing without ever putting boot to ground. The Chicago Hotel held its annual Procession of Game dinner that November. The menu featured deer, mountain sheep, black bear, buffalo, opossum, elk, coon, jack rabbit, hare, squirrels, redwing blackbirds, wood ducks, blackbirds, sandhill cranes and a couple of dozen other wild bird species.

And here at home we too kept directing traffic over the cliff of extinction.

1750 — The Sable Island Atlantic walrus. Gone.

1872 — The Labrador duck. Gone.

1908 — The Dawson caribou of the Haida Gwaii. Gone.

1911 — The Newfoundland wolf. Gone.

1920 — The Banks Island timber wolf. Gone.

1945 — The Eskimo curlew. Gone.

1970 — The Great Lakes blue pike. Gone.

1985 — The Great Lakes shortnose cisco. Gone.

As late as 1901 Quebec still hadn't listed the passenger pigeon as a protected species even though, it now seems, the sole wild one was shot the previous year. The last living passenger pigeon, a geriatric female named Martha, fell dead off her perch in Cincinnati's zoo on September 1, 1914. Her body was frozen in the middle of a 300-pound block of ice and shipped off to the Smithsonian to be skinned.

One of the virtues of this little island on the Shield is that it clearly exposes the pair of thin zones on which we depend for life. The delicate membrane of topsoil nestled in rock hollows supports everything from tiny microbes to giant pines and the few thousand feet of oxygen-rich air generated by those plants allows us to breathe. We should be tiptoeing through such fragile delicacy but we're not. Instead we've abused both and now we're about to pay for that neglect.

And we're still in the species annihilation business. Now our target is the most brutal one of all — us. We now hurry along a path of self-destruction. My longtime friends still mindlessly eat their fellow mammals, own several cars and houses, take frivolous airplane trips and consume disposable everything. All that environmental apocalypse stuff is for their children to worry about — not them. They remind me of a clutch of new hatchlings, mouths wide open screaming, "Me, more me."

We are four on the downstream run. As the river disgorges into a wild rice wetlands I spot a sandhill crane on the flats. Then it turns out there are five of those dusky waders picking away at the first shoots of the spring. I cut the engine and we drift — closer and closer. They call one another with their strange rattling cry, a song that has echoed over the gravel flats and wetlands of North America for over two and a half million years. Soon we are close enough to see the crimson blaze on their foreheads. We are mesmerized but the birds ignore us and continue probing the reeds. Finally our skiff bumps against the low bank and stops. These most ancient of birds are barely a metre away, surviving still.

A sandhill crane on the flats

EIGHTEEN

BELIEF

". . . a fairy story for people afraid of the dark."
STEPHEN HAWKING

*"For a long time I have not said what I believed, nor
do I ever believe what I say. And if sometimes
I do happen to tell the truth, I hide it among so many
lies that it is hard to find."*
MACHIAVELLI, IN A LETTER TO A FRIEND

*"You know what truth is? . . . It's some crazy thing
my neighbour believes. If I want to make friends with
him, I ask him what he believes. He tells me, and I say,
'Yeah, yeah — ain't it the truth?'"*
KURT VONNEGUT
BREAKFAST OF CHAMPIONS

"That much, whichever, depending."
SALLY HUNT

"The meaning of life is that it stops."
ATTRIBUTED TO FRANZ KAFKA

October 2014

My Jamaican father-in-law is dying. In the course of the past
dozen years I've become very attached to this man — as have
both my sons. Once a star athlete, he has been reduced by pros-
tate cancer and his 91 years to being an invalid who spends
much of his days in bed bedeviled by disturbing thoughts and

images. His only respites are slow shuffles to the bathroom a half-dozen feet away. Frequently he doesn't make it in time. It's humiliating.

What keeps him going — something I don't understand — is faith. He's a Christian and a Quaker. His physical death will be a portal to another realm, one where he will be reunited with his wife and all the many tragedies of his beloved Jamaica will be vanquished. Even though I'm the descendent of generations of Anglican ministers I can't grasp it. I can't understand how intelligent people can hold these beliefs. Our leaders — Trudeau (Pierre), a practising Catholic? Or Paul Martin? Or even our recent leader Jurassic Steve who talked to the baby Jesus in a suburban faith temple? Bizarre! Yet it seems to work for my father-in-law.

And it works for many other people here in Jamaica. My sweet-tempered housekeeper Hermin spends her evenings reading the Bible. I have no idea what the rolling cadences of the King James version mean to her or to the many thousands of older Black women dressed in their finest who walk along muddy tracks in the hills to church every Sunday. How can they embrace a faith brought to them by the same people who inducted their forbearers into slavery? Or accept the horrors inflicted on the New World by the Spanish, the French and the Brits in the name of Jesus? They must know all this. Forgiveness isn't deserved.

It saddens me to see the millions of peoples around the globe who have been seduced, persuaded or bullied into exchanging their often perfectly effective traditional belief systems for a once minor and marginal faith from a tiny Middle Eastern village. How did they manage to sell it to so many people? What is the attraction of a god that is so often mean-spirited and vengeful? What on earth is the Trinity? Does anybody truly understand it? And what about the strange cannibalistic idea behind communion — drinking the blood of Jesus and eating his flesh? Or having dominion over all natural things and interpreting that as a licence to kill and eat our fellow mammals. And, worst of all, the idea that we are just passing through, that this life, our one and only one, is merely an anteroom to one that's eternal and better. This idea excuses bad behaviour.

Of course railing on about the Bible is like tilting at windmills. It's become a historical artifact that's completely irrelevant to most Canadians' lives. This cultural shift away from any belief has to be partially responsible for the attitude of some to practicing Muslims and Sikhs, even Mediterranean Catholics, who have immigrated. Adhering to any faith seems so ancient and primitive that the people who do may as well be cave dwellers — aliens. Yet it's a powerful thing: it helps many to get through life.

I cringe when I see Chinese Presbyterians, African Anglicans or Indigenous Catholics. The Roman Catholics would seem to have been Christianity's best marketers: they have sold it, often by means of extreme violence, to everyone from the indig enous peoples of the Americas to the Philippines. The Brits were much less successful with their breakaway church, perhaps because they were less interested. It seems that very few Hindus in British India were persuaded to become Anglicans. The Brits were keener on the trade in goods than in souls.

We bicycle across the dusty Tamal Nadu plain in cymbal-crashing heat. Eventually the earth opens like a cenote and I climb down to the bottom where a pair of dreadlocked sadhus wait. My companion C. remains above, watching me from the rim. I'm his proxy, enduring a ritual in the hope it will cure his cancer and save his life. He's too ill to do it himself.

One of the old men leads me into a low cave. We crawl in through a deep carpet of bat shit, scraping our backs on the cave roof until a hundred feet in we encounter the first lingam. I stroke the big stone penis as instructed and we crawl farther

in to the next. Stroke and repeat. Still farther in and repeat.
And repeat. A quarter century later C. is still alive.

It's an October run north under gray skies following
a month's absence. After a four-hour flat-light drive
I finally reach the reserve and the river. It's been an
exhausting month of downsizing, packing and leaving Toronto for Hamilton after more than a half
century. Stepping out of the van at the river fork one
can feel the recent past slipping away and a soft calm
slip into its place. I'm home.

2018

Our new life in Hamilton has taken an unexpected turn. There's
something about this odd fractured town that turns you to fundamentals. At my insistence we live in a very middle-class part
of the city surrounded by impeccably maintained Victorian
houses, tennis courts, coffee shops and earnest restaurants.
I'm too tired and old for gritty. But a few kilometres to the
east is another Hamilton, one of rude tiny houses behind the
steel mills, of backyard Dobermans, of choppers, needles and
tricks. Many people there still smoke. There are walkers and
wheelchairs. The streets are beaten down by heavy truck traffic. Graffitied locomotives drag tanker cars through backyards
— last week one crushed a small girl's legs. It's poor. It's dark.
It's outside time.

We cycle between these two worlds, going back and forth
on the pair of wide one-way streets, Main and King, through
broken-toothed transitions left by so different histories.

Many winter Sunday afternoons we've walked the several blocks to John Lyle's beautiful 1908 Central Presbyterian

Church to listen to music — Vivaldi, Telemann and, above all, Bach. We've sat at the back of that handsome Beaux-Arts edifice and listened to Pergolesi's Stabat Mater and Bach's St. John Passion. Both have great moments. But both are strange.

"I don't get it," says Sheila, the daughter of Quakers. And I, ending a long line of Anglican ministers, can't explain it either. The Christian story makes no sense. And the music too. Pergolesi's simple melodies and occasionally jaunty arias and duets float under horrific lyrics about cruelty and abandonment. The Bach is even more extreme, sweet harmonies on flute and oboe paired with breaking bones, eviscerations and betrayals. Jesus dying for our sins?? How does that work? What does it mean? Why do people embrace it? I'm almost 75 and I still don't get it either.

NINETEEN

FINAL FIRE

*"The truest art I would strive for in any work would
be to give the page the same qualities as earth: weather
would land on it harshly; light would elucidate the
most difficult truths; wind would sweep away obtuse
padding. Finally, the lessons of impermanence taught
me this: loss constitutes an odd kind of fullness; despair
empties out into an unquenchable appetite for life."*

THE SOLACE OF OPEN SPACES

GRETEL EHRLICH

The days of rutting and rebirth are long gone. Once
the early river mists burn off, the fall morning light
flashes cold as stainless steel. Birch and alder leaves,
dry now as paper, rattle harshly in the wind. The
season of big sleeps has begun sneaking through the
pines. Winter *soon come*. The birds and I wing south.

2014

I watch an old man sitting in his Jamaican garden, surrounded
by frangipani, guava and coffee trees, feeding his dogs bananas
as the day ends. The light has gone gold, the clouds pink, the
airs have stilled. Here, surrounded by so much tropical splen-
dour Ossie faces the end of his life — only weeks remain.
During the quarter of a century since he returned to his beloved
Jamaica he has given much of what he has away. In all this
beauty there's been so much need. His fellow Jamaicans come

daily to his gate with a sick child, a crutch, a blind eye, a dying goat. They come pleading and wait.

A distant thunder, then the drumbeat of rain.

During these final weeks Ossie has taken to sitting for hours in a chair with his back to an open window. This allows him to hear, smell and sense his garden. A cool breeze caresses him as his head rests sideways against the high back of the chair. I pull up a seat beside him and photograph his face. He looks so fragile and vulnerable that it makes me afraid. His voice has become a whisper. I lean closer to hear him.

"I'm sorry I'm taking so long to die."

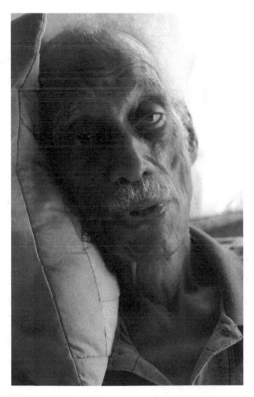

Taking so long to die

A distant drumming comes down the mountain, strides through the trees and crosses the road.

2014

During the early morning hours of his last days Ossie frequently calls Somae Claire, his second daughter, to his bedside.

"We have to make a list. Get a pen and paper." She does and sits by his side.

"Okay, Dad, what's number one?"

"Shakespeare."

She writes it down. "And Dad, what's number two?"

"Nothing to worry about." She writes that down.

"And number three?"

"That's it." He goes to sleep.

Rain has fallen like tears for five days on this little Jamaican house. Uninsulated, the wooden roof drums like my other island home. The garden is radiant.

November 2014

Sheila's father's light is faster dimming. The wear of 91 years is accelerated by the aggressive cancer he has decided not to treat. His children fly repeatedly into Jamaica from Vancouver Island, England and Toronto to succor and assist. Sheila books her fifth trip of the year when she hears that he's now totally bedridden. She will soon join her sister; both will keep watch for the remaining days until last light. It looks to be a long vigil.

The sisters Skype daily through November. Their father's decline is both physical and mental. While he has flashes of lucidity, even humour, he loses track of time, fixates on small details and is frequently confused. His dreams are frightening. I can no longer understand him on the phone.

Sister Somae Claire sends progressively dire reports. Sheila moves her departure date up and begins working overtime so she can leave. It soon becomes clear that Claire is exhausted, losing her ability to cope alone. Sheila's departure is moved up yet again. On a mid-November Friday a home hospital bed is ordered — not an easy find on the island. Sheila announces that she has once again changed her departure date. She will fly down two days hence. The next day is spent cancelling future meetings and appointments. She is relinquishing control of a project she has worked very hard setting up. Not easy.

On the day before her departure the local Jamaican doctor is summoned to set up a drip as Ossie is barely even drinking water. Doctor's verdict: he probably won't make it through the night. This message reaches Toronto while we're both on the ground floor at dusk. Our downstairs lights are not yet on. I listen as Sheila takes in this news on the phone. Her ticket will have her in her father's house by dusk tomorrow. She's just been told that he may not be there when she arrives. She hangs up and stands quietly in the dark.

"I've had to make so many decisions and changes in the past weeks. Now I know that my last decision was so wrong."

I watch her turn and begin to slowly climb the stairs to the brightly lit second floor. The light ahead and above makes a corona of her big head of curly silver hair — Jamaican hair. I've never seen her look so small, so vulnerable, so defeated and so alone.

The drumming stops.

This morning four of us began digging a hole in the red earth of the back garden. The lateritic soil is almost like clay. It's hard work. Our excavation is next to a bougainvillea partially shaded by a couple of banana trees that are in turn guarded by the enormous guango tree topping out far above our heads.

We take turns. Finally, what is essentially a post-hole, is deemed deep enough. We slide the lid of a small wooden box and withdraw a clear bag of pale powder. One handful at a time we let Ossie stream through our fingers down into the hole. We replace the earth and I cover our disturbance with a large gray rock. Ossie lies only a yard from his sister and barely a foot from his beloved wife Joan. An entire generation has now retired forever.

We have a plan to end this day with new life. A drive east along Jamaica's north coast takes us through Runaway Bay, Parsons Gully, Priory, St. Ann's Bay, Salem, Ocho Rios and Oracabessa. Not far from Golden Eye we slip through the ruined gate of an abandoned resort, skirt it and pick up a small road to the sea. It is almost dusk when we locate the waiting game warden who has taken shelter from the light drizzle in a decaying pavilion by beach. We walk the sands with him until we reach a large tree at the foot of a cliff. No X marks the spot, just a slender white rod planted upright well above

The Burial

the tide line. Under the warden's watchful eye we dig slowly with our bare hands. A foot or so down we encounter a baby sea turtle, a hawksbill, buried in the sand. His shell is little more than an inch long but already his fore-flippers demonstrate amazing strength when held between finger and thumb. We dig further and find more. Soon we have 163 flailing little hawksbills in a pail.

These little creatures are endangered. In the years before game wardens were appointed the locals would trap and kill the turtles on the beach. When those people were finally persuaded to leave them alone other predators appeared — dogs and the mongoose. One in 300 babies would make it down the beach to the safety of the sea. Our job tonight is to elevate the survival rate to 100 percent. We carefully tip the pail.

It's recess rush in a schoolyard. They're off toward the horizon's thin light and the sea accompanied by our five-person honour guard. During their dozen-minute scramble to the mother water their precise location will get forever imprinted into their brains. A hundred years from now, those that have survived to become four-foot giants will remember this place. In the meantime they will have swum through the surf, paddled to the edge of the continental shelf, curled into a little ball and ridden the great ocean currents right across the Atlantic and scattered from West Africa all the way to Islay off Scotland. Four years from now they'll have ridden currents back across and returned to this very spot.

Does this nursery effort actually work? A decade ago 300 hatchlings made it to the sea. This year the total will exceed 20,000. This is our new life for old.

Photography is part of death and grief's procession. It was once a funerary art — think of all those old glass plates of open caskets. During the days following Ossie's death Sheila's sister

Claire mounts a savage attack on the family albums stacked in the Jamaica living room. Vintage plastic pages crackle as she vaults through various three-ring binders stuffed with sheets of 3x5 inch prints with yellowed paper bases and retiring dyes. Some have blushed magenta, others have surrendered to a deathly cyan. While the few black-and-whites record early childhoods in St. Albans, north of London, life in colour begins in Toronto where Ossie was the first Jamaican consul general. The prints recording the following years as counsul general in the Bahamas demonstrate how heat, light and moisture are the nemesis of photographic dyes. Truer colours return for the retirement years in Jamaica and family visits. Claire ruthlessly excises and reorganizes the pages, purging the stack until finally only a single binder stands. It's a grief-driven exorcism whose criteria later puzzle even Claire during the calmer days that follow. The final edit of two lives now rests quietly on a little side table. A family's history has been compressed and packaged for posterity. Many doors have closed.

We return to Canada but will soon be back.

2015

We've been in the Jamaica house for a day. The empty strangeness is beginning to slip away as is the shock of seeing how careworn things are. The chairs, sofas, tables and beds; the curtains, dishes, shelves and counters all tell the same story — old people lived here. Now they're gone — Ossie, the patriarch, now for almost a year; his wife for several more. Sheila enters the room, sees me looking and reads my thoughts. "They're gone; Dad's dead," she says. "We're alone. We're the old people now."

We are now in a land of in between. I go; I return. I leave once more.

November is lumbering down from the inland head-
waters, through the bush toward the river forks. I
make a last run before my stream of stories becomes
a river stilled by ice. Snow will fall: there will be
silence. I will remain inside for months, trying to
make words flow like water.

2016

It's late November when the big airbus makes landfall just
west of Montego Bay and begins its rapid descent to Sangster
Airport. It skims the coast mountains, comes in low over the
harbour, clears runway lights at the water's edge and decel-
erates down the hot pavement. This will be my last time in
Jamaica. The house is for sale.

Paul is waiting for me outside arrivals, his face coal-black
above his neat white cotton turtleneck. We embrace and drag
my bags into the dazzling heat of the parking lot. He is first
among the many people here that I will miss. I love this island
with its many landscapes; however, over the years I've developed a sense of community and so it will be the people that I
will really miss. As I move through Brown's Town during the
next few days I get many warm greetings. In this intense market town I'm known as Mr. Murray, after my Black Jamaican
father-in-law. He was a saintlier man than I am so I take it as
a compliment. Only Paul calls me Michael and Hermin, the
housekeeper, slyly calls me No. 1. She knows where the butter
is. Many ask if I'll come back once the house is gone.

I've been alone in the Jamaica house for five days and nights.
After going to bed shortly after nightfall I quickly fell asleep.
Some hours later I wake to footfalls — slow, deliberate and very

close. A door protests; a floorboard creaks. I hear low moans. There is a sharp report. My watch says nearly midnight.

I slowly, soundlessly roll onto my back to better hear and locate the intruder. He keeps walking, directionless. Periodically something rolls. I hear a rattle, then a crash.

I'm approximately in the middle of the house — the whole building is suddenly alive. Step, roll, rattle, a ring. 12:16 p.m. More footsteps. Woodwork groans, a door creaks. Slow, methodical pacing. 12:32. It's almost the sound of my northern cabin shuddering in the wind. But this night is very still, dark, overcast and this tropical house is made of concrete. There is only one room with a wooden floor — the bedroom in which Ossie died. I am not in it.

After lying for an hour in high alert all the sounds suddenly stop. Following a few silent minutes I turn on a light to examine my watch. It's five after one. The visitation is over. The duppy, this restless spirit of the dead, has gone. The profound silence suffocates.

2016

Now that I'm past my three score and ten I've entered a valley of ghosts. My grandparents, parents, aunts, uncles and some cousins along with an entire alphabet of friends and colleagues have slipped under the waves. Several more are drowning. Life is as unstable as water. I'm now in my little ship's pilothouse at midnight. No one is on watch. The radar shows a blank sea, the chart plotter reveals no course. My vessel plunges forward, rising and falling on unseen swells. I have no memory of booking this passage. We all stand alone.

EPILOGUE

And what of Daniel Ortega, the man at the beginning of this book?

After a hiatus of 16 years he has been clinging to power for the past decade. For many of his people he has become Somoza, the dictator he replaced almost 40 years ago. He now has his own National Guard, a brutal coalition of paramilitary thugs, death squads, the police and the army. They race Toyota pickups through the streets of Masaya and the capital Managua waving guns and shooting protesters. Three hundred Nicaraguans have been shot dead in the four months since April of 2018. There have been summary executions.

Presidente Ortega himself hunkers behind the skirts of his looney wife, Rosario Murillo, who daily gives risible rants on the TV stations and in the press that she and her husband own and control. She has had government buildings painted in her "good vibes" colours — blue, yellow, purple and fushia. She has erected over a hundred twinkly 50 foot high "Tree of Life" sculptures along Managua's main avenues. Despite these measures the country remains broken and poor. The fires of the Revolution have gone out.

July 2018. 3:20 a.m.
Night of the Blood Moon

Alone in the cabin I've just gone through this little book one
last time, finally making peace with its leaks and stumbles.
Command S. The moon is full, strange backlit clouds scud and
a powerful west wind roils the waters and scatters the moon's
light. There's a veil of smoke as 10,000 hectares of pine forest
burn just a few miles north. This furious fire long ago jumped
the Key River making the hard rock land smoke like a great
volcano. The world heats and burns. Devastation and someday, perhaps, renewal.

END

ACKNOWLEDGEMENTS

Special thanks to Ken Straiton for his generous work on my picture files and for once again supplying the author photograph. The late Doug Clark's son Anton, Geoffrey James and Elizabeth Willing also made contributions to the photo files. At ECW Jack David encouraged me to write this book, Michael Holmes supported it, and Jen Knoch patiently saw it through a protracted process. Thanks to you all. I'm also very grateful to the advance copyreaders. And, as always, thanks to Sheila and Bill the Cat for putting up with me and the chaos. Bill's pal Ziggy refused to move to Hamilton and won't acknowledge me so he gets no mention. I won't talk to him either but I do miss him. He's a very special cat.

A graduate of the University of Toronto and Ryerson, Michael Mitchell returned to Toronto after working in Mexico as an archeologist. Mitchell's work has appeared in many national magazines, including *Weekend, Saturday Night, Descant* and *Canadian Art*. As well as working as a teacher, he was on the curatorial and acquisitions committee for prints, drawings, and photography at the Art Gallery of Ontario and a founder of several enduring arts organizations. Mitchell's photographs are in the collections of Sweden's Museum of Modern Art, the National Gallery of Canada, the Portrait Gallery and the Art Gallery of Ontario as well as many private and corporate collections.